Flight For Control

After a ten-year leave, Kathryn Jacobs has been invited back to the N.T.S.B to investigate a series of unexplained airline crashes. But her husband, Captain Bill Jacobs, has his concerns. While her twin daughters are off at camp, and Bill is actively campaigning for the Pilot Union Presidency, Kathryn secretly begins her investigation. What she learns will shock the nation.

Flight For Control is a thriller that reads like a mystery. But to Kathryn, there is no mystery on the condition of the airline industry—it's broken. Planes are crashing. Pensions are lost. Pilots are financially and emotionally bankrupt due to fatigue, furloughs, and loss of seniority.

It's time that someone takes control before it's too late—unless it already is.

Your life is in your pilot's hands. Do you know who's flying your plane?

Flight
For
Control

Inspiration. Motivation. And Plane Stuff.

By Karlene K. Petitt

at

Flight To Success

www.KarlenePetitt.com

KARLENE PETITT

Flight For Control

JET STAR PUBLISHING INC.
SEATAC WA

ISBN 978-0-9849259-1-9

www.JetStarPublshing.com

Printed in the United States of America

DEDICATION

This story is dedicated to my kids—Kalimar and Dylan, Kayla and Ryan, Krysta and Torrey. And to my grandchildren—Kadence, Miles, Kohyn, Carter, Ellis, and Anthony...

> *"Anything is possible if you dare to dream, embrace hard work, and never give up. Be the protagonist of your story called life, you are the hero. Remember... the sky is not the limit."*

And to the many families who've lost loved ones in an airplane crash. While this novel is fiction, the numerous airline accidents throughout history are not—your loss is heartfelt. With the power of the pen, and the truth in fiction, we can create change.

In Memory of Captain Jack Sallee, and his dream—Coastal Airways. A legacy lives on with his family, aviation, and the Sequim Airport.

Flight
For
Control

PROLOGUE
FLIGHT 39 INBOUND JFK

THE STORM raging outside the cockpit window reflected the nightmare Sandra called her career. It was 11:00 p.m., and fatigue tugged carelessly at her eyelids. She wanted nothing more than to be tucked into her warm bed and then wake up the next morning to a home-cooked breakfast. Instead, she was living the dream—flying all night, followed by a hotel bed and a Zone bar scavenged from the bottom of her flight bag.

Instead of grinding through an East Coast storm, she wished she were still at her grandparents' fiftieth anniversary party. Her entire family was so proud that she'd become an airline pilot. She didn't have the heart to tell them she was a starving pilot who couldn't afford to miss a flight. She was also exhausted.

Sandra's commute to Chicago had always been tough. But the morning had wiped her out more than usual, and that was the easy part of her day. A 3:00 a.m. wake up, a five-hour commute, an attempted catnap in an old Lazy Boy with a spring up her butt, and then she reported for work. Due to the late arrival of the incoming flight, they had a three-hour delay then needed to de-ice their aircraft. Passengers were pissed, and she was tired. But they had finally got underway. Unfortunately, and to make matters worse, she had serious doubts about Grant.

Captain Grant Madden sat to her left, outwardly flying the

plane, but it was clear to her that his mind was elsewhere. He was on autopilot, doing what was expected, and being a major prick. He wouldn't engage in conversation beyond checklist responses, he wouldn't look at her, and at one time she'd thought he was about to cry. Maybe he was exhausted from his Seattle commute, too. Or maybe she'd done something to upset him. Either way, he needed to rein in his oversized ego, and get his head into flying the plane.

Shifting her attention from Captain Numbnuts, Sandra stared out the windshield. Snow attacked the glass creating a warp-speed effect, as if they were piloting their Boeing 737 through her starscape screen saver. She was out of her element tonight, and thanked God that she wasn't the captain. She only wished someone other than Grant was in command. Last time they'd flown together he'd been a sweetheart. But currently he was being a jerk, and she was too tired to deal with his shit.

The instruments jumped erratically, and despite the warmth inside the flight deck, a chill wormed under her skin and crawled deeper. Grant had assured her that everything would be fine, but she now realized that her first instinct had been right. They should've canceled the flight. But he was the captain—a check airman, no less—and it was his call. It was always *their* call.

The radio came to life. "Regional three-niner. Cleared direct to HOGGS intersection, descend and maintain flight level one-eight-zero. You can expect the Canarsie approach to one-three-right."

She picked up their initial clearance into JFK and responded to air traffic control while keeping a watchful eye on Grant. "Have you ever flown in weather this bad?" She needed him to say yes and that he'd flown in conditions like this a thousand times. Instead, he glanced at her without response.

They were flying one of the most challenging approaches into

New York's JFK airport, and she hoped to hell that he would snap out of his funk.

Sandra tuned the second radio and listened to the weather report. The airport conditions decomposed faster than their plane could fly. Visibility decreased by the minute, braking action was poor, and unyielding winds heaved. They needed to get on the ground, and fast.

She copied the information to a scrap of paper and set it on the console. "I hope we can get in before they close the airport."

Grant glanced at the paper. "Tell ATC we want to descend to eight thousand feet."

What? An early descent would take them off their profile and put them in the heart of the storm. They needed to stay at 18,000 feet until they intercepted their path. Sandra picked up the microphone, but she didn't speak. The plane pressed forward.

"Get us a descent to eight thousand," he repeated. "Now!"

Sandra called ATC with Grant's request, double-checking the flight management computer as she did.

A descent now would put them ten thousand feet below their profile, far too low for the distance remaining. She almost questioned him, but decided that might not be in her best interest. Fighting with Grant would be far worse than his dicked-up decision to go down early. Besides, she'd be damned if she'd give him the chance to trash her reputation by claiming she was a bitch. He'd do what he wanted regardless of what she thought.

She didn't have a problem taking a stand, but this wasn't the time. Pick and choose your battles, her dad had always said, and this was a battle she wouldn't fight. Standing up to a check airman was career suicide. She swore she'd put Grant Madden on her no-fly list.

Air traffic control approved their request, with hesitation. Grant reset the mode control panel for their lower altitude and started the aircraft in an initial descent.

Outside the windshield, ice adhered to the wiper bolt. If it were on the bolt, it would be on the wings changing the aerodynamics and disrupting airflow. Each icy flake diminished their options. Too much ice on the wings and the plane would stop flying.

Ice accumulated rapidly, and the sting of their situation slapped her in the face. Experience and knowing what to do were overrated. Without the confidence to take action, neither mattered. Sandra should have spoken up before takeoff. She could have walked away. But could she? No. She knew that better than anyone.

Her fear was their reality as the plane staggered through the heart of the storm. Their aircraft would no longer climb; further descent under the weather was their only option. But the buildings below wouldn't allow that. They needed to get over the water. They needed to get the Boeing to a lower altitude in warmer air. Hell, they needed to *land*.

"Flaps one," Grant commanded.

Sandra moved the flap handle into position. Grant called for flaps five. She continued to configure the airplane. He reached up to the mode control panel, hesitated a moment, then turned the selector to reduce their airspeed.

"Grant, we need to get out of here. Maybe get vectors over the water so we can get a lower altitude and—" ATC interrupted her with a clearance to turn south. *Prayers answered.* Obviously the controllers were watching the cell on their radar. At least *they* were being proactive. She glanced at the slip of paper she'd written the weather on.

The visibility had dropped to two and a half miles at the airport, with blowing snow. Minimums for the approach. All runways were closed except 13 Right.

The wind tossed them like a toy. The flight instruments bounced with the aircraft, shifting data into an unreadable blur. A thousand white daggers attacked their airplane, and the altimeter indicated they were flying dangerously low. Sandra's heart raced with the speed of the engines. If they could just maintain altitude a few minutes longer, they'd be over the water. But massive ice accumulation left them with minimal leeway. They weren't holding altitude.

Sandra confirmed their location against her charts and kept an eye on the airspeed.

"Flaps ten," Grant commanded. She fumbled with the flap lever as he slowed the aircraft.

"Regional Air three-niner, state your altitude."

"We're passing through five thousand feet. We're unable to maintain altitude due to heavy ice buildup!" Sandra responded, louder than she'd intended.

"Tell them we'll be able to level off at three thousand and would like to continue vectors for the Canarsie approach."

She complied, but she doubted his assessment on the altitude. Ice was accumulating too fast. ATC cleared them direct to ASALT intersection with a descent to three thousand feet.

"Gear down, flaps fifteen," Grant commanded.

Sandra took her eyes off her flight instruments as she reached for the gear handle and hesitated, questioning his call for gear extension. She glanced at the speed tape then yelled, "Airspeed!" Their airspeed had dropped five knots below a safe range and the trend arrow indicated it would soon be twenty below.

Grant did nothing.

Adrenaline shot through her veins as she transitioned from

fear to survival mode. Hyperaware on all senses, she yelled again. She realized that the auto-throttles were off—*manually deselected.* Then she noticed the wing anti-ice was off, too. *What the hell?* She reached up to turn on the anti-ice, but Grant's hand flew overhead and knocked hers away. At the same time the aircraft pitched its nose forward to prevent the impending stall. Their eyes locked for a split-second. Then he pulled the thrust levers to idle.

The airspeed indicator flashed its warning. Sandra aggressively pushed the levers full forward. They needed power and they needed it fast. Grant reacted by clicking off the autopilot and pulling back on the controls. Sandra countered by pushing forward.

He's intentionally stalling the plane!

Sandra continued to fight him, but when he yanked the thrust levers to idle the second time, with the nose held high, he nailed their coffin closed.

"No!" she yelled, and with all her strength continued pushing forward on the control yoke in an attempt to prevent the aircraft from stalling. But Grant held back pressure, fighting both her and the plane. He was winning.

The 737 shook violently while the stick shaker screamed in defeat with the impending stall. The passengers screamed. Their fear sliced through the cockpit door. The aircraft fell.

Sandra grabbed the flashlight in her flight bag and swung with all her strength, slamming metal it into the side of Grant's head.

"You son of a bitch!"

Not once, but three times she slammed her flashlight against his head, knocking him unconscious. She would not die this way, not tonight.

Taking control, Sandra simultaneously rolled the wings level and guided the aircraft's nose down, then pushed the thrust levers forward. The aircraft leveled off. Almost. They had lost an additional two thousand feet of altitude, she was flying in the blind, and there was ice on the aircraft. Lots of ice. They had only six hundred feet to play with and were in a shallow descent.

Her body trembled combatively, mirroring what the aircraft had just experienced. Cries echoed from the cabin, and ATC pleaded with her. Was she okay? What altitude were they at? Did they need assistance?

Hell yes, she needed assistance. But it was all she could do to maintain control and couldn't respond. Her hands and mind were overloaded. They were going in, and she hoped it would be in one piece.

Passing over the Canarsie VOR, she turned to a heading of 041 degrees. The right quartering tailwind didn't help. At 2.6 miles she turned the plane, looking for the lead-in sequencing lights that would guide her toward the runway. She should have been at eight hundred feet until DMYHL intersection. But now, passing through four hundred feet, she was having difficulty maintaining altitude.

Only two miles from the airport. A faint light glimmered hope somewhere beyond the blanket of snow. They were going to make it.

On final approach, Sandra made that one essential call.

"Tower, Regional three-niner on a two-mile final, emergency aircraft, landing One-three Right." They needed to know she was coming in and landing.

Landing clearance was received, but it didn't matter. She had no other option. Visibility was decreasing, and yet the glow beckoned to her. The snow distorted her perception of what was beyond. Still the lights reached out, guiding her to safety.

With sweaty hands, she held tight to the control yoke. Then glanced at the gear—not an option. The drag would further an unwanted descent. They would be landing gear up and she had no way to brief the flight attendants. *"Please, God, help us reach the runway,"* she whispered.

She glanced at the flap indicator—10. Their speed would be fast, but the runway was long at fourteen thousand feet, and then—What the...

Her instruments told her she was left of course, but moments before she'd been spot on. Confused, she confirmed the course was set correctly then realized the wind was stronger than reported and it had blown her left of final. There were lights in front of her, but the instruments now directed her to turn right. She was looking at the left runway that paralleled 13 Right.

"Shit."

The left runway was only ten thousand feet long, and closed. She had no choice. They would land on the closed runway. She would land on a taxiway if she had to. She just needed to clear the...

Then her aircraft became very heavy, settling below the glideslope.

"What the fu...?" She looked down. Grant's hand was on the flap handle. He'd raised the flaps and killed their lift. Sandra knew what was ahead.

The aircraft barreled through the hotel that sat one hundred and eight feet high off the approach end of the left runway. She closed her eyes during impact, but her mind stayed alert.

The 737's skin ripped from its frame. Pain stabbed through her abdomen, radiating into her chest. A thousand bullets attacked her in the form of glass shards. Her eyes remained closed, but that didn't stop the attack on her remaining senses.

Sandra's death-grip on the thrust levers and control yoke kept her grounded in reality.

Wing spars snapped beyond, and hotel beams bludgeoned and

beat the aircraft sending shock waves through Sandra's bones as they, too, fractured. One thundering explosion followed another in the back of the aircraft. Incredible heat swept over her body, and a melting uniform worked its way into her skin. Pain held her body hostage as her mind and soul were tortured.

Her rapid breath sucked thick air into her lungs igniting a fire within her chest. And just when the volume of her dying breath was too much to bear, the assault on her senses slowly retreated into nothingness.

When she opened her eyes, distant sirens had replaced the screaming. The plane was motionless. The overhead panel hung within inches of her face. Other than the occasional snap of electricity, the silence of death surrounded her. Crackling flames lapped hungrily at her seat. The instrument panel pressed into what was left of Grant's body. Head hanging, his barren eyes stared in her direction.

Sandra felt nothing but fear. She couldn't move. Flames darted about the flight deck. There was no light to walk into, and no family to pay their last respects. Sandra had never been so alone, or her heart filled with so much regret. She couldn't accept the fact that she'd been unable to save the flight and the hundred lives she'd made an unspoken promise to. She couldn't even save herself with a metal rod pinning her to the seat.

Death stood at the cockpit door, and the question of 'why' slithered into her mind.

CHAPTER 1
FRIDAY

"I Never Thought I'd Be So Happy" echoed through her kitchen as Kathryn beat the eggs into submission. She set the frying pan on the stovetop then grabbed a potholder and pulled cinnamon rolls from the upper oven, humming with the music. Unfortunately the morning pick-me-up melody didn't replace the disquiet murmuring in her heart, or the rolling of her stomach. She dipped a finger into the icing and stuck it into her mouth. Closing her eyes for a moment, she covered her mouth with her hand.

As if on cue Princess came to her rescue purring, while nuzzling between her legs. Kathryn knelt and picked up her aging friend, and kissed her.

"Princess, why can't I do it all?" she asked opening the fridge. She located a carton of cream and filled a dish. Kneeling, she set the cat down for her morning treat and stroked her gently. Kathryn's heartbeat slowed with every touch.

She couldn't believe her luck. John McAllister had called, and her dream was becoming a reality. She'd planned on finding a job while the girls were gone for the week. But as hard as she tried she couldn't get her mind off the National Transportation Safety Board and what she'd left behind, diminishing any potential satisfaction of an ordinary job. Unfortunately nobody had ever been called back after they'd quit the NTSB—or so she'd thought.

While Princess cleaned her dish, Kathryn stood and washed her hands.

Not a day went by that she didn't miss the career she'd tossed aside. Keeping busy with the house and the girls gave her moments of reprieve, but lately, those moments were few and far between. Perhaps it was that the girls were growing more independent, or maybe it was Bill's busy schedule. The numerous airline crashes didn't help matters, reminding her daily of what she'd given up.

She was consumed to the point that it was making her sick. She picked up a spoon and stuck it in the bowl while humming, fighting the nausea that grew worse daily.

Kathryn was spreading gooey icing over the rolls when her daughters' laughter hit the top of the stairs. She closed her eyes and took a deep breath. Moments later they bounced into the kitchen.

"Good morning, my darlings." She grabbed Jennifer's hand and spun her in a circle like she had when the girls were five, then pulled her close and hugged her tight.

"Mom, you're so weird," Jennifer said, laughing and pushed her away.

Before Jessica could escape, Kathryn pulled her into a bear hug and kissed her cheek leaving a smudge of icing behind.

Jessica pulled away and wiped her face with the back of her hand. "What's with you?"

"What's with me? Nothing. Can't I just be happy?"

"You and Dad have sex or something?" Jessica asked, raising an eyebrow.

"Jessica Anne." Kathryn's eyes opened wide. "You and I are going to have a serious talk, young lady. Go sit down." They definitely *would* talk about the mouth she had developed, but not today. Nothing would ruin this day.

When the phone rang Jenny skipped across the floor and grabbed it. "Jacobs' residence… Aunt Darby!" Jenny's eyes sparkled as she told Darby about her upcoming camping trip. Darby wasn't the girls' aunt, but Kathryn's best friend, and the girls loved her. Everyone loved Darby. Well, almost everyone.

Kathryn took the phone from Jenny and cradled it on her shoulder while she dropped bread into the toaster.

"You'll never guess what happened yesterday," Kathryn said, picking up the spatula.

"You got laid?"

"Jeez Darb." She knew exactly where Jessica got the mouth and shook her head at the days to come. "John McAllister called." She turned her back to the girls, who were arguing over something or other, and whispered, "He wants to have lunch today and talk about my returning to work."

"Awesome. What'd Bill say?"

"I haven't told him yet."

"You're learning."

"What's that supposed to mean?" Kathryn pushed the scrambled eggs around the pan then turned down the burner.

"Kat, your husband's a dick."

"I hope you called for something other than to piss off my perfectly good day," she said, opening the fridge.

Darby laughed. "Yeah. I actually did. They're having a press conference in D.C. on the findings of the Regional Airlines crash. Could you tape it for me?"

"Of course." She and John had planned on watching it together after lunch. "Jenny, stop playing with your food," she said pouring orange juice into Bill's glass.

"Did Jenny tell you that she's bringing me a tree from camp?"

Kathryn returned the pitcher of juice to the fridge then closed the door with her butt. "Darby, I really need to go. Can we talk tomorrow?" Phone balanced on her neck, she reached for the spatula.

"What's wrong with tonight? You're going to make it, aren't you?"

"I can't. Bill and I need some… uh, alone time."

"Oh God. Please don't make me puke."

"Say good-bye, Darby."

Tossing the phone to the counter, Kathryn removed the pan from the burner just in time to save the eggs. She set the *Seattle Times* to the left of Bill's plate. His juice was in position to the right. She'd squeezed it fresh. Stepping back, she took in the scene. Everything was perfect when he approached.

"Something smells wonderful," Bill said, wrapping his arms around her and kissing her neck. "Who was on the phone?"

"Darby. She wants me to tape a show for her this afternoon."

"You girls and your soaps," he said, winking at the twins as they both jumped out of their chairs and ran to him. Jessica wrapped her arms around his waist and gave him a long hug. With a hand across her back he squeezed her tight and kissed the top of her head.

"Good morning daddy," Jenny said. He scooped her up into his arms and held her tight, and she laid her head on his chest. He rocked her for a moment before he placed her back onto her chair. It wouldn't be long until they were too big to be lifted like that, despite Bill's strength.

Ignoring his comment she poured him a cup of coffee then buttered his toast, and once he was seated, she set his breakfast in front of him.

"What's with the sleeping bags?" he asked, picking up the paper.

"Oh, Daddy," Jenny said, with a sigh. "We're going to camp Waskowitz today."

"For the whole week," Jessica added.

"Kathryn, why didn't you tell me about this?" He frowned. "We could've made the day special and gone out for breakfast."

Jessica glared at her mother.

"I did tell you. Three weeks ago." At least, she thought she had. She pinched the bridge of her nose and closed her eyes. Her memory lapses were becoming more frequent, as were the headaches and nausea. She just needed to get back to work and start using her brain again then everything would be fine.

Bill stood and filled a glass with water, then handed her a bottle of Tylenol. "Don't worry about it. We'll go out when the girls get back." He touched her back and returned to his seat.

The twins talked animatedly pulling cinnamon rolls apart. It would be the first time she'd have a night alone in more than ten years. Kathryn would miss them, but she was excited for them to go. And the timing couldn't be better to get her feet on the ground. She looked forward to slipping into her old life. Wearing adult clothes and discussing more than who would bring what snack to the game appealed to her on every level.

"Jess, stop that."

Jessica took the spoon off her nose and Jennifer laughed. Bill read his paper and ignored them all. He was lost in another world. A world he'd been visiting often.

"Okay, ladies, your bus will be here in a few minutes. Go brush your teeth."

After the girls ran out of the room, Kathryn moved to Jenny's chair and sat beside Bill. He smiled and patted her hand, not removing his eyes from the paper. She pushed Jenny's plate away and folded her arms on the table, and quietly sucked in a deep breath. Princess jumped into her lap, made a few turns, and nestled in. Kathryn leaned back and stroked her. "I've got great news." She waited for Bill to look up. When he didn't, she continued. "John McAllister called yesterday."

"What did he want?" he asked, turning the page.

"He wants me to come back to work."

"I hope you told him where to go."

"Not exactly," Kathryn said with a laugh at Bill's humor. "This is a fantastic opportunity, but I'd have to start at bottom seniority, and he said that—"

"You think this is funny?"

"No. Or course not. But I thought—"

"*I* thought we had that man out of our lives for good."

"Bill, there was never anything between us, he was—"

"I don't care. I want you to tell him, and that department, they can all go to hell." Bill folded his paper and set it on the table, turning toward her.

"But we agreed that when the kids were older I'd return to work."

"The girls are hardly old enough for you to leave them."

Leave them? She wasn't moving to Siberia. She was planning on driving into the city and becoming a participant in the human race once again. Maybe save a few hundred lives in the process.

"They *are* old enough, and besides, they're in school all day."

"This just isn't the right time, honey." He lifted his coffee cup and sipped.

What had gotten into him? He had no right to tell her she couldn't work. Besides, there were far too many reasons she needed to accept this job.

Bill returned to his paper and Kathryn stroked Princess for a few moments then said, "I can't tell him no."

"We're supposed to make these decisions together." Bill stood and folded his paper in half. "Don't do this to us," he said, and tossed it on the table knocking a glass of juice over. Princess jumped from Kathryn's lap and scurried out of the room.

Kathryn's eyes widened. She righted the glass and stacked paper napkins on the mess.

"Mommy." Jessica said, standing in the doorway with her sister by her side.

"Well, girls, it looks like your mom wants to leave us to fend for ourselves."

"Bill. That's enough." Kathryn stood and went to the girls as he walked out of the kitchen. When his office door closed, firmly, Kathryn cringed. Tears filled Jessica's eyes, and Kathryn pulled her into an embrace.

"It's okay, sweetie. Daddy's just having a bad day," she whispered.

"You won't leave us, will you?" Jessica asked.

"Oh, Jess, of course not. I could never leave you." She held her daughter tight and kissed the top of her head.

"Mom, we could skip camp," Jennifer said.

"Don't be silly. You're going to have a wonderful time, and Daddy and I will be fine."

She had never wanted the girls to see them fight like her parents had. For ten years the little skirmishes she and Bill had had were well out of earshot. But kids are smarter than most parents give them credit for. Kathryn knew that all too well. Thankfully she and Bill had created a fairy-tale life for their daughters. She didn't want to undo that now. But something had shifted in Bill. The closer the election came, the shorter his fuse.

"It's not Daddy we're worried about," Jessica said, pulling back from her embrace. "We heard you on the phone yesterday."

Kathryn glanced down the hall, then back to her daughters.

Their stares held more than question—she saw fear.

She smiled warmly at them both then tucked a strand of hair behind Jenny's ear, hoping the fear she felt wasn't as transparent as theirs.

"There is nothing for either of you two to worry about." She placed a hand on Jessica's back, and held the other out for Jenny. "Come on, you're going to be late for your bus. I'll walk you."

CHAPTER 2

ONCE BILL HEARD the door close, he returned to the kitchen and walked to the window. He slid the curtain aside and peered out. Kathryn and the girls were walking down the steps. He turned. "Here, Princess. Here, kitty, kitty." The cat didn't come.

He opened the cupboard and removed a can of tuna. After draining it, he set it on the floor in the center of the room. "Come on Princess, come to daddy."

Princess walked around the corner, eyeing Bill, then the door, and then the tuna. She sauntered hesitantly up to the can and sniffed.

"That's a good kitty."

The cat stuck her nose into the can and began to eat. Bill knelt by her side and stroked her gently. Then he grabbed her by the scruff of her neck, and the fight began.

"Oh sweetie, It won't be that bad," Bill said, carrying her into the laundry room. "This is going to hurt Kathryn, more than you." Not that his words would comfort the cat, but it reminded him to stay on task. Everything had a purpose. He was two months until completion, and that was all it would take to push Kathryn over the edge. Step two—strip her of what she loves.

He opened the linen closet, removed a pink pillowcase, and shook it with one hand to open it. Attempting to put the cat inside wasn't as easy as he'd thought. Princess had other ideas. Crying and thrashing, she scratched his arm, but he barely felt anything.

Amazing that the old cat had so much fight in her at fifteen. She was the one thing that had been in Kathryn's life the longest, and it was time for her to go.

When he finally stuffed her into the bag, he returned to the kitchen and dropped in the can of tuna. He then spun the bag to close up the neck. Returning to the laundry room, he picked up one of Kathryn's tennis shoes, and attempted to remove the lace. But holding the pillowcase with a thrashing cat, while trying to de-lace a shoe one handed was a challenge.

When he set the bag on the floor, Princess tried to escape, and he stepped on the opening. Once the shoelace was finally free, he tossed the shoe and knelt beside his package.

"Hold still baby. This has nothing to do with you." He wrapped the lace around the neck of the bag, and pulled it tight then tied a knot. "You'll just finish your tuna and go to sleep."

He opened the back door and stepped outside then walked across the yard to the flowerbed and pushed aside the garbage can lid that concealed a hole. He set the cat inside and picked up the shovel and scooped a pile of dirt on top.

CHAPTER 3

BY THE TIME they reached the bus stop, Kathryn had convinced her daughters that she was fine. She had told them about the job offer, and they were both happy for her. But that hadn't been their concern. They'd heard her make another doctor's appointment and were worried something was wrong.

She promised the girls that when she brought their suitcases and sleeping bags to school that afternoon, she would tell them everything that the doctor said. No secrets.

"I love you guys. See you at three." She hugged them both, but Jessica held on longer than usual. Kathryn wiped a tear from Jennifer's cheek and kissed her. She waved goodbye to the bus as it pulled onto the street, and then she slowly headed back home with other things on her mind.

She had thought Bill would've been excited for her, not angry. At least she'd hoped. Unfortunately he'd been flying a heavier-than-normal schedule since cutbacks began, and he was under a lot of stress with the union election. He'd been spread thin for many months. Thankfully his campaign was coming to a close. She only hoped it wouldn't put the final stake in their marriage. She shivered and pulled her coat tight.

The temperature had dropped significantly over the previous three weeks, and the trees had been stripped by unyielding winds.

She, too, felt bare. She needed the job more than she could explain, and wasn't sure what to do with Bill's reaction. She had thought Bill wanted more for her, too. They had always planned on her returning to work. Then again, maybe she shouldn't have scheduled a meeting with John until after she'd talked to her husband about it.

Folding her arms, Kathryn crossed the street to her front yard. She stood in front of the kitchen door and reached for the doorknob, but hesitated.

Every marriage had conflict, and compromise was a two-way street. But this fight was one worth having. She couldn't back down.

Taking a deep breath, she opened the door and stepped inside.

The kitchen was empty. "Bill?" she called.

The house was eerily quiet and smelled of tuna. As soon as she removed her coat a draft slinked around her neck and took hold. She wandered down the hall to the laundry room. The back door was ajar, and she reached for the doorknob. She pulled it wide open and looked into the back yard. A hand touched her shoulder from behind and she jumped.

"I'm sorry, sweetheart," Bill said. Kathryn turned and he pulled her close. "I love you so much," he said, stroking her hair. "That department. Walker and McAllister. I just don't want you going down that path again. Not after all we've built together."

Closing her eyes, she laid her head on his chest. She remained silent searching for the right words. Then he stepped back, held her face, and kissed her gently on her lips.

"Nothing will change," she whispered.

He pulled back and stared without response, then kissed her forehead and removed his hands. He returned to the kitchen, and she followed. He stood in front of the mirror and buttoned his epaulets on his shoulder straps while she gathered breakfast plates.

"Have you seen Princess?" she asked, still searching for the words that would convince Bill that the NTSB was the right move.

"I put her out just after you left. I'm sure she'll pop up soon."

Kathryn didn't like it when Bill put her cat outside; Princess was getting far too old to be running around the neighborhood. She also didn't have time to go out and find her this morning, but not an argument they'd get into, today.

"Your suitcase is by the front door," Kathryn said, setting the plates in the sink, now avoiding the discussion that was far from over. Then her body began to tremble and she held onto the counter allowing a wave of dizziness to pass.

"Are you okay, honey?" Bill rushed to her side. He placed a hand on her back then added, "Sweetheart, I left my bag down here last night when I got in. It's right there."

Following his finger, she saw his suitcase on the floor by the pantry. She could have sworn she'd brought it down and put it by the front door the first thing this morning. She turned her back to him and opened the bottle of Tylenol. Popping two pills into her mouth, she swallowed them with cold coffee.

"Can you pick up the laundry at the dry cleaners this afternoon?" she asked, while pressing fingers to her wrist.

"I can't," he said. "I've got a union meeting tonight."

She turned and faced him. "I thought we'd have the evening together." She'd planned a nice dinner hoping they could talk.

"The union meets when we can get the most people in town. We'll have tomorrow night, just the two of us. I promise." Rubbing his teeth with a napkin, he smiled in the mirror. He tossed the napkin toward the counter and missed. "Maybe you can help me get that deadbeat friend of yours to show up to a meeting sometime."

Kathryn ignored his comment about Darby and picked up the

napkin, her fingers turning white before she threw it in the garbage can. He was right—the union had to come first.

"So we're both on the same page, you'll tell McAllister no." Bill said, adjusting his tie. "Let's talk about it for a month, and if you still want to, then I'll reconsider."

They weren't even in the same chapter, let alone the same page.

"I think we should talk about this now." She leaned against the counter, folding her arms. *One month?* "This is the perfect time to start while the girls are at camp."

"Sweetheart, I don't want Walker in our lives. Not now."

"Who said anything about *Walker?*"

Bill turned and stared.

"Walker works for the Department of Homeland now, not the NTSB," Kathryn said.

"I don't care where he works. You know those two don't do anything alone. They never did. They're not your friends, babe, and they'll screw you over the first chance they get."

Kathryn couldn't remember the specifics with Walker, but McAllister was her friend and she trusted him. Bill was seriously overreacting—not something that she would point out. He'd always been jealous of John, and she suspected this had something to do with his reaction.

She turned her back to him, opened the faucet full hot and dumped liquid soap in. Now what? She wanted to scream as bubbles filled the sink. How could she take the job once he'd said no? How could she tell John that her marriage and her husband controlled her life? Something she was not proud of.

CHAPTER 4
TAMPA, FLORIDA

"SAY GOOD-BYE, Darby." The story of her life. Pushing the covers aside, she tossed her cell phone to the floor and almost fell out of the bed. The phone landed on top of the *USA Today.* The cover story read: *Regional Air Flight 39 Kills 95 Passengers, Crew, and 189 on the ground: Pilots to Blame? Findings Today.*

The industry she had once been so proud of was traveling south quickly. Unfortunately, there was nothing in the world that nourished her like flying airplanes. She was hooked. Regional's accident had been the third in the year, and no one knew why.

Rolling onto her stomach, feet hanging off the end of the bed, she closed her eyes. She thought about Kathryn and the girls, and how much she loved them. Bill was another story that she pushed from her mind as quickly as he slithered in.

The girls were growing up fast. Now they were off to camp, and Jenny had promised to bring her a tree. Nobody had ever given her a gift that special before. Where had the time gone? Soon she'd teach them how to drive a stick shift and take them to R-rated movies.

Oh, God, I need coffee. Not much sleeping had happened in her bed last night, and the day would be long. She was about to get up and get it herself when she felt nibbling at her toes. The nibbles shifted into full-blown toe sucking. "Mmmm," she moaned. "You don't have coffee down there, do you?"

"Brewing," Neil said.

Neil slid under the sheets and began to work his magic, licking his way north. Over her calf his tongue led the way, nestling behind her knee and drawing circles before continuing up her inner thigh. His hands followed, moving slowly over her curves and into the small of her back, then continued upward to her shoulders, trailed by kisses. His breath, now warm against her cheek, smelled of mint. Hers tasted of sex.

He tossed the sheet aside, leaving her open and exposed. The air-conditioning unit hummed and whirled cool air that cut through the humid room. He dipped down and kissed her skin and goose bumps covered her body.

She couldn't believe how any woman would have given up this man. Now if she could find a way to make him trust again, life would be perfect.

Neil dribbled hot oil down her legs and across her back. She moaned. The contrast of the temperatures seduced and relaxed her. His hands found her shoulders once again and kneaded the morning tension away.

"*Ohhh-God* that feels good," she said. Her body simmered under the life force his hands delivered. They were strong and he knew exactly how to use them. Layovers had never been so good since Neil had returned to her life.

He worked slowly with firm pressure, and slid them freely across her back. "Last night was wonderful. I'm going to miss you."

Every night with you is incredible. But Darby didn't tell him that. Instead, she reached back and touched his leg. He took her hand in his and massaged it, then bent down and kissed her palm. Long and slow. She would miss him, too. That's what made this relationship so stupid. They could be together all the time, if he wanted to, if only he could get over his past.

His hands moved in a circular rhythm around her hips. She loved his touch beyond life itself, but she needed and wanted so much more than layover sex. Not that layover sex wasn't incredible, it was. But she wanted someone to come home to at the end of a trip.

She was wrong. There was one thing that nourished her more than flying, and that was Neil making love to her. He trickled his fingers between her thighs, sending an electrical charge through her body. She closed her eyes.

Squeezing her butt, he bent down and kissed her left cheek and then the right. Neil was the only man she knew who could arouse her with nothing but a touch and a kiss. He was also the only man who could make her laugh when she wanted to cry, and who understood her completely. She gave herself freely to him.

He slid his fingers up her back and then returned to her hips. The softness of his touch deepened as he stroked her back. Then his hands were on the move again. This time they slid between her abdomen and the sheets.

He was lying on top of her, on her back. His hands slid under her body. God, she loved the sensation of his skin against hers. She loved feeling his erection grow against her. She would have him— forever. She couldn't imagine life without him. He continued to move his hands, and she knew exactly where his fingers were headed.

His hands came together over her abdomen and slid south. They cupped her mound and dipped inside her. She was wet, and Neil's reaction pressed firmly from behind. The weight of his body pressed against hers. She buried her face deep in the pillow, clutching the sheets.

He nuzzled into her hair until he found her neck, and kissed long and slow, then gently bit. Darby's body came alive beneath his embrace. Smoldering under his deliberate touch, she trembled when his lips touched her skin.

Her body moved with his, and she rode his hands. She purred with every lick and moaned with every movement. She slid her hands under her abdomen and placed them over his. Together they brought her pleasure. Everything and everyone else escaped her mind, and for the moment he was hers. It felt good. Right. Normal. Perfect. And....*ahhh...sooo...incredible...*

"Ohhh, Neil… my God!" She yelled, and came hard. Her body throbbed over his hands and her temperature rose. She held his hands firmly in place until her orgasm subsided.

When she released him, Neil rolled her onto her back. She watched his eyes devour her. His gaze consumed her as it worked its way up her body, until their eyes met. He bent down and gently kissed her lips.

Darby's heart raced, her body glistened, and every inch of her was in a state of arousal. Then he climbed on top. They fit perfectly together. They belonged together. Now if she could just convince him of that.

She wrapped her legs around him and squeezed tightly, pulling him deep. She ran her hands through his hair and pulled his face close enough for their lips to touch.

"I love you," she whispered. *God why did I say that?* There were far too many times her mouth led her brain, and this was one of them. She gently bit and sucked his lower lip, then took his mouth hungrily in hers, hoping he hadn't heard her words.

His tongue found a home within hers. He continued to move inside of her. She took both openly. Darby pulled him tight. She couldn't tell where she ended and he began. She sucked his tongue as he plunged deeper.

She wished their time together would never end. She needed him to stay exactly where he was, *oh yeah, right there*, for as long as he could. She wanted this moment to last forever. *Oh, God don't stop*, she thought as they moved together. She wanted him to… and then he cried out. She held him tight and kissed him softly, until his body stopped trembling.

"Sorry, sweetie," he whispered, still on top of her, but lifting his weight with an extended arm.

"Don't be sorry. We don't have much time anyway. Besides, there's coffee to be had. But first…" She knocked his arm out from under him, dropping the full weight of his body onto hers. She wrapped her legs around him and held tight. "Don't move," she whispered.

He was still inside her, spent, but that didn't matter. She pulled him close, held him tight, and used him. Darby rubbed and pressed her mound against his body and sucked him in. And now it was she who was urgent, and within minutes she came again. Her heart and body throbbed in unison, and she dropped her arms and legs and freed him.

She closed her eyes and smiled. But the smile didn't stop the pain that lurked below the surface, or the tears that formed beneath her eyelids. *That woman did a hell of a job on you.* She wasn't sure if she'd ever break though, but she'd die trying—if it was possible to die from too much sex.

Neil climbed out of bed and left the room. When he returned, he carried two cups of coffee.

"I was beginning to wonder what a girl had to do to get some of that stuff." Darby sat up against her pillow. "Thanks."

"My pleasure." Neil sat beside her and hung one leg off the bed. He took a sip and watched her.

"Can you stay and shower with me?" She asked.

"I'd love to, but my wakeup is coming in thirty minutes and I've got to get back to my room."

She knew this routine better than anyone. Most men were afraid to snuggle through the night. Not Neil. But he was definitely not one to stay long after the sun came up. She wondered why she allowed him to run off like he did. Sipping her coffee she thought about the night they'd just spent together. That was why.

Everything had a price, and hers was an emptiness that ached deep within her soul when she wasn't with him. It had only been a year since his divorce, and ten months since they'd reconnected, but their feelings grew daily. She'd never felt like this with anyone. She never needed or trusted a man like she did Neil. Her brain told her to run like hell, her body cried to be closer, and her heart was on the fence.

Maybe she'd tell him 'no more' until they became official. But she knew that there'd never be a last time with Neil, just another broken resolution in a line of many. She couldn't even give up chocolate. *But why would anyone want to give up chocolate?* The telephone rang and she spilled her coffee.

"A bit jumpy?" Neil asked with a laugh.

"Occupational hazard." She picked up the phone. Crew call. One hour until pickup.

Neil set his coffee on the nightstand and piled another pillow against the headboard. He leaned back and pulled her toward him. Wrapping his arms around her he whispered, "I do love you, too, Captain Bradshaw."

For the first time in her life, she was speechless. Now all she needed to do was shift his professed love into something more tangible like her clothes in his closet. But was that what she really wanted? She wasn't sure.

She *was* sure that she'd drive herself crazy if she didn't figure this out. Thank God their pilots' union had a free shrink, or she'd be broke. She'd call after she landed and schedule an appointment.

Now she needed to focus on her flight. Her passengers deserved at least that much.

CHAPTER 5

KATHRYN SAT in the corner chair with arms folded and legs crossed, staring at the clock and bouncing a foot. She'd only been waiting fifteen minutes, but it felt like an hour. She loved Doctor Anne, but this was the last place she wanted to be.

"Mrs. Jacobs, the doctor will see you now."

She followed the nurse through an old wooden door, and into an examination room. Today there would be no gown. They would review her test results. Sitting in the faded and worn blue chair, she wrapped her arms around her waist and waited.

A brisk knock at the door, and Dr. Anne entered. "Hi, sweetie, sorry to keep you waiting. How are you feeling today?"

"Okay," Kathryn said. She had no time for being ill, but the fear it might be worse consumed her.

"Hmm." Dr. Anne opened a file and read. "The good news is your blood work came back normal."

"So I must be crazy," Kathryn chuckled a nervous laugh.

"Sweetie, you're not crazy." Dr. Anne placed a hand on her back and rubbed.

"No, I'm losing it. I'm misplacing things. I found my car keys in the linen closet. This morning I thought I'd set Bill's suitcase in one room, and I found it in another. I just feel...off." She hated unloading on Dr. Anne, but it felt good.

"There's nothing unusual about getting busy and absentmindedly misplacing things. PTA President, twins, managing a house. None of that's easy. Sometimes I come to work just to get a break." Dr. Anne laughed. Kathryn had been listening to her laugh for as long as she could remember. But today she needed more. She needed answers.

"The headaches and the nausea can't be normal. And the nightmares… They've started again. I'm having them while I'm awake, too. They're like daydreams, but I wake up from them. Sometimes I'm in a different room when I come to."

"I'm going to run a few more blood tests. We'll figure this out."

"And if we can't?" Kathryn played with her keys. "What if—"

"Sweetie. You are not your mother." Dr. Anne picked up a pad of paper and scribbled on it. "But it's time you talk to someone."

Kathryn took the paper, and looked at the name and number. "I guess." She had been fighting the idea of seeing a psychiatrist for years, mostly because she knew what he would tell her.

"No guessing. I want you to make an appointment today. It'll be, what, twenty-seven years next week, and time you put the past behind you."

"I have put it behind me. I've created a life that I love. I'm stronger than she was." She spoke a little too sharply and was instantly sorry. The death of her mother hadn't been easy for Dr. Anne, either.

"Have you talked to your dad yet?" When Kathryn shook her head and dropped her eyes, Dr. Anne pulled a stool in front of her and sat. "Then you haven't put it behind you." She placed a hand over Kathryn's. "Honey, you cannot deal with this alone any longer. It's not healthy. If we work on what's hurting in here," she said, touching Kathryn's chest, "we may just figure out all the rest. Heal the heart. Heal the mind—"

"I know. Heal the body."

"Exactly. Now promise me you'll call."

Kathryn nodded. She folded the piece of paper and stuck it into her purse.

"I got a call from my old boss yesterday," Kathryn said, changing the subject. "He asked me to come back to work."

"Fantastic! That's the best news I've heard all month."

"I thought so too. The girls were impressed." She paused. "Bill had another reaction. To say he doesn't want me working for the department would be an understatement."

"Hmmm." This time, only one brow rose.

Dr. Anne didn't know the side to Bill that Kathryn had fallen in love with. He was the only person who listened patiently when she'd told him about what happened, and he never tried to convince her that her mother's death wasn't her fault. He understood and loved her anyway. Unconditionally.

"I'm supposed to meet him at noon for a lunch meeting. Now, I'm not so sure if it's a good idea. Bill's never reacted this way before. I'm sure he's just stressed with the election and he'll come around. It's just that—"

"Did you cancel your meeting?"

"Not yet."

Dr. Anne looked at the clock. 11:10 a.m. "I think you've already decided what you're going to do." She closed her file. "If you're going to make it, you'd better get going. First stop, the lab on the third floor. Personally, I think working would be the best thing for you. It's amazing how keeping busy with a passion can heal almost anything. Give my love to the girls." Dr. Anne gave her a hug. "And Kathryn, you need to put some weight on. You're too thin." Then she left as quickly as she entered.

CHAPTER 6

KATHRYN WALKED down Alaskan Way toward Pier 67. Fishing boats returning with their hauls found their docks, despite the fog. She paused for a moment to inhale the salt air then closed her eyes to draw in the aura of Puget Sound. Who was she fooling? She was delaying the inevitable. Yet, the moment embraced her.

The harbor air, thick with moisture, brought her heart home. The piers that fed greater Seattle reminded her why she loved the city. It had been far too long since she'd left the suburbs to visit downtown. A mixture of cotton candy and Ivar's fish 'n' chips warmed her. She'd have to bring the girls down when they returned from camp.

A Bainbridge Island ferry announced its departure with the haunting blare of its horn, and Kathryn jumped. Opening her eyes, she pulled her jacket tight to stave off the chill, and with a deep breath continued to walk.

The pier was busy, and Kathryn welcomed her anonymity among the crowds. As far as anyone knew, she was just another business-woman on her way to a lunch meeting. Within minutes she entered the Edgewater Inn. The lobby was crowded. People checking in, others sitting in lounge chairs, sipping cocktails and talking loudly. She walked past them and headed directly to the restaurant.

At the hostess stand she told the women she was meeting John McAllister, and the woman handed her an envelope and said, "Mr. McAllister said 'plans have changed' and he asked me to give you this."

Kathryn took the envelope. A wave of disappointment flowed through her as she opened it. Then a warm flush grew, and she glanced up to see if anyone was watching her. She removed the plastic key and stared at it.

She tapped it in her palm. *Why not?* She threw the envelope into the garbage can, took a deep breath, and headed for the elevator.

The doors opened on the third floor into a dimly lit hallway. She walked toward room 313. Memories of the nights that she and John had spent in hotel rooms just like this, after long hours in the field, overwhelmed her.

They'd been covered with soot, exhausted, reviewing the details of whatever crash they'd been working on. Smoke lingering on their clothes never overpowered their concentration. Minds engaged; she'd loved every minute of it. And then she met Bill, and he took her away from it all.

The National Transportation Safety Board had been her world, and for the last ten years she had been living a new life. Standing in front of the door, she hesitated, and then slid the key into the slot. "Knock, knock," she called, opening the door.

John grinned as he strode toward her. "I'm glad you're here, Kathryn." He took her hands in his, and gently squeezed. "I missed you. More than you know."

Pushing sixty, John didn't look a day over fifty despite his hair turning to silver. He looked good, and his warm hands brought her comfort. He held hers longer than she'd expected, not that she minded. She'd missed him, too.

"I hope you don't mind avoiding the office, but I thought we could watch the conference here without interruption."

His office had always been filled with chaos. But Kathryn felt a twinge of guilt not telling him ahead of time she wasn't accepting the offer, she could have saved him the trouble. She walked to the window and stared into fog that hung over the bay.

"I'm sorry to waste your time," Kathryn said, turning to face him. "When I told Bill about your offer, he wasn't happy. He doesn't want me to take the job."

"He won't let you work?" John asked. It wasn't often you could read McAllister's face. Today she saw not only surprise but also shock.

"Not exactly."

"When did you become the type of woman who allows a man to tell her what she can or cannot do?" She raised her eyebrows, and his eyes locked onto hers. "I'm sorry. That was inappropriate."

Inappropriate or not, there were so many things she wanted to say. The truth was that she didn't know. "I'm not sure. Maybe it happened somewhere between 'I do' and 'you're having twins.'"

He moved to the couch and patted the cushion beside him. "You came. You must be considering the offer." He filled two glasses with iced tea. "Sit, please."

"I came here to apologize and tell you in person I can't do this. Not now."

John's eyes narrowed. "I'm sorry to hear that. The department needs you. I need you."

"The door isn't closed forever. We're leaving it on the table for a month. As soon as Bill's done campaigning and settled, I'll approach him again. He's just…overworked right now."

She wanted to tell John how much she needed to return. A need that had smoldered in her soul for years, until he ignited it. Instead, she sat on the opposite end of the couch, accepted the glass of tea, and stared at the ice. She loved her children and husband, but she needed more. Her heart had danced through the previous twenty-four hours since he'd called and offered her a job. This was a dream she'd yearned for since the day she'd quit.

"If he's worried about the kids we could work around your schedule. We'd give you flexible hours. At this point, I think they'd be willing to give you just about anything."

"That was his excuse." She sipped her tea. "I don't believe it. I think the stress of the election has thrown him off."

"I'm sorry." John ran his hand through his hair and sighed. Silence weighed heavily between them before he spoke. "Shall we order something to eat and watch the press conference anyway?"

"I'd like that."

He ordered turkey sandwiches and a second pitcher of iced tea.

"Do you mind if I show you where we're at?"

Truth be told, she'd love to take a look at the files, but she was afraid that if she did, she wouldn't be able to push them away. She'd get sucked in, unable to turn back. But what could one look hurt? "Sure. I'd like that."

John walked across the room and retrieved his briefcase. He set it on the coffee table and opened it. "We're lost. We haven't a clue where to look next. Regional was the third in a series of accidents that have been left open, and we're no closer today in understanding why these planes are crashing than when the investigations first started. The media is throwing suppositions at us. We're overloaded with Senators breathing down our necks, and the FAA is creating regulations to pacify the public. We don't have time to figure out what's happened to the last plane before another goes down."

"I'm not sure what I could've done."

"I wanted you to visit the families, look at the files, listen to the tapes. Do whatever it is you needed to discover what we've been missing. I know there's something there. We just can't see it. We're too close and too overloaded. I know you'd find that missing link."

"You give me too much credit."

"Wrong. We never gave you enough credit."

"But you've got to have someone in the department who can review these cases."

"Nobody like you. You have experience, insight, and compassion. We need somebody with all that, plus your determination." He removed a stack of manila folders from his briefcase and set them on the table, then moved the briefcase to the floor. "The fact that you're married to a pilot could open doors with the families. I don't mean to be sexist, but wives would be more apt to confide in you, being a woman."

"May I?" Kathryn opened the top file. First Officer Sandra Evans from the Regional Air crash, the most recent accident. She was twenty-three years old when she died. Her father was deceased and she'd lived with her mother in Burien, ten minutes from Kathryn's home. She had commuted to Chicago the day of the crash.

Kathryn picked up the photo and looked into the eyes of the young woman. Sandra smiled from beneath her pilot hat. Aviator sunglasses hung from her right shirt pocket, and three stripes were displayed on each shoulder. Her long blonde hair flowed freely. Her expression reminded Kathryn of her daughters' enthusiasm for life. She'd been a beautiful girl. Now she was dead, and nobody knew why. Kathryn closed the file.

"John, will you excuse me?"

Kathryn stepped into the bathroom and locked the door. "Dammit," she whispered.

She had an opportunity to do something important. But now

was not the time to add one more thing to Bill's plate. She couldn't take the job, not after his objection. Maybe later. Closing her eyes, she could see Sandra's face. She had never looked at a file photo, or into the face of a victim, and felt the emotion that she did now. John had taught her how to stay detached, but her civilian life had undone that lesson.

WHEN SHE RETURNED, John was placing her phone and hairbrush back into her purse.

"Sorry. I knocked it off the table," he said, handing her the bag. "Are you okay?"

"Yeah, I'm fine."

John paced, rubbing his forehead. "My biggest concern is there's something we're missing that would prevent another accident. I don't ever want to put another family through a loss like this."

"I don't either." She wanted to scream. If only the timing of all this had been better. But there was never a good time for an airline crash.

John stopped pacing and turned toward her. "I have an idea. What would you think of coming back to work in an unofficial capacity? You could be an independent contractor. We wouldn't have to tell Bill."

She walked to the window and placed her hands on the sill and stared into Elliott Bay. Could she work without telling Bill? Her mind was a kaleidoscope of confusion. Kids, Bill, doubt, and fear swirled by in rapid succession. A different picture emerged each time a wave crashed against a pylon. "Is that possible?" she finally asked with her back to him.

"Yes. I think it is. I could pay you a consulting fee. You could create your own schedule. Work around the family. Kathryn, I'd be extremely indebted to you if you could help. As would the hundreds of families who've lost people they loved." He placed a hand on her shoulder and gently squeezed. "Not to mention the lives you'll save by preventing another crash."

She not only heard his words, but she felt them deep within her soul. She slapped the sill and turned. "Yes. Let's do it. But Bill can't know, not yet."

"Are you sure?"

"When the election's over I *will* tell him. But for now, I won't add to his stress."

Her heart raced. She had one week to get a jump on the case, and then she could work while the girls were at school. She didn't need anyone to know that she was involved. Stopping airplanes from falling out of the sky would be reward enough.

"This is fantastic." John leaned against the sill beside her and folded his arms. "You know, since 9/11 we've done an excellent job keeping the terrorists out of the flight deck. Mandated bulletproof security doors, airline procedures with exit and entry strategies... You know the drill. Don't get me started on airport security.

"The point is that the government has made a very good *show* of beefing up security. We know that terrorists are still riding as passengers on our planes trying to find a loophole to gain access to the flight deck. And now perfectly good airplanes are crashing and killing hundreds." John stood upright, turned, and stared out the window. "And we can't stop it."

"You think terrorists are involved?"

"I don't know what to think anymore." He turned and faced her. "What we do know is that experienced pilots made mistakes that shouldn't have been made. We know that there were a few, minor, maintenance issues, but nothing big enough to cause a plane to go down. Besides the first officers being new, the captains had all been highly educated and experienced pilots with military backgrounds. Hell, the Regional captain was a check airman."

Kathryn moved to the table and opened Grant Madden's file. He had over 20,000 hours of flight time. He'd been a check airman for the previous thirteen years. He was one of the best. And then there was Sandra. She'd been flying for six months. The media had ripped her to shreds for commuting across the country the night before her flight and flying with a cold.

"Where do you want me to start?"

"I need you to contact the families, and interview the spouses. Find out what we've missed."

"Can you get me the transcripts and recordings?"

"Yes. But without you officially on staff, it may take a while to get them pulled without anyone knowing. Until then, focus on the families and see what you can discover on the home front. Find out if any of the pilots were having personal problems that could have impacted their performance. See if you can get the wives to talk about their husbands' demeanor."

Kathryn sat on the couch and opened another folder and perused it. But her mind was on Bill, not the file. She hoped she wasn't making a mistake.

"I'll only be able to work when Bill's out of the house. My ability to travel to their homes will be limited. Dangit John, I may have lost my touch."

"I highly doubt that. In fact, I'm betting on the opposite." John stood and pointed the remote at the television, turning the power on.

Kathryn felt nauseous, and another headache was starting to grow. She squeezed the bridge of her nose and shook her head.

She was digging through her purse when she realized John was watching her.

"Are you feeling all right?"

"Just a little headache." She smiled. "I couldn't be better." She opened the bottle of Tylenol and swallowed one, then handed him a blank disk and asked him to record the conference.

He was her ally, and together they'd figure this out. She glanced to her right and John was smiling.

CHAPTER 7

"*W*HILE *the recent accidents appear to be random, we have identified a single thread of commonality…*"

John sat silently with Kathryn as they listened to the United States Attorney General speak. There was nothing he wanted more than to stop these tragedies, but he hoped they'd found nothing new. He needed time—time to solve these crimes himself.

"They appear to be due to the complacency towards known threats… primarily inclement weather and maintenance. Over the preceding twenty-four months we've experienced five major airline accidents, three in this year alone… This is the worst home-grown disaster our nation has faced in years…"

When John realized the attorney general didn't have any new information, he smiled. The doors of opportunity remained opened. He knew what Kathryn was capable of better than anyone, and with her help he would succeed. He also knew Walker would be furious when he learned of his and Kathryn's arrangement. But it was the best he could do, despite Walker's orders.

"He hasn't said anything we haven't already heard," Kathryn said.

"No, he hasn't. Looks like it's all up to you."

She gave him a sideways glance then returned her attention to the television.

"…While we have yet to determine if any aircraft malfunctions were the source of these accidents, airline executives, in conjunction

with the FAA, say that all aircraft are inspected within regulatory safety
standards as they age…"

"This guy is a puppet," Kathryn said as she reached for her glass.

"It appears that way." John folded his arms and leaned into the
couch. The attorney general repeated what his advisors wanted the
nation to hear. They were no closer to understanding the perplexity
of these accidents than they had been three months prior.

"…We assure you, these accidents have been all but…"

When the attorney general finished his speech he requested a
moment of silence for the lives lost. Then questions began. Was
it true that the first officer had commuted all night? Was it true
she was sick? Was it true she was talking when she shouldn't have
been? Was it true that other flights had landed in that storm?
John frowned in disappointment. The media's need for ratings
overshadowed the truth, as always.

Channel Five News cut from the attorney general and played a
clip of the voice recorder shortly before impact from the Regional
Air crash. The only distinguishable voice was the first officer Sandra
Evans. When the regularly scheduled show returned, Kathryn stood
and turned off the television. She removed the disk, placed it in the
plastic case and walked to the window.

"I can't believe they played that recording again," she said,
staring out the window. When she turned toward him, passion
burned in her eyes. "Everyone assumed it was the girl's fault for
commuting all night and being sick. They blamed her for being
inexperienced. It's not right."

"One of the problems is commuter airlines *are* putting kids
with low flight-time in planes. The FAA is currently working on
legislation that will require first officers to have fifteen hundred
hours before they're allowed to fly commercially."

"What about the captain's, are their requirements increasing too?"

"No."

"That's ridiculous." Kathryn placed her hands on her hips, and tapped her fingers. "So the captain and the first officer are both required to have fifteen hundred hours? Two fifteen-hundred-hour pilots do not make three thousand hours of experience."

"You're preaching to the choir," John said, forcing concern to remain on his face. *Kathryn is back.* "Another FAA reaction to a problem that they don't know how to solve, just to appease the media, and the public."

"So they're blaming these accidents on the first officers?"

"Appears that way," John said.

"Another reason to find the truth. If I worked for the FAA things would be a heck of a lot different under my watch."

"Wait a minute, young lady. We may have let you go to become a wife and mother, but there is no chance in hell I'm losing you to the Feds."

Kathryn had always been a protector of the truth, and a defender of the dead. But she'd never shown emotion for those she protected before. Passion for the job, yes. Not for the people affected. He liked the new side to this woman, a side that might be beneficial. But he'd be damned if he'd lose her to the Federal Aviation Administration. She'd never fit in within their bureaucratic walls, anyway.

John, now, had two concerns—Regional Director Walker and Captain Bill Jacobs.

CHAPTER 8
FRIDAY: LOS ANGELES

BILL LAZILY extended his legs across the chaise lounge, making himself at home. His uniform lay on the bed inside the house, and he wore nothing but his boxers. With hands behind his head, eyes closed, he relaxed in the warmth of the afternoon sun. Moments like this were few and far between, by his choice of course. He was two months away from completion then the control would be his. His heart beat a little faster at the thought.

The fog had dissipated before his arrival, and a comforting haze encased Los Angeles. A forty-minute cab ride, and he was in Beverly Hills. He loved this schedule—a short flight, and an eight-hour payday that left him five hours to conduct business before he returned to Seattle. He'd make phone calls and deal with union issues.

His iPhone chirped. He glanced at the message. Union members were aligning forces with who they thought would win the Airline Pilots Organization presidency. Word was out that he was the man and the election was just a formality—of course he was. "We're almost there Dad," he whispered.

Bill had always understood the power of an airline crash. But when American Airlines buried a Boeing 757 into the hills of Columbia in '95, and the entire world learned it was due to pilot error, Bill knew what he had to do. It wasn't the pilots' fault they'd been trained puppets that had lost their situational awareness. It was at that moment Bill realized his destiny.

Control over an industry would be his. He closed his eyes and thought of the years of work it took him to get to this point. His patience and strength were paying off. To his surprise, the surge of energy and power that came with control had been an added plus. He breathed it in.

Bill's vision had always been with a single-minded focus, locked onto running the union and controlling his airline. His union was the first step. In a couple years, he'd be the head of all pilot unions, and respect would return to the airline industry. Then it was only a matter of time until he'd be invited into the government where he could control his industry. Airlines—the one group that connected the world, and flew potential weapons of mass destruction into every city.

Bill closed his eyes and visited his father's grave to update him on his progress. *It won't be long until the companies pay for what they're doing to our pilots. For what they did to you. I'm so close Dad. I wish you could be here to see it. You'd be so proud.*

BILL STOOD with his ear against his parent's bedroom door and listened. His mother was crying and screaming at his dad. His dad had been crying too—a first. He was saying something about loving his job. Bill knew how much daddy loved to fly. Why would he cry? But then his dad yelled, "I can't even send Billy to college! Don't you get it? They fired my ass! We have nothing! We'll all be on the street within the month!"

"William, don't do this!" His mom yelled. "Stop!"

Bill pulled the door open slamming it against the wall and yelled "*Daaaddy!*" when he saw the gun. His eyes locked with his father's a moment before the explosion occurred. His daddy's body crumpled to the floor and there was nothing but a hole where his face had been. Bill ran to his father and pressed his body against his chest. "Daddy! Daddy! No!" he cried.

"Billy. Stop!" his mother yelled. She pulled him back, but he broke free and lay on his dad again, grasping his father's chest and hanging on tight. Then rage surfaced within him. He pushed back and pounded his fists onto his father's chest, as he sobbed.

Over his mother's tears and her yelling at him, a man's voice yelled, "Stop! Put your hands up."

"Why daddy, why?" Billy cried harder, as he pounded. Then he noticed the gun. As he reached for it something slammed into his back, shooting pain down his spine, and smashing his head to the floor. His arms were yanked behind his back and his face pressed into a pool of his father's blood. He began to choke as he breathed thick ooze into his lungs, tasting the warmth of his father's life as it flowed through him.

He heard the crack first then pain shot through his neck as they jerked his arms behind his body. Cold metal wrapped around one wrist then the other and pulled tight, cutting off his circulation. Then he—

"WHAT ARE YOU DOING in my house?" a voice growled as a hand grabbed his forehead, and a knife's blade pressed against his throat.

Bill jerked, and then he froze.

"I was invited," he said. Then his phone rang.

"Don't."

He gently set it on the ground.

"Who do you think you are? Acting like you own the place."

"Nobody was supposed to be home," he said.

"Plans change. You should know that better than anyone."

Bill glanced toward the backyard. The landscaping was well maintained, but mature. There was no way the neighbors could see anything from where he lay. His attention returned to the cold metal against his flesh.

"You don't have the nerve. Put that thing down before you hurt someone."

"Don't test me. Hands back. Now," she whispered.

This could be fun, he thought. He hesitantly extended both arms behind the back of the chair, and Kristen tied one wrist. Perspiration beaded on his forehead. But when she secured his second arm, and pulled tight, he saw red. The pounding of his heart rate shifted to an unbearable beating in his head.

"Release me. Now!" Bill roared.

"What's your problem?" Kristen said. He didn't respond, but when she looked into his eyes, she quickly yanked the knife against the nylon, and freed one of his hands. "I thought you would like to have a little fun," she said, dropping the knife onto the patio beside him. She turned and ran to the pool then dove in.

Bill rolled onto his side, picked up the knife, and slid it through the bondage with shaking hands. Standing, he gripped the knife tight, and watched Kristen swim toward him. He walked slowly to the edge of the pool to meet her when she emerged. But she did a flip turn and swam away. He closed his eyes.

His body continued to tremble but he sucked a deep breath, and took his mind down to the place that protected him. He dropped the knife, opened his eyes, and turned toward the house.

HE RETURNED naked sipping a beer, as Kristen hung on the edge of the pool and stared.

"Don't you have to fly back to Seattle tonight?" she asked.

"I do." He turned a patio chair toward the pool and sat. Spreading his legs wide, he touched himself as he sipped. He calmed his heart rate with each solid stroke.

Kristen climbed out of the pool and wrapped a towel around her waist. When she passed him he grabbed the towel and held her in place. "Where are you going?"

"To make some lunch," she said, attempting to pull from his grip.

"Did I say you could go?" He tossed his beer into the pool and used one hand to rip the towel from her body. The other hand grabbed a handful of hair. He pulled her face close to his. "I do believe it's your turn to be punished."

"Shit, Bill, that hurts."

He laughed and stood, holding tight to a fistful of hair. He pulled her toward the chaise lounge and threw her face down. She cried out when her face hit the frame. When she tried to rise, he put a foot on her back.

"Not yet."

"Let me up you asshole," she cried, fighting him. "This isn't funny. You're hurting me."

Bill laughed and pressed his foot into her back. She was quite the little rodeo queen and had a mouth to match. But she loved the rough stuff, and that worked well for him. Something he'd never had with Kathryn. He waited her out—five minutes and she was completely still. A record.

He lifted his foot, and within seconds she was on her hands and knees trying to escape. He grabbed her hips, held her tight with both hands, and plunged deep inside her from behind as she screamed. His smile and arousal grew as he tightened his grip.

"WHERE'S THE REMOTE?" Bill yelled from the living room, as he called his voicemail. He'd missed three calls. Kristen walked into the room, pointed the remote at the television, turned it on, and tossed it at him.

"Do you want mayo?" she asked, holding an ice bag on her cheek.

Bill shook his head and waved her off with the back of his hand. He listened to the first message. Kristen stood in place for a moment then left him alone.

Money he'd spent on the private detective paid off. He knew Kathryn would take the job despite his saying no. Her desire to solve airline crashes overpowered anything he'd tell her. He chuckled. Little did she know, but she was nothing more than his puppet. He just had to put the game in motion and pull the strings, she'd do the rest.

Once Kristen was out of earshot, Bill pressed speed dial.

"Jacobs here. What do you have?"

"She's gone into the Edgewater Inn, been there an hour. What do you want me to do?"

Bill glanced at his watch. "Make sure she doesn't leave the city until after three."

"How do I do that?"

"That's what I'm paying you to figure out." Bill whispered with severity that made his message clear. He closed his eyes and shook his head. Patience. He needed to make sure Kathryn stayed away from the school until the bus was gone.

Kristen returned to the room, but didn't speak. *What does she want now?* "Hold on," Bill said to the detective. He put the call on hold and waited. Kristen stood in the doorway. "What is it sweetie?" he finally asked.

Arms folded, she leaned against the doorframe. "I'm not waiting until December. I'm quitting this week."

CHAPTER 9

"OH MY GOD!" Kathryn yelled looking at her watch. She was supposed to be at the girls' school by 3:00 p.m. It was 2:30. She grabbed her purse and dug for her phone. She pressed speed dial and paced.

"Are you okay?" John asked.

Kathryn nodded, then held up a finger when her friend Jackie answered. "Thank God you haven't left. Could you swing by my house and pick up the girls' stuff and meet me at the school?"

"Sure. Where are you?"

"I'm on my way, I'll be there in twenty-five minutes."

Kathryn closed her phone and dropped it into her purse. She pulled on her jacket. How could she have lost track of time?

"Everything all right?"

"It is now." She threw her purse over her shoulder. "But I came close to winning the worst mother of the year award. I have to run."

"You've got my cell. Make sure you use it," John said. "There's enough information in here for you to get started." He handed her the folders and opened the door.

"I will. Thank you."

She gave John a quick hug then ran down the hallway. She took the stairs instead of wasting time on the elevator, and then ran out the main entrance of the hotel and down the sidewalk. Flying past the piers, racing toward her car, she dodged bodies, apologizing in the wake of people that she bumped. She was amazed that she hadn't broken her neck in her high heels.

Twenty minutes to get out of town. It was almost rush hour, but she could make it. She ran across the street and horns honked. A black Tahoe laid on its horn so loud that she thought she'd have a heart attack. *What a jerk.* She was easily three car lengths from him.

Keys in hand, she opened the door quickly, climbed into her car, and backed out of the parking lot. Within minutes she was on Alaskan Way and headed towards the viaduct. This route was a quick connect to 509 and an easy escape out of the city.

Then she slammed on her brakes. Four cars ahead, a hood was raised—the black Tahoe. It served him right, but she didn't need this. She tapped her hand on the steering wheel. "Come on. Move!"

There was absolutely no reason she couldn't make it if she could just get past a few cars. If everyone would go around that idiot, she could still see her daughters off. She looked left to see if she could cut across the divide, but oncoming traffic prevented that.

She slapped the steering wheel again. "I can't believe this." She blew the horn like an impatient fool. Then put the car in park and hit the steering wheel three more times. "Dammit! Dammit! Dammit!" She glanced at her watch and dialed Jackie's cell.

"Kat, where are you? They've almost finished loading the buses."

"I'm stuck in traffic behind a stalled car. Are the girls there?"

"Yeah."

"Can I talk to them?"

"Mom, where are you?" Jenny cried.

"Honey, I'm so sorry. I'm stuck in traffic and I'm not going to make it." The silence that ensued killed her. "I'll make it up to you, sweetie. Jenny…"

"No Mom, it's me, Jess. Why's Jen crying? Did something

happen at the doctor's?"

"No. I'm fine. The doctor said all my tests looked great. But I can't make it to see you off. I'm stuck in traffic. Baby, I'm sorry."

"That's okay. I'm glad you're fine. We were really worried. Jen will get over it. Don't worry Mom. We love you."

"I love you too, sweetheart. Give Jenny a hug for me."

She dropped her phone on the seat, but not before she heard Jenny yell that she hated her. A thread of guilt wove into her heart. She'd been a nightmare as a teenager and hadn't given her mother an inch.

Closing her eyes, she fought off a wave of nausea and dropped her head on the steering wheel. She wasn't sure which was more heartbreaking—Jenny's yelling, or Jessica's understanding.

CHAPTER 10

KATHRYN PULLED into her driveway and stared at her quiet home. Her headlights illuminated the fog that drifted around the corners. The feeling that someone was about to jump out of the bushes raised hairs on her neck. She pulled herself from her car and quickly unlocked the front door. She'd never let her daughters down before. They'd get over it, but she still felt horrible. Maybe a "nobody's perfect" lesson was long overdue. She closed the door, then removed her coat and kicked off her pumps.

This was the first time she'd lost track of time and hadn't been there when they needed her. She hung her coat in the entryway, and walked silently to the living room. She dropped the files on the coffee table then flipped the switch to ignite the gas fireplace. She held her hands in front of it, and rubbed. Then she glanced over her shoulder. The folders called to her, and she had no choice but to answer.

Contemplating where to begin, she sat on the couch and fanned the folders out over the mahogany coffee table. It didn't take her long before she ran to Bill's office and found the essentials. Paper. Pen. Post Its. She copied each crewmember's name on a legal pad, leaving space under each for an address, phone number, the airline where they worked, and spouse's name. Sandra, like the other first officers, wasn't married.

When she finished categorizing the names, she picked up the

phone and dialed the first number.

"Hello?" a female voice answered.

"Hi, my name is Kathryn Jacobs. I'm working with the NTSB and we're—"

"Can't you people just leave me alone? Haven't we been through enough?" The woman slammed the phone down.

Mouth open, Kathryn listened to the dial tone for a moment. "Okay, that went well." She dialed the second number, but this time the answering machine picked up on the first ring. She left her cell number and a short message. The third and fourth numbers went directly to voicemail, and the fifth and sixth numbers were both disconnected.

She pulled a couch pillow over her face, leaned back and screamed. *Nobody said this would be easy.*

A deep breath, and she dialed again.

"Hello?"

"Mrs. Evans, my name is Kathryn Jacobs. I work for the NTSB. She paused. "I was wondering if I could talk to you about your daughter's accident."

"Did you find something new?"

"I'm sorry, we didn't."

"Then what's there to talk about?"

Excellent question. Kathryn wanted to crawl into a hole. Sandra was young, had no bills, no insurance, and was at the beginning of her life. The photo of the young lady filled with life smiled at her from her coffee table. Kathryn felt foolish calling Sandra's mother. What could she possibly learn?

"I'm contacting the families to see if there was anything or anyone unusual in the crewmembers' lives. We're still trying to put the pieces together."

"There was nothing in Sandy's life that was unusual. We all loved her. I miss her so much, but she's with her father now."

"I'm sure your daughter was a good pilot, and I'm going to find out what happened. I know that it won't bring her back, but maybe you'll find some comfort in knowing she did everything she could."

"That would mean a lot. I only wish I'd never let her go to work that night. She hadn't been feeling well."

Kathryn sank into the couch and closed her eyes. "There are many pilots flying sick these days, not just your daughter. I don't know if you could have stopped her, even if you tried. There's too much pressure on showing up."

"Do you have children?"

"I do. Twin daughters. They're ten."

"Love them as much as you can, and don't take them for granted. You never know how little time you have." Mrs. Evan's voice cracked.

"Mrs. Evans, do you think maybe we could have a cup of tea sometime? I would love for you to meet my girls."

"I'd like that. Thank you."

They said their goodbyes. Kathryn pulled the pillow close and rolled over onto her side. Then her phone rang—a number she'd just dialed.

"Is Kathryn Jacobs in? This is Linda Madden."

"This is she. Thank you for returning my call," Kathryn said, sitting upright. "I'm investigating your husband's accident. I was wondering if we could get together and talk."

"I'd like that."

"Would you be available tomorrow?"

"How about two?"

Kathryn confirmed Mrs. Madden's address and said goodbye.

She'd doodled a fluffy cloud around Mrs. Evans's and Mrs. Madden's phone numbers, while she talked, with lightning bolts between all the numbers. Five of the seven numbers were 206 area codes, Seattle. One was from 509, Yakima, and the other, 360, Olympia. Three different airlines. Accidents in two different countries and three different states. But all the pilots involved lived within a two-hundred-mile radius of each other.

She was writing herself a note to ask John about earlier accidents when the phone rang. Jackie's number flashed across the face. Kathryn closed her eyes, preparing for a lecture.

"Darby told me you couldn't make it tonight. Please come. I made lasagna. I really need to talk to you both." Jackie blew her nose. "She also said that I was supposed to make you show up or she'd be, and I quote, hunting your ass."

"An ass-hunting sounds fun, but how can I pass up lasagna?" Besides, Bill wasn't coming home after his flight. Her house suddenly felt too empty.

"Greg won't be home until late." Jackie blew her nose again. "He says he's got a *union* meeting after he lands."

"Jackie, there *is* a union meeting tonight. Is everything all right sweetie?"

"Yeah. Fine. I'll see you in an hour." Jackie hung up the phone before Kathryn could say good-bye or thank her for helping with the kids.

Chapter 11

O N AUTOPILOT, Greg Jameson pressed the button that would carry him to the tenth floor. It was shortly after 5:00 p.m. in Seattle, but his body was convinced it was after midnight. He'd just arrived from New York, Tokyo the day before, and all he wanted to do was go home and peel the uniform off that had been part of his skin for the previous two weeks. He needed a cold beer and a warm bed, and he wanted to sleep for a very long time next to Jackie.

He'd been awake since 3:00 a.m., compliments of jetlag and multiple time zones. The end to the twelve-day trip from hell. During the flight home he'd mused over the days and laughed. His captain had asked him what was so funny. "It's either laugh or cry," he'd answered. The bemused expression on the captain's face made Greg laugh even harder. He eventually told the captain to ignore him. It had just been an exhausting trip, and he was losing it.

The elevator stopped, and the doors unveiled a dimly lit hallway leading to Doc Adams's office.

Everyone had already gone home for the night. Greg was thankful Adams worked odd hours to accommodate his schedule. He entered the reception area.

His two-hour appointment would finish in time for him to make the union meeting. He glanced at his watch and figured with luck he could be in bed by midnight. Unfortunately, luck hadn't been in his corner for a long time.

Greg glanced at the chairs and the end table. He'd read all the magazines. Besides, if he sat, he'd fall asleep. Instead he walked to the window.

The office overlooked SeaTac Airport. Five planes formed a line for departure with a northerly flow. The tail of the Boeing 767 he'd brought in from New York sat at the gate. She would come and go, and in another thirty-four hours he could be gluing his butt to the seat once again.

He turned his attention to the south end of the field, and frowned. A corporate 747 was positioned on the general aviation ramp with her interior lights glowing. At one time he'd known that aircraft as intimately as the bird he now flew for Coastal Airlines, but she'd never found her way to Seattle before. He wondered why she was here now, and if his friend Amir had brought her in. It had been a month since they last spoke and they needed to talk.

"Good evening, Greg," a familiar voice said.

Familiarity didn't prevent Greg from jumping. In addition to fatigue, his nerves stood on the fringe of bankruptcy and fought for solvency daily.

"Hey, Doc." Greg said, turning from the window.

"It's a beautiful evening," Adams said, extending his hand. "How was the flight?"

Adams used both hands as he shook Greg's. One hand gripped his firmly, the other covered them in protection of the confidences they shared. It had taken Greg a while to trust Dr. Adams, but he was thankful he could.

"I'm here," he said with a forced grin.

"That bad, huh?" Adams held the door to his inner office open.

"Twelve days of hell that included delays, wind shear, two missed approaches, an engine failure, a security breach, an improper fuel load, and a passenger who had a heart attack. But other than that, I had a ball. Y'know, just livin' the dream." Greg smiled. "Sorry, Doc."

Maybe counseling after a long trip and jetlag wasn't such a good idea. He hated sounding like a whiner. That was the single most annoying thing about work—listening to captains bitch for hours on end about how bad work was. He refused to become one of them.

"No apologies. This is your safe zone."

"I'm just tired." Greg settled into the comfort of the leather chair and scanned the walls. Every time he took this seat he admired Dr. Adams's accomplishments.

Parchment certificates filled the walls, indicating Adams's training had been at the best schools. Books, some of which Adams had written, lined the shelves. It didn't matter how many times Greg sat in the hot seat, Dr. Adams's life's work continued to impress him. There had been a time when Greg thought he was something, being a pilot, but compared to Dr. Adams, well, he knew otherwise. In addition, Adams couldn't be more than five years older than Greg.

There had been a time when being an airline pilot was a respected profession, a time when pilots made an excellent living. There would always be pilot jobs. Someone was needed to monitor the planes. But nothing they could call a profession—not the pay, the days off, or the respect that once belonged to an airline career.

Those times were lost with an industry gone astray. He, and most of his friends, had become bondservants to a dying profession. Their passion had morphed into a need to survive, with a vestige of memories to keep them company on layovers while their families were home. All he wanted to do anymore was be home with Jackie and his son, Chris. But that wasn't an option.

Adams removed Greg's folder from the cabinet and turned pages.

He set the file on his desk, closed his eyes, and raised steepled fingers under his chin. This behavior had once made Greg uncomfortable. But now he enjoyed the quiet time to relax, and to allow his mind to wander with no expectations.

Dr. Adams had worked with their pilot's union for eleven years. The Airline Pilots Organization had an exclusive to his time and talent, and Adams was based in Seattle.

Greg appreciated him more than he could express. Adams had guided him through many dark nights. But this time, he knew there was nothing that Adams could do or say to make it better.

When Adams opened the folder the second time he found a fresh page, then picked up a pen. "Besides the lousy trip, how are you feeling?"

"Good." Leaving out exhausted, frustrated, used, and hopeless.

"Everything okay at home?"

He glanced away. "Yeah. Nothing major."

"Nothing major?"

"Jackie put in her paperwork to go back to work."

"*Really?* How do you feel about that?"

"It's killing me, Doc. Staying home and taking care of Chris is her life. She loves the PTA, carpools, and being there when he comes home from school. She'd have had a dozen kids if we could've afforded it."

"What has *she* said about her return?"

"Nothing, of course. Which makes it worse."

"Do you think that helping her family will give her a sense of self?" He spoke softly now. "To be needed is a powerful thing."

"She is needed," Greg said abruptly. "Chris and I need her." Selfish, he knew. But who'd be there for Their son when they were both out of town? The only way to make this work was if they bid opposite schedules, and then he would never see his wife. No, her returning to work was not a good thing.

"And Chris?"

"He left for camp today. And I may be gone before he returns. I won't see him for three weeks." He paused. "I did everything I could to get the time off."

"I'm sorry." Adams folded his arms over his chest and leaned back in his chair. "Last time we spoke, you mentioned you were working on something to pay off the mortgage. How's that going?"

Greg glanced toward the window. "Still in progress. But I'm good for the next month or so."

"Status on the captain upgrade?" Adams raised an eyebrow as he asked.

"There won't be one. They're furloughing two hundred first officers at the end of the month, with more cuts on the horizon. Deep cuts."

"I hadn't heard. I'm sorry." Of course he hadn't heard. Bill hadn't told anyone except Greg. But Adams would hear about it soon enough when the line formed at his door.

Greg's stalwart exterior deluded everyone except Dr. Adams. This chair was the only place he could disclose his fears and vulnerability. Jackie knew times were tough, but she had no clue as to the tar pit that immobilized them. How could he tell her? How could he tell Chris that his dad the airline pilot couldn't pay the bills and was losing their house?

He closed his eyes to avoid Adams's stare. He'd jumped the gun when he purchased his captain house prior to his upgrade. Shortly thereafter, the union negotiated pay cuts to keep the airline afloat but the airline furloughed regardless. His upgrade was postponed indefinitely. It wouldn't be so bad if they hadn't heard about the millions the CEO had pocketed.

He not only lost the pay increase to captain, but he took an additional thirty percent pay cut with all the pilots. His only option was to work more hours, see his family less, and become a slave to the job. For all that, he was still unable to make ends meet. He had no clue how he'd send Chris to college.

"Bill has big plans if he gets elected. But then I suspect we'll have to take four or five steps backwards before we make any headway," Greg said. "I think he's prepared to take a stand against the company."

"What do you think that'll do to the morale on the flight line?"

"It won't be pretty. But if they think there's hope, maybe the guys will suck it up."

Everyone was suffering, and the mood in the cockpit had shifted from oppression to fury. He'd tried to explain to the doctor what it was like on the flight line. Distraction was the one word that encompassed it all. But it was the constant complaining that was driving him out of his mind. If he didn't start a trip depressed, he certainly was after nine hours of another pilot's bitching.

"How will you deal with the backslide?"

"The jury's still out." Greg drummed is fingers on his leg. More silence.

"Tell me about that heart attack."

Greg hesitated a moment before he spoke. "We were flying out of Osaka and not yet halfway to San Francisco when the lead flight attendant told us there was a problem." He continued to drum his fingers on his leg. "There's not much more to say. The lead did a good job and found a doctor who worked with him. They used the defibrillator." He stopped speaking, and closed his eyes, pausing for several seconds.

"He died." Greg opened his eyes, pain weighing heavily within them, and stared at Dr. Adams. "They moved him to an empty row and we didn't tell anyone. The poor guy was traveling with his son. They lied to the little guy. Told him his dad would be fine. We allowed everyone to think that he'd died after landing. I could hear his son's cries from the cockpit. He was Chris's age, and as it turned out, had no family in the States. He didn't even speak English."

"Hmmm." Dr. Adams wrote in the file.

"The guy was Japanese. He was on vacation. Had we returned to Japan we would've had to fill out a horrendous amount of paperwork. The captain would still be writing." When Adams didn't reply, Greg added, "Pressing on was a no-brainer."

"What happened to the little boy?"

"I don't know. Waiting to be shipped back to Osaka, I guess." Alone. The weight of that had haunted him for days. He rubbed his hand over his face and looked up at Adams. "We should've turned back like we were supposed to, and taken that little boy home. I'm not sure when they sent him back, but imagine his fear."

"How are you feeling about this?"

Greg shrugged. It wasn't just this. It was everything.

"I could give you something to relax, and a write a note for some time off."

"Thanks, Doc. As nice as that sounds, with the new work rules we only get paid 75% of regular pay on sick calls. I can't afford to take time off."

Adam's wrote a prescription, then scribbled on a sheet of paper and handed them both to him. "Hang onto these, just in case you change your mind. I really think you should reconsider taking some time off to rest. Be home when your son arrives. Spend some time with your family. You can't afford not to."

Greg took the paper and read the note, then stood. He walked to the window and glanced at the Boeing 747.

"I know you're right, Doc. If only I could."

Chapter 12

THE DOOR was unlocked and slightly ajar, and Kathryn slowly pushed it open. "Jackie?" There was no response so she let herself in. A fire crackled in the river-rock fireplace, candles flickered on the mantel, and something jazzy murmured in the air. But no Jackie. Italian spices wafting from the kitchen filled her nostrils, and her stomach growled.

"Jackie, it's me, Kat," she yelled. She walked through the living room and into the empty kitchen, then heard something crash in Greg's office. A chill flashed over her body. She ran down the hall. When she opened the door Jackie was on the floor.

Kathryn rushed to her side. "Are you all right?" A drawer was overturned, and the contents lay scattered everywhere.

"Jeez, Kat. You scared me," Jackie said. She righted the drawer and attempted to get it back on track, but when she couldn't, she dropped it. The clamor echoed throughout the room. Then her tears began to flow.

"Let me give it a try," Kathryn said. Within seconds she had the drawer back in its proper place. "Good as new."

Jackie gathered papers and stuffed them into the drawer, then slammed it closed. "It will never be good as new. Nothing will ever be right again," she said, with emotion spilling from her eyes.

Kathryn wrapped her arms around her friend. Jackie's sobs came in jagged heaves.

"Whatever it is, it's going to be okay." Kathryn stroked Jackie's hair. Jackie never shed tears unless they were of joy. She had the perfect marriage, perfect husband, and perfect life. Apparently everything wasn't what it appeared to be. Kathryn's heart ached for her, and whatever torment she was going through.

When her crying jag subsided Jackie stood, dabbed her eyes with a tissue, and returned the final scraps of paper to the drawer. "Let's get dinner ready. Darby will be here in a few minutes." She stuck the used tissue into her pocket and, with a forced smile, said, "I hope you're hungry."

"Starving." She followed Jackie into the kitchen and peeked in the upper oven. Lasagna bubbled. French bread browned below. "Everything looks great."

Jackie poured them each a glass of merlot, pretending that nothing had happened. If Kathryn hadn't seen the tears, she wouldn't have thought anything was amiss.

Kathryn sliced a pile of vegetables that lay on the cutting board. Jackie pulled the ingredients from the fridge for her 'world famous' dip. Green beans steamed on the stove. The two friends worked in silence, the air thick between them. Whatever was bothering Jackie, she obviously was not ready to talk about it.

Kathryn was pulling plates out of the cupboard when the front door slammed. She jumped. She and Jackie then shared a knowing smile—Darby's here.

Chapter 13

Once inside, Darby pulled the door closed. She hadn't meant to slam it. But closing doors firmly was a habit she'd developed the hard way after accidentally walking in on her fiancé years ago. Some habits were hard to break.

"Is there a paaarrrteee in here?" she yelled, entering the kitchen.

Due to excessive headwinds, and a late arrival, she'd driven directly from the airport to Jackie's house, with a slight detour to the market, and was still wearing her uniform. Her flight bag was in one hand, and a bag of limes in the other. "Put the lime in the tequila, and mix 'em all up," she sang. She dropped her flight bag on the floor and swung the bag of limes onto the counter.

Hands on hips, she looked back and forth between her two friends. The room had a bit of chill despite the temperature on the thermostat. She tapped a manicured nail on her hip. Tonight they were burgundy to match her lipstick, but that wasn't the point.

"What's going on ladies?"

"Not much." Kathryn said, hugging her then whispered, "I'll tell you later."

"Everything couldn't be better," Jackie said, nudging Kathryn away for a hug of her own. "Okay, ladies, I'll get dinner out of the oven and join you in two minutes." Jackie handed a wine bottle and a glass to Darby, piled plates and silverware into Kathryn's arms, and shooed them out of the kitchen.

They didn't go far. The main floor was one large living space. The only thing separating the kitchen from the dining room was a black marble counter. There was nothing between the dining room and living room, other than a fireplace on the far wall. Darby kicked off her shoes and headed toward her favorite spot.

She filled her glass, set the wine bottle on the bar, and then plunked her butt on the couch, while Kathryn set the table. She'd been sitting for the previous seven hours, but something about the cush of a couch made all the difference—her butt was finally happy. Then she thought of Neil and—

"Are you going to stay in that uniform all night?" Kathryn asked, placing silverware on the napkins.

"Hell no. But first things first." Darby took a drink then put her glass on the coffee table. This party needed a kick-start. Kat would fill her in on the details of whatever was up later, but for now the mood needed changing. With a deep breath, she theatrically forced herself from the couch. She took Kathryn's glass and set it aside. "We need to have a toast, and wine won't do."

Darby glided to the kitchen, ripped open the bag of limes with her teeth, and cut them with precision into small wedges, swaying to Billie Holiday. She opened her flight bag and removed a fifth of Patro'n. "Tequila, anyone?"

"Sweet. And *exactly* what I need," Jackie said.

"Compliments of a Tampa layover," Darby said. But when did Jackie need alcohol?

"How'd you get that through security?" Kathryn asked.

"Uniform, baby. While I'm wearing it, I can bring in any liquids I want."

"Are you serious?" Kathryn said. "What if some idiot wore a fake uniform to get through security and brought a jug of gasoline on the plane?"

Darby rolled her eyes. "What's the difference if he brought ten three-ouncers? None. So get me some glasses, and focus on the point—drinking."

Jackie produced three shot glasses. They all moved to the living room and sat around the coffee table. Darby filled their glasses and passed the bowl of limes.

"I forget, is it drink, lick, then suck?" Kathryn asked Darby.

"Whatever makes you feel good," she replied.

Darby licked her hand and sprinkled it with salt and Kathryn and Jackie did the same. She'd been trying to teach the girls the finer art of doing shots for a couple years now. Some things were a lost cause, but these two were worth the effort. Kathryn had been her rock for ten years, and there was nothing she wouldn't do for that woman. And Jackie, well… she'd do anything for her too. Yep, these were her friends and she loved them.

"To good friends, and to love." Darby extended her glass. "And Kat, I am so glad you're with us instead of that putz tonight." She wanted nothing more than for Kathryn to know the truth, but it wasn't her place to tell it. When Kat was ready, she'd discover it on her own.

"New opportunities." Kathryn raised her glass.

"To liars." Jackie extended hers.

Kathryn glanced at Darby then looked down. Far too much eye darting for normal cocktail hour behavior was occurring in this room. But Darby knew better than to try to pull anything out of Jackie, the shots would take care of that. Kathryn, on the other hand, had always been honest with her. If she wasn't talking, there was a reason.

They held their glasses together as they did every month—each occasion, a new toast. They licked the salt, downed their shots and bit the limes. Jackie closed her eyes and shook her head. Darby and Kathryn laughed. Jackie had never been much of a drinker. One shot was her limit, but that always meant more for Darby when Jackie pushed hers away.

"Okay, just one more, and then the entertainment." Darby poured three more shots, and was surprised when Jackie sucked down number two. She was glad to see Kathryn visibly relax, her shoulders melted before her eyes. Something she hadn't seen in a long time.

Darby changed the CD and turned up the music. "Girls Just Want to Have Fun" blared over the speakers. She unbuckled her belt, pulled it out of the loops, and tossed it on the floor, in time with the music. Then she slowly unzipped her pants, allowing them to fall. There was more than one way to brighten the mood.

"Oh baby!" yelled Kathryn, laughing.

"Come to mama," Jackie said, and then whistled.

Darby danced to the music, which manifested in more of a bounce. She removed her tie then held it between her legs and moved it forward and aft, a new move she'd just developed. Some things came more natural than others. The ladies were laughing so hard that tears streamed down Jackie's face.

"I think I wet my pants." Kathryn said.

"Too much information," Darby said, covering her ears and closing her eyes.

Kathryn laughed then yelled, "Take it off." She put a dollar in Darby's panties and said, "I'm not sure if these legally count as underwear."

She was right; they were nothing more than a piece of string.

"No kidding, somebody stole the bumcover," Jackie said.

Bumcover? Darby choked down a laugh. "A captain has her standards and panty lines are so unprofessional." She swung her hips and spanked her butt. Then slowly unbuttoned her shirt. She turned her back to them and opened it wide. She glanced over her right shoulder, then her left, and then she threw her shirt across the room.

"Ahh… Do they let you fly without a bra?" Kathryn asked. "Cute socks, by the way."

Darby looked down to her feet, forgetting what socks she was wearing. Her favorite red wool socks wiggled below her butt thong undies.

"The flight ops manual says nothing about a bra as part of the uniform," Darby said, joining in the laughter, then bowed. She'd taken her bra off before she came in, but she wouldn't tell them that. She winked, then skipped out of the room and got dressed. She returned wearing a red tank top and her Wonder Woman boxers. "Who first?" she asked.

"I think we need to hear about liars," Kathryn said. She glanced at Jackie, who stared into an empty shot glass.

"Liars it is," Darby said. "But I'm starving." She was the first to find her seat at the table, and curled one foot under her butt, the other leg dangled. And she waited for her friends to tell her who the hell the liar was. Liars were on the top of her least favorite list.

Jackie put another log on the fire, topped off their wine then sat next to Kathryn. Once they were all seated and plates filled, Jackie held up her wine glass. "I am so glad you guys are here. To friends."

"To friends," Kathryn and Darby said in unison.

Jackie sipped her wine, her eyes shifting between Kathryn and Darby over the edge of her glass. Darby pretended not to notice, and stabbed her lasagna then raised her fork. A long string of cheese hung, and she used her finger to wrap the strand around the fork then she stuffed the bite into her mouth. Kathryn picked at her salad.

"Okay, what's up?" Darby finally asked. "There is definitely something going on here."

Jackie swirled a green bean in the dip. "I think Greg's having an affair."

Darby looked at Kathryn, back to Jackie, and then started to laugh. Within moments Kathryn joined her. Jackie stuffed the bean into her mouth and glared. Then she, too, laughed.

"Shut up, you guys. Okay. I know it sounds stupid. But he's been so *off* lately." Tears filled Jackie's eyes, and her laughter stopped.

"You think your *perfect* husband is cheating?" Darby asked. She didn't want to minimize Jackie's concerns, but there was no way Greg would cheat. He loved his family. Greg and Jackie were good together.

"We haven't had sex for five weeks," Jackie said, overly serious again. "He says we're broke. He's gone all the time." Tears escaped and slid to her cheeks, and she wiped her face with the back of her hand. "On top of everything else, I've been snooping through his stuff, and I found, well, let's just say he's been keeping secrets from me. Huge secrets. And I can't tell him I know, because he'll know I've been spying."

"Oh, sweetie, that's a wife's job. You're supposed to spy on him." Darby patted her hand. "He'll get over it."

Kathryn handed Jackie a clean napkin. "Five weeks without sex doesn't mean anything, he's just under stress. I mean the poor guy is probably overwhelmed with the cutbacks."

Jackie stuck her fork into her salad and asked, "Okay, if he's not having an affair then what?"

"Male menopause," Darby said. "Don't worry, he'll get over that, too."

Jackie rolled her eyes.

Kathryn smiled and tossed a cherry tomato at Darby. "What's with the love stuff?"

"Neil had the nerve to tell me he loved me this morning." She allowed the weight of that statement to settle on the table. "I'm thinking about packing my bag and showing up on his doorstep. Or leave him until he's ready to commit." She sucked a bite of lasagna into her mouth. "The problem is… he's like a good buzz," she said with her mouth full. "The more I have of him, all sense disappears and the more I want. He's intoxicating. But the morning after, it sucks when he disappears. I'm beginning to wonder if the guy's a vampire."

"You need to break up with him," Jackie said. "If he's not willing to commit then he doesn't deserve you. Besides, Mr. Right will come along if Neil's out of the picture."

"He is Mr. Right. Mr. Right Now, that is."

The truth was, he was so much more than Mr. Right Now. He consumed her every thought, and gave her reason to hope and dream. He'd enabled her to fall in love again. A part of her she'd thought was gone forever had come alive. And being in love was so much fun.

Kathryn lifted her glass to her lips and sipped, then said, "Darby, if you're happy that's what matters. Just keep your eyes open and make sure you're getting what you need out of this relationship. But one day you *are* going to have to let us meet him."

"I'm working on that," Darby said. "Tell me, did Bill let you meet up with John?"

"That's where you were today? Jeez, Kathryn," Jackie said.

"Who's John, anyway?"

"He's my old boss from the NTSB," Kathryn said. "I met with him, but Bill doesn't know." She picked at a piece of cheese that had dried to her plate.

"You didn't tell him," Darby said. "Smart girl."

"No, I told him. And he didn't like the idea."

"I told you he was a dick, and—"

"Tell her the rest," Jackie said interrupting Darby. But before Kathryn could speak, Jackie continued. "Kat missed saying goodbye to the girls today and we almost didn't get their camping stuff to them in time because she was downtown." Jackie's silverware hit the plate with a clank. She was seriously overreacting.

"Come on, Jackie. This was an isolated event." Kathryn said.

"There is nothing more important than being there for your kids." Jackie pushed her plate away.

Jackie's reaction was major overkill. Darby now wished she hadn't mentioned the meeting.

"You know how much I love my girls. But there's no reason why I can't work." Kathryn spoke with alcohol-induced confidence, a confidence that Darby liked to see. "And I don't want Bill to know. Not yet. Not until after the election, so please don't tell him."

"What happened today is exactly why you should *not* be working," Jackie said, folding her arms. "Besides, when did you start lying to your husband?"

"That's not fair, Jack. She didn't lie to him, she just didn't tell him. Big difference." Darby stood and refilled Kathryn's wine glass, then placed a hand on her shoulder. "Besides, kids are important and it's great that you're there for them, but mothers need a life. Mothers are someone else's kids.

"If it's all about what's best for the kids, then those mother kids need what's best for them, too." Darby scrunched her brows together. "Shit. I've had too much to drink." She laughed and took another sip of wine. "You guys might have to cut me off." Not. She was glad that she could come to Kathryn's defense, for all the times Kat had stood by her.

After a moment of silence passed, Jackie spoke. "I'm sorry, Kat. I didn't mean anything." She put her face in her hands and shook her head, then sat up straight. "I'd just give anything to be in your shoes and not have to go back to work."

"You're coming back to work?" How did she miss that memo? Darby loved working with Jackie. They'd always had a great time on their layovers. This was great news. They should celebrate.

Jackie nodded. "Let's not talk about me working." She returned her attention to Kathryn and said, "Tell us what happened today."

"Well, to start with, I met John at the Edgewater Inn."

Darby's mouth dropped opened. "You slut!" Then she started laughing. "Kiss and tell."

"We didn't *do* anything. It was a working meeting. He wanted to watch that press conference. Oh, and we recorded a copy for you."

Kathryn began sharing the details of her meeting, trying to enunciate her words with a tequila-and-wine-saturated tongue. Darby initially laughed at the presentation. Kathryn definitely needed more practice drinking. Hell, if Darby had been married to Bill, she'd have already been an alcoholic. Kathryn amazed her in so many ways. She respected her on every level.

Kathryn continued, and Darby sobered as she listened. When Kathryn finished, she sighed and folded her hands in her lap.

"It's kind of scary," Jackie said, "not knowing why they crashed."

It would be scarier for Jackie being a flight attendant. She had no control over the outcome of a flight, and thought Greg, as a first officer, had less control than Bill or Darby had as captains.

"I don't know about scary, but I want to know what the hell is happening," Darby said. "This is seriously nuts."

"I keep wondering if the next accident will be Bill's," Kathryn added, then choked on her wine. "I didn't mean that the way it sounded." She covered her mouth. "Oh God, I've had too much to drink, too."

Darby couldn't allow the 'slam Bill' opportunity to slide. "So what would it take to buy him a one way ticket on one of those flights?"

"What's wrong with Bill?" Jackie asked. Darby rolled her eyes.

"Nothing," Kathryn answered. "He's just busy with his life. He's on a mission and feels compelled to save the world. We're just running parallel lives right now. But when I get working for the NTSB fulltime, we'll have more than enough to discuss. Just like when we first met." Kathryn sipped her wine, and then added. "He has one of the most brilliant minds. Quite honestly, he's missing his calling being a pilot. No offence Darby."

"None taken." She was right. Bill was brilliant. But that gave him no excuse to be cheating on Darby's best friend. She sometimes wondered if Kathryn knew, and just didn't want to acknowledge it.

"Besides," Kathryn said. "He absolutely adores the girls. You should see them together. The feeling is mutual, and it warms my heart to see so much love."

"Ohhh," Jackie cooed.

"Enough of the father daughter love crap," Darby said. "Is your former boss a hottie?"

"You *are* about to be cut off." Kathryn pulled Darby's glass away from her, splashing some of the contents onto the table. "Do they still say 'hottie'?"

"Don't avoid the question."

"He's cute." Kathryn replied, with that smug look of hers. "He's tall and he has these really dark brown eyes, the kind that stare through you. And he listens when you talk, like he cares about what you say."

"Sounds too good to be true," Darby said. "Did he get any?" She knew that Kathryn would never stray from Bill. As much as her husband was an ass, that didn't change Kathryn's behavior. But Darby still loved to tease her about the possibility. Some sport was just fun.

"Of course not, it's not like that. But he did hug me."

"He sounds nice." Jackie picked up her plate then tripped over a dishtowel, and dropped it onto the floor. Food and glass splattered everywhere. She froze, then looked up and started to laugh. "I know I've had too much to drink."

"Definitely, but we have only just begun." Darby slid her chair back, knocking it over, but catching it before it hit the floor. *Lightning quick reflexes.*

"How about we clean the dishes in the morning." Kathryn held a hand out to Jackie, and they stumbled into the living room together, laughing.

Darby filled their shot glasses. Kathryn raised an eyebrow when Jackie sucked down not only her own, but Kathryn's as well. Darby laughed. Somebody is going to be very sick in the morning.

Jackie's attempt to sit in the recliner, ended up with a butt slide down the front landing her ass on the floor. She began to laugh. Then her laughter turned to tears.

Kathryn swung her leg wide and sat on the recliner behind Jackie and rubbed her shoulders. "So what *did* you find in Greg's office?"

Chapter 14

GREG STOOD in the doorway. A near-empty tequila bottle sat in the middle of the table. Cards were flying. Clothes were scattered everywhere, and laughter filled the room. The women were obviously feeling no pain.

"I'll see you a pair of panties and raise you one shirt," Darby said.

"You're going to be butt naked," Kathryn responded. "You sure you want to do that?"

"Oh yeah." Darby set her cards on the table face down, then dug through her suitcase and produced a shirt and a pair of red panties.

"That's cheating," Jackie said. "But I'll call you on that. I totally love that shirt."

"Love it from a distance, Sugar Pie, cuz you ain't gettin' it!" Darby waved the purple fabric over the table.

"Excuse me, can anyone get into this game?" Greg asked.

"Jeez, Greg. Give us a heart attack," Darby said, tipping back and landing on her butt.

Jackie jumped up and tripped. She fell into his arms, and hung on his neck. Darby peeked at Jackie's cards.

"Did I ever tell you how much I love you?" Jackie asked, kissing his cheek.

"I love you too, sweetheart," he said. Then kissed her on the lips. She tasted of lasagna and booze. Not a pretty combination, but Jackie wore it well. She was the most incredible woman he'd ever met, and he was lucky to be married to her.

Then there was Kathryn, whom he loved dearly. He'd been the brother she never had. They'd played marbles and ate marshmallows by a campfire as kids, and they had shared their deepest secrets for more than thirty-five years. Greg had been at her side during the happiest moments of her life, and the saddest, too. He would always be there to protect her, but consumed with his own life he hadn't been doing a very good job lately. Thankfully she had Bill and the love and security that marriage gave her.

"I'll be right back," Greg said when he noticed the chill of Jackie's skin. He left the room, only to return moments later with three robes. He handed one to Kathryn, tossed another to Darby, and helped Jackie into hers. Darby pulled the white fuzzy robe on inside out and left it hanging open, a Darby move if there ever was one. He glanced at the kitchen table, and food enough to feed ten remained. Obviously more drinking than eating had occurred here tonight.

"Come on, ladies, how about something to eat?"

Jackie wrapped her arms around his waist. "I love you. Did I tell you I love you?"

"Yes, you did," Greg said, guiding her into the kitchen.

"Can we have coffee?" Darby asked, uprighting herself on a bar stool at the kitchen island. "I love coffee. Don't you just love coffee?"

"I love cocoa," Jackie said, climbing on a stool between Kathryn and Darby. "Can I have cocoa?"

Greg laughed. "Yes, sweetheart, you can have cocoa. And no coffee. For anyone. You ladies are going to..." His voice trailed off as he walked around the counter, looking at the ceramic pieces and food spread across the floor.

"We had a little accident," Kathryn said. "Sorry."

"I can see that." He smiled, then opened the cabinet and

retrieved a dustpan and broom. When the floor was safe to walk on, he chopped an onion and dumped it into a pan, added bacon, and fried the mixture before he cracked the eggs. He dropped whole wheat bread into the toaster, and then he made cocoa for everyone. He buttered toast, filled their plates with eggs and set their midnight snack in front of them.

"Whipped cream?" he asked. Three hands went in the air. Darby stuck her finger out for a direct hit, and Greg complied. The white blob fell off her finger and onto her eggs without making it as far as her mouth. She didn't notice, and stuck her finger in her mouth anyway.

The ladies were talking, and Greg was washing the frying pan when the tune from Jaws rang out. The women laughed.

"Mine." Kathryn raised her hand. "Bill." Greg handed her the purse and she dug through it in search of her phone. She found it quickly, but fumbled with the cover. Greg held out his hand to take it.

"Bill, Greg here."

"Where's Kat?'"

"The girls had a little too much partying. They're all sleeping now." He placed a finger to his lips. "Why don't you enjoy the night and I'll send her home in the morning."

"Sure. That sounds like a good idea. Did you get the message about the meeting change?"

Bill said he had rescheduled their union meeting last minute due to two delayed inbound flights caused by a snowstorm in Denver. Greg knew he'd rescheduled it because of media availability in the morning. Regardless, it had given him the opportunity to return to the airport and speak with Amir. Then he'd signed his life away.

"I did. Tomorrow should be a great turnout," Greg said.

"See you then," Bill said. "Have a good night."

Greg closed the phone. "You girls say anything to Bill, I will deny it. And personally kill you. And no more whipped cream."

They all laughed. Jackie held her stomach and swayed, and he hoped he only had to see the scrambled eggs once tonight.

"Mum's the word." Kathryn placed a finger to her lips.

Greg sat with them while they finished eating, and chattered on. The kitchen scene reminded him of the many late nights he'd spent with his sister years ago. She'd always included him in her after-parties. He'd make food. They'd talk. He'd listen. Then he'd climb out his bedroom window and run next door to hang out with Kathryn. Friends for life. That had never changed. But there was never a day he didn't miss his sister. It was times like this that brought her memory close.

When the eggs were gone, he cleared the plates, rinsed them, and put them in the dishwasher, then wiped down the counters. He dried his hands then held one out to Jackie. "Now, ladies, if you don't mind, I am going to take my bride to bed. You girls make yourselves at home. You know where everything is."

ONCE THEY WERE ALONE, Greg touched Jackie's face gently and looked into her eyes as he trailed a finger down her cheek. He placed his hand behind her neck and pulled her close, and their lips touched. He kissed her lightly as he removed her robe. She wore only a bra and panties. The last thing she would've been wearing in the poker game raising with a pair of twos. He smiled. Not at her poor card skills, but at her beauty.

He unhooked her bra and let it drop, then knelt in front of her and slid her white panties down to her ankles and lifted one foot, then the other. She balanced with hands on his shoulders. He guided her to the bed and she sat, then leaned back and propped herself up on her elbows, smiling.

He unbuttoned his shirt and tossed it on the chair, then removed his pants. She reached out and touched him. *Incredible.* His body trembled while he leaned over hers and kissed her once again. He helped her up on the full length of the bed, and joined her.

It had been too long since they'd made love and he didn't know why he'd waited. Guilt perhaps. But one day rolled into the next, and then there would always be tomorrow. Tomorrows were running out. He slid his hand up her abdomen and gently squeezed one breast, then the other, and bent down and took a nipple in his mouth.

He entered her slowly, enjoying the warmth and moisture of her welcoming body. She responded to his touch and his movements, and gave of herself freely and openly as her body devoured his. She was the most beautiful woman in the world, and he the luckiest man. Somehow he'd lost sight of that over the previous few months. He'd allowed the clamor of life to intrude, and Jackie had been the victim. There was so much he needed to tell her, life choices she should've been part of.

His guilt burned deep, but tonight was not the time to ease his conscience. Tonight was about Jackie and he would give her everything, he would give her his love. It may be all he had to give, but he would show her how special she was. How perfect they were together. Everything else would come with time.

GREG HAD ONLY SLEPT for four hours when he awoke to Jackie kneeling over the toilet. He sighed and held her hair back while she emptied her stomach, wrinkling his nose at the smell. Once she stopped, he brought her a Coke, some crackers, and two aspirin.

Still partially intoxicated, Jackie allowed him to help her brush her teeth, and then they both went back to bed. His body gave up on sleep and left him staring at the minutes clicking by on the clock for the remainder of the night.

His eyes fluttered open again some time later when he heard Darby and Kathryn giggling on their way out the door. Jackie snored gently in his arms. Morning had finally arrived, but they wouldn't see the sun. Not today.

Everything was out of his control. There was nothing he could do to stop or alter the outcome of what he'd done. He couldn't pay the mortgage. He couldn't send Chris to college. He was also on the verge of losing his job. There was no way to get out of the grave he'd dug, and he only hoped that he wouldn't drag Jackie and Chris down with him.

Jackie wouldn't be pleased knowing he'd reactivated his life insurance policy. Premiums they couldn't afford. Now he was officially worth more dead than alive.

He was a coward. When he told her they were broke, she'd said, "that's okay, I'll just go back to work." He doubted she believed him, and he couldn't bring himself to tell her the brutal truth of how bad the situation was. Maybe he'd write a letter. She would eventually understand. She had to. But now he only hoped that one day she'd forgive him.

CHAPTER 15
SATURDAY

KATHRYN OPENED the door to an empty kitchen and was thankful that she was alone. Bill was somewhere in the house, but now all she wanted to do was snuggle with her cat. She had a lot to process, and although her double tall vanilla cappuccino gave her the caffeine fix she needed, Princess in her lap would help her think. She put a bowl of food on the floor, opened the door, and called for her. She disappeared often, but was never gone for more than a day. She glanced around the back yard, then moved the bowl to the porch and closed the door.

She and Darby hadn't been quite sure what to say when Jackie told them how broke she and Greg were. Pay-cuts and backsliding were no mystery among the pilots, but Greg was in more trouble than most. Jackie had thought he'd been spending their money on another woman. But he'd borrowed against his house, pulling out equity to invest in the stock market that didn't pan out. Their only out—selling their home. Seattle wasn't as bad as some cities, but now they weren't able to sell it for what they had invested. Losing it in a short sale would be their only option.

It was shocking how deep Greg was stuck. Jackie had every right to be scared. Kathryn herself was a little angry that Greg hadn't told her. Then again, she hadn't told him about her medical concerns, either. Neither one wanted to worry the other. But Greg was more than her friend, she loved him like a brother, and this secrecy needed to change.

She located the bottle of Tylenol and swallowed three, then walked quietly down the hallway and paused at Bill's office, his cave. The door was open, lights were on bright, and his computer was up and running. She tiptoed further down the hall to the adjacent room. The door was closed and she listened. "I got my finger on the trigger, but I don't know who to trust…"

Bruce Springsteen, "Devils and Dust." He was working out. His grunts overpowered the clatter of weights and the music. Bill had an amazing body that never seemed to age.

There had been a time when they had worked out together, but those days had long since passed. She raised a hand to knock, and then thought better of it. Door closed, he wanted privacy. Instead, she returned to the kitchen and started his coffee. She cut and cleaned a papaya for him, placing half in a dish and setting it on the table, then climbed the stairs to their room.

After turning the faucet to hot she removed her clothes and tossed them in the laundry basket, then stepped into the shower. She thought of Greg cooking for them in the middle of the night, and was happy for Jackie. They were a good pair. Kathryn couldn't have picked a better wife for him, had she tried. Despite their financial struggle, she knew that Jackie and Greg could handle anything together.

The hot water cascaded over her body, and she tipped her head back, soaking her hair. Jackie's pride and secrecy had been washed away with a bottle of Patro'n, and she'd broken down and told them everything. It had been Darby's idea for her to win enough in a game of poker so she wouldn't have to go back to work. At the time, strip poker made sense. Kathryn smiled and turned her face into the spray.

She washed her hair and thought about the meeting she'd scheduled with Mrs. Madden. She wasn't looking forward to it. How in the heck could she possibly see a pattern with a total of one interview? She couldn't.

Besides, her experience had been in the field trudging though debris, connecting the remains of broken planes and painting pictures of the final moments. Not with the families. Her comfort was with the dead, not the living. The dead told secrets, while the living played with your mind and clouded reality with their perceptions of what they wanted or needed you to believe. In the long run, they did nothing but fill your head with superfluous junk that confused and sidetracked the issue.

She needed the tapes. She also needed to tell Bill what she was doing. Going behind his back was not a good option. The question was, how and when.

Kathryn rinsed the conditioner from her hair and the soap from her body then stepped out of the shower. She wrapped her hair in a towel, and body in another then walked into her bedroom. Her heart added a couple extra beats when she saw him.

Bill was sitting on the windowsill, eating his papaya. Waiting.

"I didn't hear you come in," she said.

He didn't speak. He just stared and ate. He was in a mood, and her head ached—not a good combination. She returned to her bathroom and pulled on a robe.

"Have a good time last night?" he asked, when she returned to the bedroom.

"Yeah. It was nice." She unwound her hair and began to dry it with the towel. "How was the union meeting?"

"Cancelled. So where were you yesterday?"

"What do you mean?"

"I called, you didn't answer. Where were you?"

"You called? It never came through."

He couldn't possibly know. Her mind whirled. Guilt mixed with caffeine increased her heart rate and goose bumps sprouted. But she hadn't done anything wrong. "Downtown," she finally said.

"What were you doing?"

"What is this, an inquisition?" She laughed, attempting to make light of the conversation.

"Just curious what my wife was doing downtown. That's a reasonable request."

"I went to meet a friend for lunch."

"Who?"

"What's the big deal?" Irritation swept over her. He didn't own her. She was married to him, not enslaved. Guilt, combined with a hangover, put her on the defensive. "I'm stuck in this house every day taking care of you and the kids. You would think that I could have one day with a friend without getting an interrogation."

"You're sure pissy this morning. Is it that time of the month or did you drink too much last night?" Bill winked then grinned the smile that she'd fallen in love with. Somehow it was losing a bit of its charm as the years passed.

"Definitely drank too much," Kathryn said opening her dresser. "So, what'd you do in Los Angeles yesterday?" She asked over her shoulder.

"Not much. Just got caught up on some union work."

She turned her back to him and stepped into her underwear and dropped her robe, then pulled a sweatshirt over her head. When she faced him, he was smiling.

"Come and give me a kiss. I missed you last night."

She went to him, and when she leaned forward he placed a hand on the back of her neck and pulled her mouth to his. He wrapped his arm around her, and pulled her body close. He skimmed the back of his fingers up her thigh and slipped them inside the line of her panties, and she closed her eyes and melted into his hand.

"What are you doing today?" he asked, removing his lips and his hand casually, but just as quickly as they touched her.

She held her breath wishing he'd put his hand back where it had been, and finish what he'd started. It had been too long. Instead, she stepped back. Schedules, kids, and her not feeling well seemed to leave romance on the back burner these days.

"I'm going to have lunch with Darby," she said.

"You just spent the night with her."

Kathryn shrugged.

Bill pulled her onto his lap and wrapped his arms around her, and nuzzled into her neck. "I just don't know what's wrong with me. I'm sure it's the election. When it's over, we'll get back to just you and me." Then he pulled her mouth to his, and his tongue found a home in hers.

When he came up for air, she swung a leg over his lap. Straddling him, he pulled off her sweatshirt. Her nipples were hard. A flash of another time aroused her. Despite their hectic schedules, she wanted to find time for him. She ran her fingers through his hair and brought her lips to his once again.

His erection grew between her legs, and his mouth was moist, his lips soft. His hands moved to her waist and he held her tight, returning the kiss she longed for. When he pulled his lips from hers, he pressed his face to her breast. He took one nipple in his mouth. *Oh God. Yes...*

And then he freed the nipple as easily as he'd taken it, and lifted her off his lap. "Babe. I'm sorry, I didn't realize it was so late. I've got to get out of here. Union meeting today and the press will be there. I need a shower."

She picked up her sweatshirt and held it to her chest, then turned her back to him as she pulled it over her head. He infuriated her when he built her up and didn't follow through. She had a lot to do, too, but enough was enough. She was beginning to wonder if he had a physical problem, but everything appeared to be working properly.

Bill reached out and touched her shoulder. He turned her toward him. Cupping her chin, he brought his mouth to hers and their lips touched. Then he stepped back and turned toward the closet. When he came out, he carried a white dress-shirt and pair of black slacks.

"Jackie wanted to know if we could have dinner with them tonight," Kathryn said, sitting on the bed.

"That'd be nice. I'll be back by four-thirty, we can drive together." He pulled her close and kissed her long and slow. "I love you, sweetheart," he whispered. Then he walked out of the room.

Kathryn sat on the bed and stared at the door, and the room began to spin. The files could wait a few minutes, and she pulled the comforter around her body. But the warmth didn't diminish the chill that sliced through her soul, nor hide her frustration of how her feelings had changed with Bill.

Her job would close the distance between them. Bill would find renewed respect for her. More importantly, she would find renewed respect for herself. They would find their way to reconnect for the girls, and for their marriage as a whole.

Their passion for aviation safety had brought them together, and their commitment to each other and their family would take them into the future.

They had met at an airplane crash and their ensuing discussions had enthralled her. But it was that first night of sex with Bill that held her captive. *Incredible.* Kathryn smiled at the memory, and then wondered if lust had blinded them both.

The downstairs shower echoed through the walls. She pulled the comforter closer and envisioned joining him.

CHAPTER 16

KATHRYN HAD BEEN REACHING for Bill when the door slammed. She opened her eyes, and it took her a moment to bring the numbers on the bedside clock into focus. Forty minutes was all the time she'd lost. She rolled out of bed and stumbled to the window just in time to see Bill's red Porsche pull onto the street and disappear into the fog.

She Braced herself on the windowsill to catch her balance, then turned and padded into the bathroom.

Staring for a moment, she shook her head before she splashed cold water onto her face. "Everything is going to be fine," she said to the ghost in the mirror.

Returning to her bedroom she knelt on her side of the bed and removed the files from underneath the mattress then carried them downstairs. She would tell Bill what she was doing after the election. If he wasn't elected, she wasn't sure exactly what she'd do. But lying to him wasn't a long-term option. Neither was their lack of intimacy.

Downstairs, she poured herself a cup of coffee and sat at the table with a legal pad and pen, and stared at a blank page. She bounced her pen on the paper, her mind gaining momentum with each tap. She pushed the files aside. The solution didn't require a folder.

Kathryn dialed the number like it was yesterday.

"Transportation Safety Board, how may I help you?"

"Aviation Department please, Samantha Schafer."

"Is this regarding an accident, ma'am?"

"No."

"Standby."

She held the phone to her ear and paced the kitchen floor. One hurdle complete—Sam still worked there. The next question— Would she help?

She and Sam had worked together for years and had maintained a solid friendship during that time. Sam had attended her wedding, and brought baby gifts when the girls were born. And then Kathryn never saw her again. Different life choices.

They'd been hired within a month of each other. Kathryn had been there first, and when Sam arrived the harassment shifted from Kathryn to Sam. But Kathryn had always stood to her defense. They'd been quite the team that everyone soon loved. Sam brought humor and brains to their group. The two of them had spent many nights working together, discussing various details of how the plane burned and or some fact they'd pulled off a black box. When Sam couldn't sleep Kathryn had sat with her through the night, on many occasions.

"Schafer. How can I help you?"

"Sam, it's me, Kat."

"Oh my God. How in the heck are you?" Samantha's voice reminded her that she'd lost more than the job when she had quit. Marriage and children had taken her a different direction—A busy road, but lonely.

"I feel bad only calling when I need something."

"Oh my God, are you kidding me? Anything at all. Except babysitting, I'm really not good with kids."

Sam wasn't good with living things, and her job suited her well. It was Kathryn who'd cared for Sam's plants, and her kitten. Then she thought of Princess.

"No. I don't need help with the girls. But how is Muffin?"

"Alive. She figured out when her bowl is empty she'd better catch me while I'm asleep. I wake up to the proverbial pussy in the face most mornings."

"And plants?" Kathryn asked, after she stopped laughing.

"Dead."

"Sorry."

"Well, you know, some things never change." Sam sighed. "So how in the heck have you been? I've missed you so much. Dang, girl, it's about time. Life is definitely not the same without you covering my butt."

"That was the best part of the job," Kathryn said. "Are you ready to take a step back in time? I'm investigating for McAllister, and I need some help."

"Oh my God, that's great."

Kathryn was surprised that they had gone nine years without a call and still nothing had changed between them. Sam was genuinely excited for her.

"John gave me the personnel files to a few accidents, but what I'd like to see are the actual reports from the investigations, the first view stuff. He can't pull them right now, because nobody is supposed to know I'm working. I can't do a anything without them."

"Which ones do you need?"

"Regional Air Thirty-Nine. Skylark Eighty-Two. And Global Thirty-Two. And could you pull me a copy of the recordings?"

"No problem. The boys owe me a few favors. Give me your email address and I'll punch the cockpit voice recordings over the wires right now. But keep this quiet. I'd get a major butt whipping if they knew I emailed these reports. If they found their way to

YouTube, holy shit, makes me shudder to think."

"Thank you, and mum's the word. On both ends."

Kathryn gave Sam her email address and they exchanged cell numbers. Sam and Kathryn had always shared everything, and they'd had a motto—*It's easier to beg for forgiveness than to be told no.*

She opened her laptop, then stood and stretched. "I'm back!" she said, punching the air. A different angle from what she'd done before, but that didn't matter and she felt remarkable, better than she had in years.

Kathryn signed in to her email account. Just as promised, the files waited for her. She pulled the recordings off the server and saved them to a personal file, then deleted them from her account. She plugged her headset into her laptop and placed headphones over her ears. Every detail was important. Focus essential.

San Francisco was first. The recording was noisier than she remembered. Static crackled loudly, but she could still hear papers rustling in the flightdeck. Controllers spoke clearly over the radio, providing clearances to other aircraft in the same airspace. She fast-forwarded to the landing.

Face in hands, she leaned on the table and listened.

"Skylark Eighty-Two, you're cleared for the ILS approach runway one-niner left, contact the tower over SHAKE." Approach control was handing Skylark off to the control tower for landing.

"Roger NORCAL, Tower at Shake with information Bravo." A young voice responded to their clearance. The captain was the pilot flying and the cadet worked the radios.

More papers shuffled and then, "You okay?" a voice asked. It was old and raspy. Fifty-nine-year-old training captain, Walt Miller, stared at her from the kitchen table.

"Yeah, just pissed… babysi…" another voice responded. This

was followed by the captain's laughter.

Kathryn paused the recording, backed it up and listened again. Someone was pissed about babysitting? The voice was distant, not as clear as the captain or the first officer. It had to be the other first officer who'd sat in the jumpseat. He was pissed about babysitting, and the captain found this humorous. Kathryn pressed pause and scribbled on her pad, babysitting? Then pressed play.

"Flaps one." The younger voice responded, then gears moved.

Kathryn visualized the wings changing shape as the leading and trailing edges extended. The aircraft would be slowing.

"Coastal One-Eight, you're cleared to land." The tower controller could be heard clearing a plane to land in front of Skylark. *Bill's flight.* She'd forgotten that he'd been there, landing just prior to the crash.

It was eerie hearing his voice on the recording.

"Flaps five." The crew was performing a scripted play. The pilot flying commanded, the other pilot performed. Everyone was on the same page playing his part. They selected ten degrees of flaps. More gears groaned and the aircraft continued to slow. One hundred and seventy knots or so, she estimated.

The first officer, Jeff Martin, had 350 hours of flight time and was a cadet in Skylark's training program. Twenty-two years old, fresh out of college, and he was a first officer on the Boeing 737-800. *Ahhh… The first officer in the jumpseat was babysitting the new guy.*

Airlines were using cadets as first officers at minimum pay to help keep costs low, and Jeff Martin was one of them. In return, those who signed these long-term contracts were able to get flying experience that otherwise wouldn't have been available.

Despite the public's lack of knowledge, this type of training was being conducted on revenue flights. Had the new regulations been in place last year Jeff would still be alive. But Kathryn suspected someone else would be dead in his place.

With the new regulations these young, inexperienced, U.S. pilots would go overseas to fly in China to get their flight hours. Would they gain quality experience from those foreign carriers? She wasn't sure. Kathryn ran a finger over Jeff's photo.

"Tell the tower we're with them for landing."

"Uh, San Francisco Tower, Skylark Eighty-Two is… uh, sixteen miles to landing runway one-niner left." Kathryn pressed pause.

She ran to Bill's office, grabbed his charts and located the San Francisco section and opened to the SFO 19L ILS approach plate and checked the distance from the runway to the intersection they called 'SHAKE'. *10.4 miles.* They'd been directed to call *over* SHAKE, yet the captain told the first officer to call at sixteen miles. She made a note and then pressed play.

"Roger Skylark Eight-Two, cleared to land runway one-niner left, altimeter is two-niner, niner-eight, wind calm." The power reduced. There was nothing unusual or out of the ordinary. Other than the early call, which the Tower didn't seem to mind. The winds were even calm.

"Uh…cleared to land runway one-niner left, Skylark."

"Flaps fifteen."

Gears grinding indicated the flaps had been moved.

The report stated that during the communication with the tower, the radio altimeter flag on the aircraft had come into view— the plane thought it was on the ground. The thrust levers responded accordingly and had come back to idle, reducing the power to stop the airplane on the runway. The problem was that the aircraft was still in the air.

"Gear down, flaps twenty-five."

Another standard response and more noise filled the flight deck along with the landing gear dropping into place. She pressed pause. The final report attributed the accident to faulty equipment. But why was this case still open?

She moved the audio back to the moment where the flag had produced itself on the instrument—the exact moment that the captain commanded the landing gear extension. She selected play and started the timer on her watch.

"Flaps thirty, landing check."

The first officer moved the flap handle and then read the landing checklist and the captain responded. Altimeter, landing gear, and flaps were on this check. She stopped her timer and pressed pause. That took thirty seconds. *Were they too busy to notice the flag?* The captain must have been looking at the instruments. *How could he not see the altimeter flag, or the power reduction?* She pressed play, and continued to time the approach.

Another sixty seconds elapsed. After the entire ninety seconds had passed she paused the recording and looked at the chart, the location of impact. Something didn't make sense. She scribbled another note to herself.

Nobody had been prepared for what came next, and she'd forgotten the overwhelming impact of audio. She closed her eyes and listened. The sounds and voices painted a clear picture of the terror that prevailed.

"Skylark, go around!" That command came from the controller.

The first officer did not respond. Instead he yelled, "Shit!" Then an immediate increase in power as the engines roared to life. The ensuing noise sliced through her kitchen. It sounded like a giant sledgehammer had crashed into the side of the aircraft and resonated throughout the fuselage. Then the tail slammed into the water with full force.

Magnified screams carrying the pandemonium of death through the aircraft found their way into her kitchen. The second blowout, much louder and closer to the flight deck, erupted as the fuel tanks exploded.

Between explosions and screams from the cabin, she identified a faint voice, "I'm…s…" and moments later, silence.

She replayed that last segment five times in attempt to pick up what was spoken, to no avail. Each time she listened, her heart raced and she prayed the outcome would be different. Her prayers were never answered. There was always an explosion obscuring the screams of fear that fueled the passengers' last breaths, followed by the silence of death.

One hundred and thirty-two passengers, six lap-children, four flight attendants and three pilots had been on board. The silence impacted Kathryn far more than the explosions. Tears filled her eyes, as the faces of the flight crew stared at her from her kitchen table, smiling, knowing the secret, but unwilling to tell.

CHAPTER 17

GREG STOOD in the back of the room watching the show—an exceptional performance. Bill was a man with a mission, and a man whom he grew to respect more with each passing day.

"My fellow pilots, my brothers and sisters of the industry, thank you for being here this morning." Bill's voice was deliberate, strong, and methodical. Greg had coached him well. Not only did he pause for emphasis, but he also scanned the audience as he spoke.

"As you know, our industry is in a rapid decline," he said, shaking his head with a subtle droop of his shoulders. "Not only have we faced extensive job loss, leaving far too many pilots on the streets, but CEOs have been cutting our pay with a hatchet." He stood a little straighter. "And now they're stealing our pensions, too."

The audience rumbled and Bill continued. "Their business decisions have impacted the safety of our industry. The stress, it's killing our fellow pilots. I know you feel powerless. But I assure you on my father's grave, it's not too late." The group clapped loudly.

Bill looked directly into the camera. Channel Five News was filming. Bill raised a hand, and the audience quieted. "We are experiencing one of the greatest crimes of all times. It's not only a crime against the airline industry, but it's a crime against humanity. The safety of a nation, and the security of our pilots and their families, are in jeopardy. It will be a fight, but one I will not lose. I assure you, we *will* take back control!"

The audience roared.

The cameraman smiled broadly. Greg had no doubt that Bill's pledge would find its way beyond the local station to the national network. He suspected the man behind the camera knew that, too.

Tuning Bill out, Greg glanced at his watch and stifled a yawn. He'd heard this speech many times. Hell, he'd written it. His mind drifted back to the incredible night he'd just experienced with his wife.

He'd allowed his fears and frustration to release into a passion that had been a stranger for too long. He took Jackie's willing body with everything he had. Granted, she'd been drunk, but she hadn't been drunk this morning when they'd continued their reunion. Maybe a little weak and hung-over, but he did his best to take her mind off her headache. As an added bonus, with Chris out of town and their guests out the door, they didn't have to be quiet.

They say tequila makes a woman's clothes fall off. They were right. Walking in on their strip poker game was a first. Had he arrived ten minutes later, he would've had an eyeful. He grinned at the thought. But cheap thrills weren't his thing. Jackie was more than enough woman for him, in every way.

His attention returned to Bill who spoke of work rules. He was the third and last candidate speaking today, but the speeches were only a formality.

Despite the facade, Greg knew better. Bill was the new president. The union bylaws enabled anyone to run for office and speak at this forum, but the selection was accomplished behind closed doors. This outcome had been decided weeks prior to the actual election. The members just thought they had a say.

The representatives at each pilot base were wined and dined, and then told as a group who to give their vote to. If a union representative voiced his opinion, voting against his base, he was politically castrated.

Seattle was the largest pilot base at Coastal Airlines. They had all the power, and Bill held this group in the palm of his hand. He had the respect of most, and the fear of the others. What Seattle wanted, Seattle got, and they wanted Bill.

Greg scanned the room for Darby, but doubted she'd be there. He was glad she wasn't. She rarely came to these things. Not only was she openly against this process, she was smart enough to know that these guys were not ready for a woman who spoke her mind.

He worked his way across the back of the room toward the door, squeezing between bodies as he walked. The back five feet of the auditorium was standing room only, and every chair up front was filled.

Greg's plight was nothing more than what the other pilots faced. Granted, some were single and others had businesses on the side. But those who focused solely on their airline profession and had families were hit the hardest. They had no secondary income. At one time they'd been the safest pilots, focusing only on the job. That was no longer the case. Now they were the most distracted, with fear of losing their pensions and all they'd worked for during their careers. They were not only distracted, but the most dangerous.

"Take it back!" yelled a voice from the center of the room. Bill smiled and held up his hand. He was the preacher and his flock followed his lead silencing to a low rumble when he spoke.

"Our pilots have taken a thirty percent pay cut, and now we are some of the lowest paid in the industry. Not only are we the lowest, but we're making thirty-six percent less than industry standard. Now management is threatening to furlough an additional 497 pilots. We *will* say no. No more!"

Then Bill lowered his voice. "We've lost five airliners in the previous two years, three of them this past year. Planes piloted by our union brothers are falling out of the sky. Those accidents never should have happened. We don't know what happened on the recent three, and we may never know. What we do know is that our brothers and sisters are overworked, and they're fatigued. We're all facing the same stresses they were. They were losing their homes, but instead they lost their lives. They deserved better than that. We all do."

"You know it," someone from the back of the room yelled.

"Please, join me in a moment of silence for those lost in these tragic accidents." Bill lowered his head and closed his eyes, as did everyone except Greg and the cameraman who swung his camera wide scanning the group. Then the cameraman bowed his head slightly, but the camera continued to roll.

Greg stopped short of the door. He closed his eyes and willed a silent prayer to the lives lost. Not only to the crews, but to the hundreds of passengers who had placed their lives in the pilots' hands as they stepped aboard the aircraft, and to the families left behind. They'd given their trust to the flight crews, but it was the industry that had failed them. He had to continually remind himself of that fact.

There was a bigger reality than his. They all had to sacrifice in one manner or another. He'd finally accepted Amir's offer to buy their home. The ultimate sacrifice of the life, a symbol of safety and security, he had worked so hard to provide his family. But in the long run, there was no other option. One step forward and three back.

When all eyes were open, everyone like puppies waiting for their master to throw them a bone, Bill spoke. "You have an important decision today, and that's to elect a new president. We need someone who's not afraid to take a stand, and I promise you that I, Bill Jacobs, am that man, because I get it, and I *will* take that stand!"

"You got my vote, Bill," yelled a voice in the crowd.

"Thank you," Bill said. "Now, if I can get the support of more than Tony here, then we'll be getting somewhere." The pilots laughed openly.

"You got mine!" someone yelled from the back of the room, and applause broke out.

Bill allowed the clapping to continue. When the volume decreased he raised his hands with the illusion that he had quieted the crowd.

"This affront to our careers is personal to me. Many of you know that my father was a captain for Universal Airlines. Hank Dyer not only took that airline into oblivion, but he also took my father's career and his life in the process. We've watched our friends and families suffer, eaten by the corruption of the industry, and we've watched many airlines disappear. Eastern, Braniff, TWA, and Northwest, to name a few. Whether our destroyers are insiders, CEOs like Dyer, or outsiders, I will not allow Coastal Airlines to follow in the wake!"

The clapping began strong and turned into a standing ovation. Greg clapped loudly.

He'd instantly liked Bill the day he'd met the man, and Bill had proven him right on many occasions. Greg had walked Kathryn down the aisle; proud to walk her to one of the most honorable and passionate men he'd ever met. Kathryn was obviously in love, and he was happy that she had finally found the love she deserved. Someone true who would be with her through the end.

Greg had been working overseas, and it was Bill who'd persuaded him to come to Coastal and work for what he called a "real" airline.

Greg jumped at the chance to be close to Kathryn again. Despite his many setbacks and pay cuts, Coastal being the largest, he'd never regretted what he'd given up when he'd accepted Bill's offer to join the airline. Kathryn was back in his life, and on top of that, he'd met Jackie.

Had he remained overseas, Jackie wouldn't be part of his life. He loved her more than he'd ever loved anyone or anything. And when he held Chris in his arms that first time, his life and love for Jackie grew tenfold. It was ironic that the people who gave his life meaning were also the reminders of what a failure he'd become.

The clapping continued and Greg locked eyes with Bill, who nodded. Greg returned the nod and smiled.

"Ladies and gentleman, when you vote today, remember one thing. A vote for Jacobs is a vote for the success of your career and quality of life for your families. And for all of you who won't be flying today, we'll be taking this party to suite eleven-forty at the Doubletree for sandwiches and adult beverages. I'll be available to answer questions. Thank you."

Bill walked off the stage, directly toward the cameraman. He placed an arm over the guy's shoulder, leaned in, and spoke. They both laughed, and the cameraman nodded.

Greg turned and walked out of the room, the roar continuing behind him. He followed the dimly lit hallway through the basement of the terminal. Punching the code into the security panel, he glanced down the hall then opened the door to the crew room.

Hundreds of black flight bags lined the walls and filled the shelves. His was one of many falling apart at the seams. A bulletin board covered with posts of boats, airplanes, and homes for sale, created a collage. The lives and dreams of his fellow pilots hung on the wall in a fireside sale. He pulled his flier off the board, wadded it up, and then threw it in the garbage can.

Shaking his head, he glanced at his watch. There was only one thing left to do now, and he hoped it would be enough.

CHAPTER 18

KATHRYN SLIPPED into a warm sweater to stave off the chill that had crept under her skin. A rawness that had nothing to do with the damp air hanging outside her window, but everything to do with the death of hundreds, clutched her body. The last words of any crash were something that she'd never gotten used to, but the silence after was unbearable.

She poured herself another cup of coffee and sat. With headphones over her ears, she pressed play. This time New York came alive. She closed her eyes and listened.

"Regional Air Three-Niner cleared direct to Hoggs intersection descend and maintain flight level one-eight-zero. You can expect the Canarsie approach to runway one-three-right."

These pilots were easier to identify than Skylark's. There were only two, and one was a woman. Sandra. The reception was static free, and if she didn't know better, she could have sworn she could hear the wind howl from outside the plane.

Sandra responded to the clearance and then asked, "Have you ever flown in weather this bad?" The captain's initial response was nothing, followed by commanding her to request a lower altitude. When she didn't react, he'd yelled at her.

Unfortunately, the audio didn't capture a complete picture. There were signals, head nods, and expressions alive in the flight deck that went undetected on the audio, and she hoped the captain had acknowledged, but his lack of response followed by his angered demeanor spoke volumes. The captain was ignoring and verbally attacking his first officer—but why?

The weather report blared over the radio in a robotic tempo. The automatic terminal information service provided the weather, and its computer generated voice projected loud and clear, cutting through the background noise. The wind had been gusty and blowing snow. Braking action had been poor.

"Grant, I think we need to get out of here. Maybe get a lower altitude and vectors over the water so we can…"

No kidding. She pressed pause, then opened Grant's file. *What's he doing?* Kathryn was a low time pilot, and it had been years since she'd flown, but even she knew that you didn't descend early into the crud in icing conditions if you didn't have to. She opened his file and turned the pages.

Grant was a check airman. The best of the best. *This doesn't make sense.* She pressed play once again.

The crew continued to descend and configure their flaps. Air traffic control yelled for them to state their altitude. Sandra cried for help. They couldn't maintain altitude.

"Tell them we'll level off at three thousand and would like vectors for the Canarsie approach," the captain spoke, calm as ice and in control.

"Gear down, flaps fifteen," Grant commanded. Sandra didn't respond, nor did gears move. Roles had shifted and Sandra ignored her captain, until her voice screamed over the audio.

"Airspeed!" she yelled. Not once, but twice.

Thrust levers slamming forward and the engines roaring to life followed her cry.

Kathryn pressed pause, and squeezed the bridge of her nose.

She stood and paced. The flow of this crew—their actions, their dynamics—was a recipe for disaster in the best of conditions. They both should've known better. She leaned over the table, pen to paper, and scribbled. Perhaps they'd been having a relationship, a lovers' quarrel that they carried into the flight deck. If that were the case, and his wife knew about it, Kathryn could have that answer by late afternoon.

She'd never experienced a case when victims became people, with names and faces, families and stories. Everyone had a story. But in the field they weren't people, just bodies, and she liked it better that way. Objectivity and detachment were much easier than feeling.

Kathryn sank into her chair once again and pressed play, but she wasn't prepared for the haunting exclamation that followed, or the emphatic clacking as the aircraft stalled.

"No!" Sandra screamed, and the clacker wailed due to a lack of speed. The noise sounded like a machine gun, and it might as well have been because the aircraft would fall out of the sky just as if it had been shot down.

And then, "You son of a bitch!" Multiple thuds followed a whopping sound, like someone hitting a baseball bat against carpets as they beat the dirt out. Then there was silence, except for ATC's continual plea for contact.

But the aircraft had continued to fly. There were clear signs of life as papers rustled in the flight deck. *Why didn't they contact air traffic control?*

And then Sandra's voice broadcasted loud and strong. They were landing on 13 Right. But they had crashed short of the left runway.

Kathryn closed her eyes and waited for the ending she knew would come, but still hoped, like she did with all sad movies, that this time it would be different. She braced for impact.

"What the fu…?" Sandra spoke, distant but discernible.

Kathryn paused the recording and then played segment again. And again.

"What the fu…" But it wasn't Sandra's words that bothered her. It was the sound of grinding gears that screamed foul play.

CHAPTER 19

"GODDAMMIT, JOHN. First you screw up hiring Jacobs, and now your employees are emailing confidential documents over the damn Internet!" Walker yelled, as he stormed into John's office slamming the door behind him.

Walker's veins bulged in his neck. His bald head reddened, and John envisioned a tomato ready to explode. His eyes were set too close together, and he looked like a snake about to strike when he wasn't shouting.

Dick Walker was the Director of Homeland Security, west coast division, and 'reptilian' was a good look for him.

John leaned back in his chair and listened to Walker yell without interruption. In time his fuse would fizzle down to a manageable size to where they could talk. *Patience.*

Despite Walker's allegations, which were more than likely true, John was surprised his staff broke confidentiality, especially via the Internet. They knew better.

"It's bad enough your contracted assistant called someone in your department and requested copies of active reports. But to have your people openly send them over the Internet is grounds for termination."

John attempted to swallow the smile that tugged at his lips. He'd wondered if Kathryn had maintained contacts within the office, and now he had that answer. At least she saved him the time by pulling the tapes herself.

"I have to say that I'm not surprised."

"Mrs. Jacobs was supposed to be working for the department, and you screwed that up." Walker paced. "What the hell are we supposed to do with her in an unofficial capacity? And now you say you knew this would happen?"

"I didn't say I knew, I said that I'm not surprised."

"Goddammit, John. I cannot have these files leaking to the outside world. Do you know how far my ass is hanging out?" He stopped pacing in front of the window and placed his hand on his hips with his back to John. "This has put me in quite a position."

"Which is?"

Walker turned and glared. "A major security breach. We have to pull the plug on your employee that leaked that information."

"Who was the leak?"

"Samantha Schafer. And you *will* take care of this."

John didn't want to compromise Sam, but Walker was right. Files should not have been leaving the department, especially via the Internet. When the time was right, he'd deal with it. But now was not that time.

"Did you hear me?" Walker asked. "Do something before this gets out of hand."

"Before what gets out of hand?" John leaned back in his chair and folded his arms. Walker glared at him. "You wanted her to work for the department, and she is."

John knew that Walker wanted to watch Bill via Kathryn, and it didn't matter if she was in an official capacity or not. But there was more to this story than Walker divulged.

"She's here and we need her," John said. "And I wouldn't worry about her sharing anything with anyone. She's not the type. Those files are as secure as if she actually worked for the department."

Walker stared at John for a moment then sarcastically asked, "What type is she?"

"She's the type to honor the confidentiality contract that she signed twenty years ago."

"In case you've forgotten, we don't have the ability to hire contract agents."

"She doesn't know that." John leaned forward and rested his arms on his desk. "She'll keep quiet, and maybe she'll find something we've been missing."

"I hope you're right," Walker said, glaring. "But you will deal with Schafer."

"If Sam believed Kathryn was working with us then she wasn't doing anything wrong."

"Bullshit!" Walker stood in front of his desk with hands on the surface. Spittle sprayed when he spoke. His eyes burned holes in John's. "She violated procedure."

"She's not the only one." John returned the glare holding his position. He knew better than to throw anything in Walker's face, but enough was enough. "If we say anything to anyone about Sam, then we'll have to divulge how we knew this transpired. I don't think you want to go there."

Walker ran a hand over his forehead. "This better not bite us in the ass."

"It won't."

"You better be right. You're buried as deep as I am."

John was sure there was something Walker wasn't telling him. Walker mandating John to hire Kathryn had both surprised and pleased him. He should have known there was more to the story. He'd seen this look on Walker's face before. They'd been friends far too long for him not to know when Walker was up to something. Time would tell.

John took a deep breath. He'd had enough of this conversation. He stood, walked around the desk, and extended his hand. Walker accepted it. His head was a normal color and bulges had receded, but his eyes were still too close together and his hands were sweaty.

"When she said no, you should have left it at that," Walker said. "Bugging the house would have been enough. I hope you don't screw this up."

"Nothing is screwed up."

"For your sake, I hope not."

Their eyes met in meaning, and John allowed the insinuation to pass. He'd taken out insurance against his friend, so his threats meant nothing.

"We've just begun," John said. "I'm sure you'll hear far more than you bargained for."

"I should have known twenty-four years ago that I'd never have another day of rest."

"You did know," John said, as he opened the door then watched Walker leave.

He told his secretary that he needed a few moments alone and he was not to be disturbed, then he closed the door. He returned to his chair, retrieved a key from his briefcase and unlocked the bottom drawer. He removed a handheld GPS receiver and watched the green glow blink. Kathryn was still at home.

John had set up surveillance for Walker in the Jacobs' residence, but Walker didn't know that John, too, had an ear to the taping, or that he was making copies of all recordings, creating leverage that would be used if, and when, the time came. Nor did Walker have any idea that he had placed a tracking device in Kathryn's cell phone.

Not only could he monitor her movements, but her conversations were recorded as well. He only wished that he'd listened to the events that set Walker off before his visit.

The best part of all this magic was that it was bought and paid for by the Department of Homeland Security. There were definite advantages of ongoing terrorist investigations. Everything could be grouped into the 'terrorist' category with no questions asked, and it was classified. They could get away with pretty much anything they wanted to, and did.

CHAPTER 20

STATIC FROM THE AUDIO did its damage on the inside of her head while the pressure of the headset worked on the outside. It was the content, though, that was the root of Kathryn's growing headache. She held the bottle of Tylenol and tried to remember how many she'd taken. She set the bottle down and pressed play. Global Air Freight, flight Thirty-Two came to life.

"Global Airfreight Thirty-Two cleared for ILS two-four right MAYAH transition."

"Jack, why don't you…the landing".

"Kid, you're going to have to…one day. Wouldn't you rather… here the first time?"

"I'm on probation…if I screw something up…it will be my…"

"Not to worry, kid. You'll do fine. I can put…after we land… They can blame it…"

This communication was more difficult to decipher, not only due to the static, but also because of the many missing words and voice similarities, despite their age difference. At least the "kid" comments helped. She continued to listen to the pilots configure the aircraft for landing. The flaps moved, grinding into position, and the landing gear groaned as it dropped into place.

In control was Global's most senior captain, with thirty-two years of experience. He was flying with a junior cadet who was in his first month out of training, only this time the "kid" was flying the airplane. In the previous crashes the captain had flown.

"No worries. This isn't wind shear…normal play…turbulence. You're doing great…"

No worries, and not wind shear.

The first officer had to be looking at the fluctuating airspeed, and the captain schooled him. The winds were thirty knots and gusting to forty, which would push the limits of most aircraft, and pilots, but they pressed on. There were no wind shear warnings broadcasted in the flight deck. *But with conditions so bad, why didn't the captain fly?*

The next sixty seconds were the eeriest, and Kathryn visualized the controls and equipment being manhandled as they pushed, pulled, and banked the aircraft. She had seen the video of this approach, machine against weather, on television, and she now replayed that picture in her mind, matching it to the noises coming from her computer.

She listened through the end of the audio, then minimized the window and looked up the crash on YouTube. Someone had recorded the final approach, and it had aired on national television for millions to witness. It wasn't often that she had a video in addition to the audio, and it was priceless.

Since she'd left the department, however, video equipment in the control towers had become more common. They were finally catching up to the value of a picture.

Bill, Darby, and Greg had all voiced opinions after seeing the clip, but Kathryn pushed them from her mind to make room for objectivity. She set up the video of the approach in conjunction with the audio to play the two simultaneously.

The video quality wasn't the greatest, but she clearly saw the approach and the aircraft's control surface movements; a rare but priceless opportunity during an accident investigation.

This particular footage had been taped because it had occurred in Asia. It was a common occurrence for the locals to take pictures and shoot videos of all departures and arrivals, in addition to the airport videos.

The aircraft flew sideways into the wind, crabbing, as it should, twenty degrees to the right toward the camera, but still tracking toward the runway. In the flare, the nose changed position as the rudder moved left and aligned it with the runway centerline. The ailerons simultaneously rolled into the wind. Then the sun glared into the camera, creating a flash of light that made the aircraft difficult to see.

For no apparent reason the plane rolled to the left, digging its wingtip into the runway. The aircraft cartwheeled, and Kathryn felt a rise of nausea as she watched the MD-11 explode.

All reports stated that the wind had shifted, and in an attempt to regain control, the pilots had over-corrected. She'd assumed the same. If the wind had sheared from left to right and then back again, that would explain the lack of a wind shear warning. Perhaps it was that simple. *But why then was the case not closed?*

The control deflections were quick and violent. The left wing burst into flames upon impact. After one turn in a cartwheel, the fuselage tumbling over the cockpit, the right wing hit, creating a secondary explosion. The tail struck the asphalt with force. The aircraft landed upright on the taxiway, skidding left. Thank God ground control had been flowing departures on the right side of the runway. There had been six aircraft awaiting departure in what was nearly an unsuspecting death march.

The pilots never had a chance to die from smoke inhalation. They'd burned alive.

She closed the window to the video, returning to audio only, and replayed the final minutes with a fresh visual in her mind. The broken sentences made more sense the second time through, but the static was insane. Impact was moments away, and then she heard those final words—"What the fuck!" Impact. Multiple explosions. Silence.

She stopped the audio, removed the headset, and leaned back in her chair. What happened to the good old days when the pilot's final words were shit?

What was it with these accidents? All three aircraft had had highly experienced captains on board. And if the wind was too strong to land, or if maintenance or icing issues existed, then why had they continued? Why hadn't this captain taken the landing?

She was thankful they had the recordings. When the European carrier had lost its Airbus 330 somewhere over the Atlantic, it took them two years to locate that plane—and its black box. But the delay hadn't stopped the FAA from mandating regulations, making it appear to the public that they were doing something to fix the problem of heavy rain causing water to enter the pitot-static system, and messing with the instruments. Airplanes need airflow and pressure for their flight instruments to work. When the system is blocked, or filled with water, the readings are erroneous, or in some cases, non-existent.

That particular pitot-static system had caused a problem with all aircraft—not isolated to the Airbus. It was also not enough to take down a plane. That accident went beyond equipment failure. Pilot error and lack of training took them to their deaths.

They should have taken care of the equipment problems years earlier, or at the very least trained the pilots to fly with the failure of their instruments. But they never expected that the pilots wouldn't be able to fly if they lost their automation. Now they knew. But what were they doing with that knowledge? Nothing.

A chill gripped Kathryn.

This lack of ability to fly, due to the reliance on automation, would not be a one-time event. This was just the beginning of a system-wide universal problem. She also doubted the airlines would budget the necessary training unless the FAA dropped the hammer on their current training programs. She wouldn't hold her breath for that one either, since she knew the FAA was signing off on the airlines to cut training, not increase it.

Unfortunately, the FAA only mandated regulation after an accident occurred, not before, and that particular problem had never caused a fatal accident until now. The pending legal battles also kept them from reacting to the real issue—proficiency. The companies involved were so busy postulating and positioning for release of liability, that everyone lost sight of the fact that this could happen again. It would only be a matter of time.

If she could change anything in the industry, it would be to make the FAA more proactive. But that accident, as with all, was due to more than just one isolated problem. There was always a combination of events, and nobody was seeing the big picture.

She tapped her pen on the table and read her notes.

Was there something wrong with this plane? What did they miss? What were the events that made this plane uncontrollable?

Her cell phone rang and she jumped.

"Can you meet me at our old spot for lunch?" Samantha asked.

Kathryn had forgotten about their spot, one of those memories tucked away until Sam unearthed it, and for the second time that morning she smiled. She had forty-five minutes to get there, and saved the audio recordings in a file titling it 'Tuesday chores.' When the investigation was over, she would delete them. She pressed the power button on her laptop and was closing the lid when a glare caught the screen. She looked over her shoulder at the light hanging over the kitchen sink, then back to her computer. The glare. There was a glare hitting the tail of the plane in the video just before the crash. *But why?*

She opened her laptop and pressed the power button, bringing it to life once again. Relocating the video, she watched the crash one more time. This time she paid closer attention to the tail of the aircraft, specifically to the stabilizer and the rudder.

Narrowing her eyes and focusing on the aircraft, she located the basic flight control knowledge buried deep within her brain. The stabilizer provided stability to the aircraft, while the vertical stabilizer specifically prevented a side-to-side yawing motion during flight. Attached to the vertical stabilizer was a hinged, movable, section—the rudder.

They initially flew the approach into the wind. Then on short final they used the rudder pedals to move the aircraft's nose to point straight down the centerline, just as they should have. But the rudder suddenly moved in the opposite direction, picking up the glare from the sun.

The ailerons and wings moved violently, rolling to counteract the directional control. But the rudder, once positioned where it shouldn't have been, stayed in that *incorrect* position. Everything happened quickly, and it looked like the wind had done the damage. Still, the glare remained constant throughout the crash.

The poor quality from the video was due to that glare shining into the camera's lens. She added, "check the rudder's airworthiness" to the top of her notes. If there had been an indication that the rudder had been faulty, she'd dig into the maintenance records.

Unfortunately, with non-scheduled freight operators, those

records were often scarce or destroyed by unexpected water damage or unexplained fires.

Maybe the rudder had run away on them. Kathryn, however, wasn't familiar enough with the MD-11 to know if the rudder had a tendency to move on its own as some of the earlier Boeing 737s had. Her dad would know.

It had been years since she'd spoken to him. She'd thrown him out of her life because of his part in her mother's death. Who was she kidding? The real reason was she needed someone to blame besides herself. He was an easy target. Despite what Dr. Anne had said, she wasn't sure she could go there, yet.

CHAPTER 21

KATHRYN WAS SITTING in the restaurant parking lot, but she couldn't remember driving there. She wiped sweat from her brow and checked the time seeing that she was only five minutes late. She shook off the dread and chalked it up to too much on her mind.

Anthony's was busy. Nestled on the waterfront just south of the marina, the restaurant buzzed with activity. She climbed out of her car and stared across the water. The fog had lifted high enough to see Vashon Island. A lone sailboat drifted quietly across the bay, and she watched it for a moment before making her way inside.

Laughter bombarded her as guests attempted to talk above each other. She glanced around the lobby. The scents of seafood, grilling butter, and fresh bread overwhelmed her in a good way. The hostess asked to take her name, but she declined and made her way to the bar. She walked past the open seafood counter and turned right. A woman waved and yelled, but she was waving at a man behind her. Kathryn entered the bar and scanned the room.

Samantha sat in a corner booth. Their booth. The moment their eyes met, they both smiled, and Kathryn was transported back a decade. Sam slid out of the seat and they embraced. Her hug was strong, just like Kathryn remembered.

"It is so good to see you," Sam said. "I mean like really good."

"For me too."

Sam looked great. The years had been good to her, and it felt like it was just yesterday that they'd sat in this exact same booth and joked about married women. Now Kathryn was one herself, and Sam thrived in the life Kathryn had given up.

"How's work going?"

"It's okay. I'm pretty much behind the scenes these days. The office is really quiet when everyone's out at the crash site, then I get slammed." She hesitated. "They've been out a lot this year."

"This is insane. We never had this many airline accidents when I worked there."

"No kidding. I'm thinking maybe it's your fault for leaving." Sam buttered a chunk of bread. "Or maybe destiny. They say when it's your time to go it's your time to go. Unless it's the guy in row 5B's time, then you go with him." Sam popped the bread into her mouth.

Kathryn laughed. Sam had always lightened the mood when things got tough, it was her survival mechanism. All the same, she'd been fun to work with. When Kathryn had returned from a crash site with death soaked into her skin, it was Sam who'd spout something stupid and make her laugh. She always eased the pain. If it hadn't been for Samantha, Kathryn may not have made it through that first year.

The waiter interrupted them and took their orders. They each ordered an iced tea and a bowl of clam chowder. When he left, Sam leaned forward and whispered. "I'm not sure what's going on, but Walker stormed into the office today and slammed McAllister's door." She scanned the crowd and lowered her voice. "Then I passed him in the hall as I was leaving and he looked at me like he was going to pounce."

Samantha had always been a conspiracy theorist and the best thing to do was smile and nod, not indulge her illusions, then get her back on track.

"Did you bring the files?"

Sam nodded. Her job was transcribing the audio into text after she'd listened to each tape. That process took hours, days, and sometimes months. Kathryn had renewed respect for her after the few short hours she's spent with headphones on that morning.

Their food arrived, and they were silent until the waiter left, then Sam looked suspiciously around the room. Confident that nobody was looking, she slid a Wal-Mart bag across the table. Kathryn placed it in her briefcase. She loved Sam's theatrics. Mostly she loved that they were partners once again.

"Did you read them?" Kathryn asked.

"Million times. Duh, I wrote them."

"I mean recently."

"Of course."

"And?"

Sam had excellent intuition. She'd notice details that everyone else often missed. She pretended she didn't know their significance, but Kathryn knew it was Sam's way of staying off stage and behind the scenes.

Glancing around the room, Sam leaned in and whispered. "The pilot sitting in the jumpseat in Skylark actually lived through the accident. He burned to death while he was awake. The controllers watched from the tower and could see him trying to get out. Nobody could get to him because of the security door. The crew was locked in."

"My God. They didn't say anything about that on the news." Kathryn put a hand on her chest. "There's supposed to be a security release after power loss."

"Apparently the juice continued to run until it was too late."

"That makes me sick." Kathryn spoke a little too loudly.

Another government-mandated security blanket that resulted in unnecessary deaths. The only way for those doors to be effective was if they were never opened. Anytime the pilots left the flight deck to use the lavatory, they were open to attack. Not until aircraft manufacturers built private quarters for the crew would the flight deck be inaccessible, and that wouldn't happen until the FAA forced the issue, something else she wouldn't hold her breath for.

"The guy watched his own plane crash. He survived. Then he burned to death." Samantha slowly stirred her chowder. "Not a good way to end."

Kathryn touched her briefcase. No, it wasn't.

Samantha caught Kathryn up on the office gossip, and they chatted about the kids while they finished their chowder. Easy, light conversation, and they laughed often. It felt good.

When Sam excused herself to the ladies room, Kathryn glanced around the bar, then opened her briefcase and retrieved a folder. She opened the Regional file and scanned the pages. Sandra had died from smoke inhalation, and 75% of her body had been burned. She'd been pinned to the seat by a piece of the hotel that had impaled the aircraft. Otherwise, she might have escaped. Kathryn continued to turn pages, and there it was.

Both of Sandra's thumbs had been broken. That answered the question of who'd been flying. Whoever had their hands on the controls upon impact would have broken thumbs—one hand on the thrust levers, and the other on the control yoke. Somewhere during the flight, control had shifted from Grant to Sandra. She had been flying the plane when it crashed.

Flipping pages, Kathryn located Grant's medical information. The entire lower half of his body was burned, melted beyond recognition, but the upper torso, arms, and head were identifiable.

Multiple layers of skin had been melted, but the skeletal structure was in place. Dental records positively identified Grant as the captain. Then she read something interesting.

Grant had cranial swelling, and cracks in the side of his head that were not compatible with the plane crash. He wasn't wearing his shoulder harness. His head hung. Cracks across the frontal faceplate indicated he'd hit the control yoke with his face, undoubtedly upon impact; that made sense. However, nothing indicated that he'd been hit by anything on the top of his head during the accident. Clearly he'd had a fractured skull. *Was he flying with a head fracture? Or did it occur when—*

"Do you mind if I bail on you? My supervisor just texted me to come in and see him," Sam said, and Kathryn nearly jumped out of her skin.

"No, of course not. I'll walk you out." She put the files back into her briefcase, left some cash on the table, and then she and Sam walked to the parking lot.

They hugged goodbye and promised to keep in touch, then went in opposite directions to their respective cars.

A breeze drifted across the bay slipping a chill through Kathryn's jacket. She climbed into her car and watched Sam pull out of the parking lot. A black 4Runner that had been parked on the side of the street turned on its lights, and pulled out behind Samantha.

Kathryn's heart sped up. Obviously paranoia was contagious.

CHAPTER 22

"TIME TO WAKE UP, sleeping beauty," Kathryn said when Darby answered her phone. Kathryn was on her way to meet Captain Madden's wife, but too many unanswered questions irritated her, and she needed Darby's help. She wished she'd kept up with her flying, but there was always another reason not to while raising a family. Tomorrow never came.

"What time is it?" Darby asked.

"Just before two."

"Holy shit. I must have slept through my alarm."

"Can you make it to dinner at Jackie's tonight?"

"I'm gonna take a raincheck. I've got a lot to catch up on," Darby said. "What I really need more than dinner is a wife. Jeez, my place is a mess. I haven't paid my bills for weeks, and my dirty clothes are playing rabbit."

"Do you have time to talk tomorrow?"

"Of course. But why don't you get your butt over here now? You can clean and talk. I'll listen."

"I'd love to, but I'm minutes away from meeting the only wife of one of the pilots who'd crashed, that hasn't hung up on me."

"I can't help you on that one. I'm no good at talking to pilots' wives. Tomorrow it is. Give me a shout."

Kathryn closed her phone and dropped it into her purse as she pulled into the Madden's driveway.

The Madden's home was a gorgeous two-story colonial. Stones paving the face accentuated its beauty. She'd lived in a similar home many years before. One major difference was that this house was located in a great neighborhood with a spectacular view of Lake Washington. Hers had been in a working class neighborhood. The taxes had to be horrendous here. She parked in the driveway next to a black Suburban, and got out of her car.

Standing frozen in place, she tried to relax. But her heart raced and her palms were sweating. She'd never had a physical reaction like this to an interview before. She glanced toward the second story, and just off to the right a curtain moved back into place. There was no turning back now.

Where would she begin? What should she say? Anything she said would remind Mrs. Madden of all that she'd lost. This house held the sorrow from a tragic ending, and it would be haunted with visions of what should have been. In many ways it was just like the home Kathryn had left behind. Different neighborhoods didn't change the reality of death.

She felt lightheaded and leaned on her car to steady herself before she headed up the path. She lifted and then dropped the heavy lion's head that served as the doorknocker. The door opened within moments, and Kathryn found herself starring at a woman close to her age. She was shorter than Kathryn by at least four inches, with short blonde hair. Emptiness filled her dark brown eyes, but she smiled warmly at Kathryn.

"Mrs. Madden, I'm Kathryn Jacobs."

Extending her hand, the woman said, "Call me Linda. Please, come in." Her handshake was strong.

She guided Kathryn into the open entryway. They headed left through the dining room and into the kitchen. Hardwood floors sparkled, but the kitchen instantly overpowered them. *Gorgeous.* Stainless steel appliances, a Sub-Zero fridge, and granite slab counters met her eyes. High ceilings and a wall of glass faced Lake Washington.

"I made some coffee. Would you like a cup?"

"That'd be nice, thanks. Cream and sugar if you have it."

Linda's home was immaculate as well as beautiful, but loneliness drifted along the walls like a cold fog. Silence hung in the air. The only sound was a clock ticking. Kathryn wrapped her arms around herself and gave a squeeze.

A plate of cookies sat on the table, and the women nestled into the kitchen nook, with their coffee. They were talking about the weather when the door slammed. Linda cringed, and her expression changed losing the forced smile.

A petite girl, about fifteen, dressed in designer jeans and a sweater with Abercrombie across the chest, and headphones stuck in her ears, entered the kitchen. She threw her backpack on the table, and stopped when she saw Kathryn and Linda sitting in the corner.

She pulled her headphones off and tossed her iPod onto the counter. "Who are you? Another one of Mom's death squad pals?" she spat sharply, then opened the refrigerator as if she had said nothing out of the ordinary.

"Francine!"

"Hanging out with the wives of dead guys isn't going to bring Dad back," Francine said over her shoulder.

"That's enough. You apologize this instant."

"No." She slammed the refrigerator door. "You can't make me. This is a bunch of crap, Mom. Dad's gone and all you do is run a friggin' halfway house for pilots' wives. I'm so sick and tired of it." Tears began to form, but she wasn't about to back down.

"Francine!" Linda looked at Kathryn. "I'm sorry."

"Sorry? You're apologizing to *her?*" Tears flowed freely now. "For what? Jesus Christ, Mom, you're pathetic."

"Go to your room right now."

"I was going anyway. I hate you!" Francine yelled. She ran out of the kitchen. Moments later a door slammed on the second floor.

"I'm so sorry," Linda said, looking away. "Do you have any children?" she asked, wiping a finger under her eye.

"Twin daughters. They're ten, and at camp right now." Kathryn sipped her coffee, then set her cup on the coaster and gazed out the window. She didn't know what to say. Teenage hormones. Dead parent. She knew exactly how Francine felt. And now she knew how her mother had felt, too. Then she looked at Linda. "Teenagers. I'm going to have my hands full pretty soon, too."

"I'm so embarrassed. She's just been so…angry. I've taken her to therapy, but nothing seems to help."

"Time and patience," Kathryn said, placing her hand over Linda's. "She'll come around."

The phone rang and Linda answered it. Speaking softly, she turned her back to Kathryn. Then she covered the phone with her hand and said, "I need a minute. Do you mind?"

Kathryn shook her head. "Of course not."

Linda walked out of the kitchen, and Kathryn returned her gaze to the lake. A black lab ran across their yard and down to the dock. She was lifting her cup when she heard something behind her and turned. Francine.

"I'm sorry I talked to you that way." She had changed her clothes, and was now wearing a baggy sweatshirt and sweatpants. Her long hair was pulled into a ponytail. Her eyes were red and swollen, but the tears had stopped. She stood in the doorway.

"Apology accepted, Francine." Kathryn lifted the plate of cookies and extended it.

Francine glanced at the plate, then came close and took one. "Frankie," she said, as she sat.

"I'm Kathryn Jacobs. Kat. I work for the NTSB."

Frankie's eyes widened. "Wow. That's cool."

"Thanks. I'm really sorry about your dad." Francine shrugged in response. The daggers Frankie had thrown at her mother were filled with pain, masked as hatred. Frankie and Linda were headed down a dangerous road—one without an exit, one that Kathryn had traveled down herself. She knew it well, and didn't wish that journey for anyone. She also knew there was only one way to break through to this girl.

"I know what it's like to lose a parent," Kathryn said, and Francine rolled her eyes sliding her chair back, and stood. "My mom died when I was seventeen. She killed herself."

"What?" Francine slowly sat.

"I was the one who found her," Kathryn said. She glanced out the window. "She'd been having a hard time with life. I guess, as a teenager, I wasn't the easiest to live with. Then one day she just decided to end it.

"When someone leaves that quickly, there are so many things left unsaid. I wish I could've had one more day." Kathryn turned toward her. "Your dad dying in a plane crash must've been horrible." When Frankie didn't respond she added, "I lost my brother and uncle in a small plane crash, too."

"Jeez." Francine put a hand to her mouth. "I'm so sorry."

"It was a long time ago. I think the hardest part is when it's sudden. Unexpected. Maybe if someone's sick, you have time to say goodbye."

Kathryn never spoke of her past, but if she could help reach Francine before it was too late, she had to try. Understanding her pain on a parallel level was the only way.

"It's not fair. I hate him for dying." Tears filled her eyes. Looking directly at Kathryn she said, "I told him that I'd wished he were dead a couple months ago. I told him that I hated him. Then I stopped talking to him."

"Sweetie, he knew that you didn't mean it. I said some pretty hateful things to my mom before she died, too." Kathryn squeezed Francine's hand. "I felt so angry when my uncle and brother died. But years later, when my mom died, my feelings moved to pure hate, blaming my dad for everything. I haven't talked to him for, gosh, twenty-four years."

Frankie's eyes widened. "That's a long time."

Kathryn nodded. "Too long. I've been such an idiot. I was so mad at my mom that I pushed him away. I blamed him."

"Why don't you call him now?"

"I don't know what I'd say. It's been too long." Kathryn took a sip of coffee and watched Frankie over the edge of her cup. "The thing is, I never thought about how my dad felt when Mom died. All I thought about was myself. My loss. My hurting. I was so mad. I took my anger out on him, and blamed him for everything."

Tears leaked from Francine's eyes. She picked at a chocolate chip on the top of her cookie. "I've been so mean to my mom, too." She looked up. "She hates me now."

"Your mom doesn't hate you, Frankie. She loves you. The way I see it, the only way the two of you will get through this is together."

"But what do I say?"

"Tell her how you feel. Everything else will fall into place." Kathryn looked past Frankie. Linda stood in the doorway, tears streaming down her cheeks.

Frankie followed Kathryn's gaze and saw her mother. She jumped up and ran over, and wrapped her arms around her mom hugging her tight. "I'm so sorry, mom. I don't hate you," She cried. "I love you so much."

Linda closed her eyes and hugged her daughter. They swayed back and forth. "I love you too, sweetheart. Everything is going to be alright." Linda opened her eyes, tears flowing, and silently said, "Thank you." Then kissed the top of her daughter's head.

Kathryn stood and mouthed, "I'll call you tomorrow," then let herself out the front door.

She thought of her dad then glanced at her watch. If she hurried, she still had time to get home and take a shower before Bill arrived.

CHAPTER 23

BILL PULLED into the driveway. Irritation swept over him when he didn't see Kathryn's car. Maybe she was with McAllister again. He'd know soon enough. He climbed out of his Porsche, glanced at the oil spot where Kathryn's car should have been, and decided that it was probably a good thing that she wasn't home after all. She'd want details of the meeting that he wouldn't have time to provide.

Kathryn taking the job behind his back, he'd counted on. But her not telling him about meeting McAllister, after he confronted her, surprised him. Kathryn took honesty seriously. Maybe she was reacting to her medication.

When he met Kathryn, he knew he had found the perfect replacement for Darby, after Darby made it clear she wouldn't have anything to do with him. Kathryn loved the industry as much as he did, and she also had a ton of baggage that he could use when the time came. He'd been fortunate when their paths had crossed and he'd made sure to stoke the fire to her burning passion. The kids were a necessity to keep hold on her. His initial fear had always been she would give up on her dreams and fall blindly into motherhood. But the first time a plane crashed and he saw her reaction, he knew that would never be the case.

He opened the front door, then picked up the note laying on the floor.

"Gone to lunch. Be home by 430. Dinner with Greg and Jackie at 5. Love, Kat."

Nice. He wadded the note into a ball, tossed it to the floor, and headed up the stairs. He unbuttoned and removed his shirt, rehashing his day with each step, and suddenly realized he'd folded his shirt. He grinned. Some habits were hard to break. Shaking it, he turned it inside out and tossed it on the floor in front of the closet, then removed his pants and threw them over the back of the chair.

Bill had noted Kathryn's irritation the moment he'd started this behavior a month prior. But she'd yet to say anything. She just continued to pick up after him. As far as wives went, she was pretty good. Too bad he didn't need or want one.

He quickly climbed into his workout gear and pressed speed dial on his cell phone. It rang as he walked downstairs but went directly to voice mail.

It was already 2:30 when he stood on the front porch. He stretched his arms out wide, then high overhead. He had just enough time for a run, a shower, and a few calls before Kathryn returned.

The visibility had lifted, but the fog drifted lazily through the treetops. The afternoon air had a crispness to it that made for excellent running weather. He loved this time of year.

Bill pulled the door closed. Headphones in place, the beat of Shakira's "Whenever Whatever" ricocheted through his brain. He turned up the volume and headed for the street, ecstatic at how everything was coming together. The network he'd built was strong, and serving him well.

In a day the official results of the election would be announced, and he would be in perfect position for his next move. Steps had shifted, molded, and changed along the way, but he always held fast with one focus in mind—to fix the airline industry at whatever cost.

The deaths with so many crashes burned in his soul, but the reality of those accidents and how they helped his cause could not be denied. He would never be able to control the industry if planes didn't crash. The FAA wouldn't mandate policy until the public cried for a solution, and the airlines wouldn't take action until they were forced. They didn't care; they had insurance.

Bill waved and flashed a smile at the car hesitating at the stop sign for him to pass. He then continued to sprint down the sidewalk, beginning to break a sweat.

The shutdown of the airline industry would take the country, and the world, hostage. For that reason, the president of the United States had the right to stop pilots from striking. Bill's heart beat rapidly and his face reddened. *What kind of leverage is that for a union?*

His dad's airline hadn't been unionized. Had it been, he wouldn't have lost his job and blown his brains out.

With the strength of the airline unions came stability for the pilots, security knowing their jobs were protected, and safety for the public. Protection from the bean counters chipping away at work rules to increase the bottom line at the expense of safety. The union started that way, and somewhere along the journey the leaders had lost their way. Instead of fighting for what's right for their charges, they climbed into bed with management with the reward of power, prestige, and money. The union job shifted from one of servitude to one of self-indulgence. Time off, dinners, $200 bottles of wine, $50 cigars—all paid for by the pilots, compliments of their dues. There were a few good men left standing, but they were the minority and their hands were tied.

The union needed a hero to take a stand, someone like Truman who wasn't afraid to drop a bomb to win the war—"Carry the battle to them. Don't let them bring it to you. Put them on the defensive and don't ever apologize for anything." Bill didn't take those words lightly, and he'd used them as the foundation of his platform.

What he hadn't envisioned was impact that power and control had over him. Every time a plane crashed reminded him of why he was doing this—for the greater good. But the power fed his soul.

The daily decline in the airline industry emotionally financed his campaign. There were so many issues within the airline industry, and he built upon them all. Now everyone wanted answers and easy solutions, and it wouldn't be long until the public was afraid to fly.

Bill's heart pounded with force, and he was soaked with sweat when he jumped the final curb and ran up the stairs to his porch. He leaned over, with hands on knees, to catch his breath. The neighbor raking leaves across the street waved. Bill smiled and returned the wave.

His front door was ajar. He hesitated. He hadn't left it that way. Or had he? He opened it slowly then yelled, "Hello?" Then stood silent, listening. Nothing. He closed the door behind him, and headed for the kitchen, glancing into the rooms as he went.

He poured non-fat milk into the blender and added liquid vitamins and vanilla protein powder. He dumped in a handful of ice and three raw eggs, and pressed liquefy. He chugged a glass of water while he waited for the drink to finish blending.

Lifting the concoction to his lips, he noticed Kathryn's headset beside her laptop on the kitchen table. He stared at it for a moment, then opened the computer and pressed the power button. He finished his drink while the computer booted up. He pulled off his shirt and wiped his face with it then tossed it on the table. He glanced at his watch, then left the kitchen and ran up the stairs.

Bill pulled off his shorts, threw them aside, and turned the shower on. While it warmed, he brushed his teeth and stripped out a piece of floss and began to work. Steam filled the room and he wiped a circle in the mirror. Dropping the floss onto the floor, he stepped into the shower.

He was in a full lather when the shower door opened.

"Can I help you with that?"

What the...? His heart slammed against the wall of his chest. "What in the hell are you doing here?"

"I wanted to finish our discussion."

"Jesus Christ, Kristen, what if Kathryn comes home?"

"Oh, sweetie, that's what'll make this so exciting."

He'd been furious when she'd told him she was quitting early, but everything always worked out *exactly* as it should. The flow of life moved like the blood in his body—to his benefit. Pushing the timing up worked better, especially with Kathryn returning to work earlier than planned. He'd told Walker to hire her, but not until next month. To hell with Walker and his games.

Kristen slipped into the shower behind him, wrapped her arms around his waist and pressed her body against his back. She rubbed her breasts into him, and slid her mound against his leg. Her fingers slid through the soapy hairs on his chest. She played with his nipples and he became instantly hard.

She moved her hands down his abdomen and grabbed him and stroked. "God, that feels wonderful," he said. "But you can't just show up like this...ahhh."

"I'll make it worth your while," she whispered. Maneuvering in front of him, she dropped to her knees, and licked his...

"Oh God," he groaned. The thrill of her in his house *had* escalated the level of excitement. He pulled her to a standing position and took her face in his hands and whispered, "You cannot be here. You know that...right?" Then he kissed her hard without waiting for her reply.

He maneuvered her against the shower wall and pushed his body against hers. She raised a leg and wrapped it around his waist, and when he pressed inside of her she wrapped her other leg around him and clung tight.

She hung on him, legs around his waist, and he stepped out of the shower and set her on the counter, their bodies still connected. He watched her ass in the mirror, spread on the counter, and he grew within her.

"So, what are you going to do about it?" She whispered. "Punish me?"

"You have no idea," he said, pulling her hips into him so hard that her head fell back and slammed against the mirror.

"Ow," she said, touching the back of her head.

"Punish you? I've just begun to make good on that promise."

"No. Please don't hurt me," she cried, trying to push him off. When he stumbled, she kicked him hard. He lost his balance and fell backwards against the shower door. The glass cracked and she laughed.

"Shit," he said, glancing at the damage. She jumped off the counter and ran to the bedroom and he chased. Diving toward her, he knocked her to the bed, and threw himself on top of her.

"Stop. Let me go. Please," she cried as she hit him, laughing as she did. He pinned her arms above her head and held her wrists tight. The power of control fueled his erection. She struggled and bucked, kicking her legs wildly then smacked a foot on the side of his head.

"You'll pay for that," he said, laughing.

"Oh yeah? You think you're such a tough guy."

He bent down and placed his mouth on hers. She bit his lip, and he tasted blood. It drove him wild. He released her arms and stood at the end of the bed, then grabbed her legs and pulled her to the edge. He knelt at the end of the bed and put his face between her legs and returned the bite, and sucked.

"Shit! That hurts." She hit his head with an open palm, but spread her legs wider.

"I know," he said climbing on top of her. "That's what makes this so 'exciting.'" Then he entered her with force. She pressed the soles of her feet on the edge of the bed and lifted her hips toward him, and he slammed into her again holding her tight. He continued to move, quick and violent, and, with hips raised, she presented herself to him. Her arms flung wide and she grabbed the bedspread.

"Oh God. No. Stop. Stop." Then she threw her arms around his waist and pulled him close, and they rolled over and fell off the bed onto the floor. She landed on top of him, and his body hit hard, and knocked the wind out of him.

"Damn," he said, after he caught his breath.

She climbed on top of him, spreading her legs wider as she straddled him, and rode wildly until they came together. She was absolutely right. She did make it worth his while.

He rolled her off his body and looked at the clock. He had less than thirty minutes until Kathryn's return. He stood and pulled on a pair of shorts.

"How'd you get here?" he asked

"Plane. Duh." She leaned back on her arms.

"Don't be a smartass." He pulled on a pair of jeans.

"Rental car. I parked a block over," she said, standing. "Don't worry, nobody saw me."

"You can't be doing this. If you need me, we'll get a room."

"Don't get a big head," she said and smiled seductively grabbing his crotch. "I came to see Daddy, to tell him I'm quitting. I'll be in town for a few days."

"I loved the afternoon snack. But if Kathryn catches you here, then we're both screwed, and our plans are for nothing." He tipped her chin and gently kissed her lips, her brow, and then the poolside bruise on her cheek. "Is that what you want?"

"You know what I want."

"Good. Then get that pretty little ass out of here, and I'll see you in L.A. in a couple days." What was he thinking? He didn't need to wait a few days. "What if I take the L.A. flight tomorrow? Will you trip trade and go with me?"

"You'd do that for me?" she said.

"Of course. I love you sweetie," Bill said, and then he touched her chin and kissed her gently on the lips.

"Think we could we get rid of the first officer for a few minutes in cruise and have a quickie?"

"I don't see why not."

She climbed into her clothes and straightened the bed. "Good as new," she said, and patted the pillows. She picked up the picture of Bill and Kathryn on the nightstand, and stared at it for a moment. Then placed it face down, and disappeared into the bathroom.

"I'll be out in a minute," she called.

Bill picked up his phone and pressed speed dial. It was answered after the third ring. "I've got a bit of a problem here and could use your help."

CHAPTER 24

JOHN SAT in the dark room—one door, no windows—and listened. The surveillance system had been set up with an option to monitor live, in addition to record. He was live, and more than once during the previous ten minutes, as he'd been pacing, he reached for his phone, hesitated, and left it in his pocket.

The first thud and the threats had alarmed him, but he'd heard laughter. Besides, if Bill hurt Kristen, there wasn't a damn thing he could do to get to her in time anyway. The fact that he didn't have a court order to tape was the least of his worries. He loved Kristen like a daughter and wasn't sure what he'd do if anything happened to her. Walker would lose it—he loved his daughter more than life itself.

The surveillance was Homeland's baby, and under normal conditions, the department had the power to do anything they liked, including tape without a warrant. This was anything but normal. Both he and Walker would be dropped in the desert if anyone discovered the actual purpose of their surveillance. Maybe. Chances were that he'd be sacrificed, and Walker would walk away unscathed as he always had.

Despite the crack of glass, ensuing chase, and apparent fight, he'd heard laughter. Hers. He knew she enjoyed the roughness, and it pained him to listen to it now. John shook his head and wondered when she'd lost her way.

Wiring the Jacobs' home had been John's responsibility, not listening. Walker was supposed to have an exclusive on that while he monitored Bill's late night union meetings, but John knew that was a ruse. *Late night meetings in the office, yes. But the bedroom, too? Yeah, right.* Walker knew Kristen and Bill had been seeing each other for the previous six months, and John suspected that's what this taping was all about.

Distracting Kathryn took no effort while his men got into the house, but he felt horrible lying to her. She deserved better than that. He was also supposed to have convinced her to come back to work—Walker's orders—another agenda to piss off Bill.

Kathryn's working undercover was a bit more complicated. If Walker would keep his mouth shut, all would be fine. By no means did he want to cause her any problems by having Bill find out she'd lied to him. He'd witnessed Bill's temper firsthand, and that was one hole he chose not to climb into. He sure didn't want to push Kathryn in, either. John needed her, but he also cared too much for her to put her in harms way. If it came down to alliances between Kathryn and Walker, he knew who would win.

John had been Walker's right-hand-man for years. But it was damn time he took control of his own destiny. He glanced around the room and nodded. He'd found a way to do just that. He'd come close to installing cameras, too, but now he was glad that he hadn't. Watching Kristen with anyone was not a visual he wanted to invite into his nightmares.

Taking orders from Homeland Security was far beyond the scope of his duties, but for Walker he had made concessions. John wasn't sure where his life fell off the track. He was supposed to investigate aviation-related accidents and incidents, document and report. That was it. However, watching planes crash, with his hands tied, reinforced what he already knew—he had to get out of this office and into Washington. Unfortunately, to be appointed to any position out East took political connections, and despite Walker's connections, and promises, none were ever made.

It had been a long thirty-eight years. He'd moved up rapidly for the first twelve until he made director of the west coast region. Then there was no place for him to go. To make matters worse, his lifelong friend, Dick Walker, had rapidly moved ahead of him to the Regional Director's office in Homeland, a job that, in hindsight, should have been his. John had supported Walker during his career, and where had that gotten him? Nowhere.

If he were going to be more than a glorified administrator, he'd need to get one of the two upcoming positions in Washington. He needed to get noticed on a global level and he had to act now. He had to solve these goddamn accidents.

The second thud sounded like someone had been hit over the head and John touched his phone, but the following dialogue, from both Bill and Kristen, allowed his shoulders to relax and he removed his hand from his pocket, once again. He closed his eyes at the ensuing noises, and shook his head.

If Kathryn came home early, it would be over for all of them. He looked at her position on the GPS. That wasn't an issue at the moment. He wondered if Walker was listening to the live audio, half expecting the man to charge into the room at any minute. He sure wouldn't want to be in Walker's shoes right now, but he'd do just about anything to have the equivalent of his friend's DHS position in Washington.

John might have stopped the terrorists on 9/11 if he'd been given the opportunity. But nobody would listen. The Attorney General declared that case an intentional criminal act, and the

NTSB had to surrender control of the investigation. Then grew the power of the Department of Homeland Security. DHS was now the group called if an accident was connected to criminal activity. In the case of the September 11th attacks, the Department of Justice took over. Either way, he was out.

He was capable of so much more than they gave him. He needed to get out of Seattle and into D.C. if his existence was going to mean anything.

Kristen's cries pained his heart, and he closed his eyes.

Sacrificing a marriage and family, he'd dedicated his life to his job, and to his friends and their successes. He'd been a fool. As the accidents increased, more departments were created and his power diminished. He'd thought it would have been the other way around. Assisting Walker was the only avenue that could lead him to where he needed to be. This was all he had left.

Either Walker would hold true to his promise and recommend him to the U.S. President for a board position, or he would use the tapes as leverage. If Walker were listening now, he'd be on the tape at any moment, and John would have him for attempted murder. Who was he kidding? He would have Walker for murder.

He knew his friend well. Walker was an engine ten thousand hours beyond overhaul, ready to explode. Anything was possible, and he would be in position to take advantage of the situation, whatever that might be. Walker may just end up being a casualty. It was all up to him. If he was listening to this, Bill was as good as dead.

He closed his eyes and focused on the voices on the other end of the line. Kristen was off to the bathroom. A door closed, and then Bill spoke to someone. "I've got a bit of a problem here, I could use your help."

John wondered who else knew about Kristen, then opened his eyes and looked at the GPS. *No kidding you have a problem.*

Kathryn had begun moving, and she was headed home. Bill had maybe ten minutes. He watched the lights blink toward their moment of truth, and then her movement stopped. She sat in position, the green light flashed. Then the lights began movement again—this time in the opposite direction of home.

Chapter 25

KATHRYN OPENED the front door and walked through the living room, following the voices into the kitchen. Jackie was setting the table, and Bill and Greg were out back with the barbeque, their voices carrying through the back door. Bill was laughing about something. It had been a long time since she'd heard him enjoying himself.

"Hey, Kat," Jackie said as she removed baked potatoes from the oven.

"Sorry to sneak out on you this morning," Kathryn said, removing the bottle of steak sauce from a bag and setting it on the counter. She struggled out of her coat.

"I'm glad you did," Jackie said, looking over her shoulder. "Last night was incredible," she whispered. "What I could remember of it. But this morning…Well, let's just say that Greg is very, very, relaxed."

"Oh, Jackie, that's great." Kathryn smiled, and gave her a hug. She was genuinely happy for both Greg and Jackie.

Kathryn set the table, and then poured water for everyone while Jackie threw a salad together.

"Kat," Jackie said. When she hesitated, Kathryn turned to face her. "I need to tell you—"

"Knock, knock," Darby said, walking into the kitchen and interrupting Jackie.

"You came," Jackie said, hugging her and ending whatever she was about to tell Kathryn.

"Yeah, well, there was free food and my best friends." Darby flashed a grin at Kathryn. Then Greg and Bill came into the kitchen, and the air hardened.

"Hey ladies," Greg said. "Darby, I'm glad you could join us." Then he turned toward Kathryn and hugged her, holding on longer than normal. "Thanks for picking up the steak sauce."

"Darby," Bill said with a short nod and a huge smile, Darby returned the nod brusquely.

Greg opened two bottles of wine, and Jackie set an additional place setting. Everyone took a seat as Greg filled the glasses, filling his only half full. "To Bill, our newly elected chapter president." He extended his glass.

"Oh my God, congratulations!" Jackie cried. "Kat, you didn't say anything." Kathryn refrained from admitting that she hadn't known he'd won. Bill had told her the election was a month away.

Bill raised his glass. "Well, it won't be official until all ballots are counted tomorrow, but looks that way."

"Congratulations, I knew you could do it," Kathryn said. She was proud of him. She had been so caught up in her life she'd forgotten the significance of his. This was a very big deal.

"Finally, we'll have someone in there with some balls." Greg winked at Darby. "With the new contract coming up, we'll finally get somewhere."

Darby sipped her wine without comment.

"What do you plan on doing that's different?" Jackie asked Bill.

"No more pay cuts. A thirty-percent raise. Improved work rules. And I'm giving power back to the flight crews."

"Here, here," Greg said.

"How can the airlines afford that?" Kathryn asked. "With the price of fuel, aging equipment, and regulatory fees, expenses are higher than they've ever been."

"They could afford it if they re-regulated the airlines," Greg said.

"That'll be a cold day in hell," Darby said, pouring a pile of steak sauce on her plate and passing the bottle to Greg.

"Hell is about to freeze." Bill lifted his glass and tipped it toward the air before he drank. "They won't be able to afford *not to* when I'm done sticking it to them. Our union's been so worried about increasing membership they haven't noticed they're creating jobs not worth having. They've allowed work rules and pay cuts to subsidize the airline that's killed the quality of our jobs.

"Guys can't afford to become pilots because they'll never see a return on their investment in training, or time. Hell, we'll never get another college graduate because there's no way for them to pay back their student loans. Then there's some new legislation about mandating first officers to have fifteen hundred hours. That's really going to screw things up." Bill stabbed a steak and dropped it onto his plate.

Moments after Bill quieted the table with his rant, Greg said, "Pilots won't be able to get that kind of time."

"The impact will be on the quality of pilots we'll see in the future," Bill said. "Guys who don't have the grades or aptitude for college will become the new generation of aviators. Spoiled little rich kids whose daddies bought them their training. Hell, we'll be flying with a bunch of *next gen* morons. Anyone with brains and initiative will do something else." Bill emptied his glass and reached for a bottle.

"How *exactly* are you going to fix it?" Kathryn asked, picking at her vegetables. "The economy's down. People aren't flying. Load factors are as bad as they were just after the September 11th attacks.

There's no money."

"That's because the CEOs are draining the companies," Jackie answered, passing Kathryn the salad. "Right Greg?"

"Not all of them are raping the airlines," Darby countered. "Besides, you need leadership. And you get what you pay for. If management doesn't get some kind of incentive to stick around, *then* you can kiss the airline goodbye and—"

"Leadership? That's a joke," Bill interrupted. "By cutting corners and chipping away at the pilots, they'll end up paying more in the long run. Look at the numbers of planes going down. How much is *that* costing the industry?"

"You can't blame the airline industry for shitty pilots," Darby said. "That's training and standardization's responsibility. Or perhaps it's just the union's fault protecting them."

"Perhaps," Bill said.

Darby's mouth opened to say something, but didn't. Kathryn sipped her wine, thankful Darby didn't get into politics of the union with Bill. She thought about Frankie and Linda. What kind of pilot had Grant been? He was a check airman, yes, but what else had been going on in his life? Where was his mind? And how did they afford that house? She'd contemplated the impact of stress and fatigue as attributing factors to the accidents. After listening to the audios, she knew that the pilots' behaviors were anything but normal. She'd rule nothing out.

Bill filled everyone's glass. Greg pushed his aside and switched to diet soda. Kathryn continued to nurse her wine, but she felt queasy again.

"So, how will you change the trajectory this industry has taken?" Darby asked Bill.

"Re-regulation. There's no way in today's market for carriers to compete without losing money, especially if people can pay less to fly to Portland than they have to pay for a tank of gas to drive."

"I never did understand deregulation," Jackie said, breaking open her potato. Kathryn took a deep breath. *Not again.*

"Hell, deregulation was just some idiot's plan to increase competitiveness, and create more productivity in hopes of lowering prices. But the damned government focused only on the price the consumer would pay, not on the actual cost to the airlines. Legacy carriers had to modernize equipment, and—"

"Legacy carrier?" Jackie interrupted, narrowing her eyes.

Kathryn loved her friend and how clueless she was as to the history of the airline industry. To Jackie, the airline just paid their bills and took her husband away for long stretches of time. However, Bill was now in his full glory. He knew *everything*, and he loved the platform.

"The old airlines, those guys who don't exist anymore, like Universal," Bill said, stuffing a bite of steak into his mouth. He washed it down with a long drink of wine and continued.

"Fuel prices increased and airlines couldn't make a profit. It enabled anyone jump into the game, and the legacy carriers couldn't afford to compete. Their only option was to lower their fares to match those of startups, or else they'd get nobody to fly. The legacy carrier expenses were so much higher, they got squeezed tight." Bill shook his head, "It's a crying shame what they were allowed to do."

Since deregulation, nine major airlines and hundreds of smaller airlines, had liquidated as a result. Eastern, Midway, Braniff, Pan Am, TWA and Universal—all distant memories.

"Bill, didn't your dad work for Universal?" Darby asked. Kathryn kicked her under the table. She knew damn well that Bill's dad had worked there and was just being nasty. Bill's was a wound that shouldn't be uncovered.

"I loved Universal," Jackie said. "I actually wanted to become a pilot because they'd let me sit in the cockpit every time we went on vacation. I always got wings, too," She added, stumbling over her words, having drunk too much again.

"What happened?" Kathryn asked. "Why didn't you pursue a career in flying?"

"Everyone told me that girls couldn't fly. I believed them."

"Well, you can teach a monkey to fly, but that doesn't mean you can teach it how to think," Bill said, and laughed.

"Thank God for that," Darby said, choking on her wine. "Otherwise, they wouldn't have elected you president." With that, everyone laughed, including Bill.

Universal had been as much a member of Bill's family as their dog had been. His dad's life and identity had been wrapped around the title of Captain. And then he was fired. There hadn't been any protection because his airline hadn't been unionized.

There had been some incident with a passenger, and Bill's dad supposedly handled it incorrectly. He had lost his job without even as much as an investigation. They took his life.

When Kathryn first met Bill, he'd told her, over a few bottles of wine, about the father he'd loved and lost—the reason Bill became a pilot. That was the first and last time she had seen tears in his eyes, and they'd never talked about his dad again. But his passion for the airline union was equal only to his passion for airplanes and flying.

"Whatever happened to Universal?" Jackie asked.

"Dyer murdered the airline by playing with the unions. The pilots and flight attendants had called a sympathy strike for the mechanics, and he shut down operations.

"He immediately sold off pieces to his other companies. Hell, he didn't sell them, he gave them away. Universal filed bankruptcy five days later and ran the airline with non-union employees."

"Jackie. More wine, please," Darby said, wiggling an empty glass over the table. Kathryn smiled her thanks. Bill's soapbox was becoming wearing. She knew that Bill's vengeance against the industry was a survival mechanism, and a place to lay blame for what had happened to his father. But sometimes it was nice to have dinner without discussing the past.

"So how do you get them to re-regulate?" Jackie asked, still visibly struggling to understand the finer points of the conversation through the haze of alcohol. Kathryn glanced at Darby who rolled her eyes.

"The only way the government will re-regulate the industry is if true monopolies set precedence, planes keep crashing, or if we, as a union, take a stand," Bill said.

"A Universal Airlines repeat," Darby said, then sipped her wine.

Bill ignored Darby and spoke directly to Jackie. He always had patience with Jackie, as he talked down to her to get her to understand. "The pilots will establish the work rules, the pay and benefits, and we'll tell the company that it's non-negotiable."

Non-negotiable meant a standoff and strike. Kathryn felt a ball of nerves grow in her stomach. "Do you think that with today's economy, the pilots will vote that in?"

"I don't care what the pilots think. There will never be another pay cut. We'll demand our salary to be increased. I don't care if they lay off half the pilots."

Darby's mouth fell open. "Are you crazy?"

"For years the company has threatened layoffs in lieu of pay cuts, and our union has been gutless in fear of losing jobs. They've rolled over and we all took it in the ass. The union wants numbers, and we lose jobs anyway. But not before salaries and work rules are destroyed. Last year, the union signed a contract that gave a DC-9 captain the same rate as a 747 captain by cutting the 74's pay. The 9 carries a fraction of what the Whale carries, and the domestic pilots don't fight fatigue that the international pilots do. Or spend twelve to eighteen days away from their families every month. Then look at the number of passengers the pilots are responsible for on a 747 compared to a DC-9. There has to be a reward at the top for seniority, something the 9 guys could have looked forward to.

Kathryn was still back on the 'laying off half the pilots' comment. Jackie's face turned white. Greg was junior with the company. He'd be laid off for sure. With the current state of their finances, they'd be on the street within months, and Jackie wouldn't be able to return to work. They'd lay off flight attendants, too. Kathryn didn't know what to say. How could Bill do this to them?

Greg calmly set down his fork. "They'd probably furlough anyway. I'd gladly sacrifice my job for a couple months to take a stand and have a job we can be proud of. I have the lives of hundreds of people in my hands with each departure, and somebody needs to see the value in that."

"Growth is the goal of any airline," Bill said. "If we hold them to the fire and accept nothing less than what we're worth...hell yes, we'll lose a few thousand jobs in the process, but then they'll eventually have to rehire everyone if they want to grow and prosper."

Darby choked on her wine. *A few thousand?*

"A couple of months?" Jackie asked almost simultaneously.

"It could be years. We're in for a war." Bill tipped back his glass of wine until he emptied it. He reached for the bottle. "It's the only way."

CHAPTER 26

BILL STARED out the window at the airport with both palms on the windowsill. The building was dark, his office silent. Everyone had long since gone. After dinner he had told Kathryn he'd meet her at home. This detour, however, he'd forgotten to mention.

The buzz from the wine was still with him, as was the high from his speech that morning. Pure electricity sparked within, now that the end was near. Kristen's change of plans worked perfectly combined with the timing of Kathryn's involvement—a sign from his father that everything was a go.

His office, on the top floor, had a first-class view of the airport. He'd miss it when he moved to Washington He slid his hand over the eight-inch deep windowsill and smiled. He'd had many women on this spot. With planes departing into the night, traffic below, and a naked woman on the ledge, life had been good. Kristen had been the best, and he'd miss her, but there would be more windowsills and women in D.C.—all an added benefit.

Bill stood frozen in the darkness watching the lights flash in the distance. The roar of a departing jet rumbled the glass, and a siren screamed below. His heart rate increased and sweat formed on his brow as if it were yesterday.

"GOD DAMN IT Bill, we're all going to fucking die!" Grant yelled. He paced, stumbling in the brush he fell to his knees and cried,

"Those fucking gooks! They killed Jack!"

"Stay with me buddy!" Bill yelled at Grant. "Get off your ass and help me find the living. Now!"

Bill cradled what was left of Jack's head in his lap, as he watched his father die again. Unfortunately Jack was still breathing, and his one remaining eye locked with Bill's and cried for help. "It won't be long," Bill whispered. When Grant turned his back, Bill pulled his knife from the sheath, and stabbed it into the center of Jack's chest, crunching through bone and into his heart, stopping the hell that had become the end of his life. "I love you man," he whispered.

Bill slid Jack off his lap and turned toward Grant's screams.

"Over here! I found Aaron." Bill ran to his side. "Those damn gooks nailed his ass. He's going to fucking die!" Grant's hands now covered his ears as he screamed above the roar of gunfire, and explosions yards away.

Bill punched Grant in the stomach, and as Grant doubled over Bill yelled, "God dammit Grant! Nobody else is going to die! Get a fucking grip!" Bill dropped to his knees and saw that Aaron's legs had been hit with Napalm. The Vietnamese hadn't done this one. Their own pilots had. He pulled his knife out once again, and cut then ripped the burning fatigues from Aaron's body, but not before the damage underneath had been done.

"Holy fuck! Holy Mother of God!" Walt cried when he saw Aaron's legs, then turned and emptied his stomach. Brian was sitting on the ground, arms wrapped around his knees, pulled tight, crying as he rocked. Shots rang out in the distance, and airplanes rumbled overhead. Blinded by the ongoing flares, Bill now tried to focus in the black of the jungle.

They had trained them how to fire guns, but nobody had taught them how to deal with the blackness of the jungle or the power of the hole. They'd forgotten to tell them they'd become victims of claymore mines. Bill glanced at Aaron's melted legs. They also forgot to mention the reality of their own pilots dropping a death sentence upon them when the gooks snuck inside the wire. None of them were prepared to watch those they had depended upon, and had grown to love, destroyed in a war they never should have been part of. But at eighteen years old, Bill knew the only teacher would be experience.

Bill worked quickly pulling the shirt off his back and ripping it into strips to bandage Aaron's legs. Infection would set in, but if he could keep them covered and the bugs out, there was a chance Aaron would walk again.

Grant, calm now, focused on helping by holding the swatches in place. Walt handed Bill his shirt then stood nearby. Bill ripped it and wrapped Aaron. He spoke while he worked—

"Aaron, this is nothing, buddy. Hell, you've just got your ticket home. We're all going home. I promise you that," he said, making eye contact with each of the three men left standing in his troop. Then he refocused his attention on Aaron, but spoke loud enough for all to hear.

"As my father stands with God, I promise you all one thing— I will get you back to the United States of America if I have to throw you all on my fucking back and carry you out myself!"

Brian's rocking had stopped and he sat close to Bill, riveted on every word. Hope. They needed hope, and a future they could focus on. Bill knew that all too well.

"When we get out of here we'll fly. Never again will those fucking sky boys dump on us. We'll become one of them."

Bill had fought the desire to become a pilot after watching what the job had done to his dad. But the reality was, it was the flying that his father had loved and the system that had failed him, and flying was a part of Bill's soul. Times were changing, and there was a future for them all. Bill would see to it.

"To be in the sky is to be in control of our destinies," Bill said, putting the final wrap on Aaron.

When Bill stood and stretched his legs, he said, "Do what I say, and I promise you this—I will get your out of this hell-hole! We will become pilots! We will live and nobody will ever touch us again!" Bill extended his arm, with his hand in a fist, and Grant placed his hand over the top of Bill's. Brian covered Grant's and Walt placed his hand on top. Bill encased their hands with his other. "Together," he said, and squeezed.

Aaron moaned and Bill looked down. Aaron's arm was extended towards theirs. They all dropped to their knees and embraced Aaron's hand, and his life.

THE KNOCK at the door was expected, and he turned as it opened. "Thanks for coming." Bill spread his arms wide and hugged Captain Aaron Stephens, who held him in a strong embrace. They patted each other's backs.

"Excellent speech today," Aaron said, stepping back and shaking Bill's hand.

Bill closed the door and locked it, then turned, wearing a serious face. "Can I pour you a drink?" Bill asked, reaching for the bottle of scotch.

"No thanks."

"I think you should have one," Bill said, half-filling each of the two glasses with gold liquid. "I've got some bad news."

Aaron accepted the glass, eyes questioning, waiting for Bill to speak.

Bill let the moment linger before he finally said, "They're pulling you off the flight line at the end of next week."

Aaron set his glass on Bill's desk. "I was supposed to have my review at the end of next month, *after* the Amsterdam flight."

Bill pulled a hand through his hair. "I'm sorry. Honestly, I think they're doing this to get at me. Management's threatened, and they want to hurt me where it matters—my pilots. You're an easy target." Bill sat on the edge of his desk and folded his arms. "Maybe this is best."

"*Best?* Bullshit!" Aaron paced. "This is not best. They can't do this to me. Not after everything we've worked for. I won't let you and the guys down."

"There's nothing you can do. Besides, you're not letting anyone down. Sometimes things are beyond our control. I'll take the last flight. I'll take her in and then it'll be over."

"No. You're not doing this without me. If it hadn't been for you, we'd still be rotting in Nam. There is no way in hell I'll be left behind. That was not the deal. I go. Then you."

"Dammit, Aaron, sit. Please." Bill extended a hand toward the couch. But Aaron stood his ground and folded his arms. "Come on, buddy. You've been there with all of us. It just didn't work out. You can stay behind and make sure our actions weren't in vain."

"There is no way in hell I'm staying behind. Shit. They've never pulled anyone for a downed check before. I thought it'd help to tank one." Aaron began pacing again. "This is not how this was supposed to go down. I'm ready. I'm so ready it'll kill me to stand by and watch." He walked to the window and stared out.

Bill joined him and they stood in silence for a few moments.

"What if I could put you on a flight before they pull you?"

Aaron turned and faced him. "Could you do that?"

"Perhaps."

"Yes. Hell yes! Whatever magic you've got up your sleeve, do it."

Bill sat at his desk and picked up the phone then dialed the home number of the manager of crew scheduling. Aaron turned and leaned against the ledge with arms folded. Listening. Waiting.

"Brenda, Bill here." Bill leaned back in his chair and crossed one leg over the other.

"Hey, love. I understand congratulations are in order," she said.

"Soon, real soon." Bill winked at Aaron.

"I think a celebration's calling, and I'm buying."

"Oh, darlin,' I wouldn't think of you paying for anything. Have I ever let you pay?" Bill grinned. He and Brenda had had some wonderful times together, and she had served the cause well over the years, in more ways than one.

"There's a first for everything," Brenda said.

"That there is." Bill took a sip of his scotch, and then said, "I need a little help."

"What is it, love? Anything for you."

"The chief pilot is screwing around with my boys again. I need to give my buddy a line check tomorrow morning. Can you pull the crew on the early L.A. departure? Captain Aaron Stephens will be flying left seat. Put me in the right seat as the check captain."

Aaron walked around to the front of the desk and sat in one of the two chairs facing him. He lifted his glass and tipped it toward Bill, then emptied it with one swallow.

"Yeah, of course, sweetheart. Consider it done. I'll call the office as soon as we hang up."

Bill set the phone down and splayed both his hands out, palms up. "Just like magic."

CHAPTER 27

WHEN SHE PULLED up in front of their house, their driveway was empty. *Where is Bill?*

"PLEASE DON'T DRIVE. You've had too much to drink," Kathryn had said, reaching for Bill's keys. "We'll come back and get your car tomorrow."

Bill had pulled her into an embrace and kissed her hard, holding his keys beyond her reach, then winked at Greg. "I'm fine." Then he walked out the door, sauntered down the steps and got into his car. He wasn't fine; he was drunk. She also knew that he didn't like to be told what to do.

"Come on, buddy, you don't need a DUI. You've worked too hard for everything," Greg had yelled from the porch. Bill waved then climbed into his car.

Kathryn had pulled on her coat then quickly hugged Jackie and then Greg. Darby had long since gone. Kathryn had grabbed her purse, said, "Bye, you guys," and then had run out the door. If she couldn't convince Bill to ride with her, at least she could follow him home.

He had waited until she got into her car to start his own, and then had backed out of the driveway and onto the street, still pausing until she did the same. When Kathryn backed down the driveway, he had waved out his window to Greg and Jackie, then put his car into gear and had driven down the street. She had followed. Bill could hold his alcohol better than anyone, but she hated when he drove drunk.

He had been driving the speed limit, though. But when Kathryn had glanced down the road and saw the light change to red far ahead of them, Bill's brake lights didn't illuminate. Instead, he had accelerated and shot through the light. Kathryn had stopped and watched his taillights fade into the fog.

KATHRYN CARRIED a bag of groceries into the kitchen and was hanging her coat on the rack when her heart stopped.

A moment of terror swept over her when she saw her laptop open. She set the bag on the table and let her coat slide to the floor. The screen was bright. She hadn't left it that way, had she? She prayed he had not found the files.

She shut down the computer and began putting the groceries away. She had stopped by the store on the way home to give Bill time to cool off, but by the time she had emptied the bag, she was scared. She shouldn't have let him drive.

Kathryn glanced at her watch. He should have been home well over an hour ago. She opened her phone and dialed 911, but the front door slammed before she pressed call.

"Where have you been?" she asked, somewhat frantic, when he walked into the kitchen.

"I stopped by the office. What's wrong, sweetie?"

Kathryn's emotions were on edge and she couldn't answer. Instead, she put a pot of water on the burner and leaned against the counter, arms folded, and glared at him. He sat at the table and opened the mail without looking her way. Silence filled the kitchen until the teapot screamed, but Bill still didn't look up. She wanted to smack him upside the head, or shake him. Anything.

Instead, she poured boiling water into her cup, then ripped open a yellow packet of sweetener and dumped in the contents. She played with the tea bag, bobbing it in and out of her cup in time with each tick of the clock, watching Bill sort the mail, engrossed in nothing.

"I think I'll go take a bath," she announced stiffly.

"That's a great idea, honey. I'll be up in a few minutes."

Kathryn took her tea and walked slowly up the stairs. When she reached the top, she heard Bill's office door close. She hesitated, then set down her cup, and crept back downstairs. She stood for a moment and listened. Nothing.

There was one thing that would get her mind off of Bill. She moved to the kitchen, pulling her keys out of her jacket pocket, and then quietly opened the door, and ran to her car. She retrieved her briefcase, careful not to slam the lid of the trunk, and hurried back inside.

She closed the door quietly, and listened for Bill. Still not a noise. She walked up the stairs and set her briefcase on the bathroom floor, and locked the door.

Turning the faucet to hot, she added a cap of lavender bubble bath to the water and stripped off her clothes. She wrapped a towel around her body and sat on the floor. Hugging her legs and leaning against the door, she closed her eyes. *What in the heck am I doing lying to Bill like this?* Then she thought of Linda and Frankie.

She opened her briefcase, pulled files from the bag, and began to read the contents of the Regional crash. Grant had initially been flying and clearly called for flaps for the arrival. But Sandra's thumbs had been broken—she'd been flying the plane upon impact. Sandra had made the radio transmissions and later taken command. *At what point did Sandra become the pilot flying?* She continued to scan the transcript for a clue. Then she read the list of miscellaneous items loose in the flight deck. Manuals, flight bags, pens, approach charts, Sandra's purse, hats, a sweater, uniform jacket, and a flashlight—twelve-inch, titanium, three inches in diameter. She turned the page to the dimension of the fracture on the side of Grant's skull, bingo.

That's it. Sandra had hit him with her flashlight. *Had she knocked him unconscious? But why then did she crash?*

On the initial approach, Sandra had said, "You son of a bitch." The transcript further indicated three repetitive thuds in three seconds, then no more talking except for ATC until she told them her intentions to land. Then flap movement. Then Sandra's final words, "What the fu…" Then impact.

She stared at the last line of dialogue, "What the fu…"

Sandra had been surprised by something, but what? The building? Ground contact?

"Shit." Kathryn lunged for the tub, shutting off the faucet just before water overflowed. When she reached in and pulled the plug to remove a couple of inches of water Bill was at the door trying to get in. Then he began to knock rapidly.

"Why is the door locked? What are you doing in there?" Bill yelled, and then kicked the door.

Kathryn dropped her towel onto the files and put the plug back in the tub. "What do you want? I'm taking a bath." She stood naked and prayed he would just leave, but he didn't. He knocked again, this time louder than before. God, she wished he would stop drinking so much.

She pulled on her robe and placed the bag and towel into the hamper, opened the door a crack and said, "What?"

He stuck his foot in the doorway. "Why's the door locked?"

"I hadn't realized I'd locked it." He looked over her shoulder into the bathroom, and her eyes followed the path of his. She noticed the crack in the glass. "What happened to the shower door?" she asked, turning back to face him.

"I slipped," Bill said. "I'll get a new one next week." He turned and left, leaving the door open.

"I'm just going to soak for a few minutes and I'll be right out," she called after him. He didn't respond. She closed the door, then quietly put the files back into their plastic bag and gently slipped them into the bottom of the towel closet, setting her briefcase inside the cabinet under the sink. Bill was definitely getting more difficult with each passing day—or perhaps she was just noticing it more with the girls out of the house. Either way, she was glad the election was over and he'd won.

SHE CLIMBED into the hot water, closed her eyes, and replayed the flight in her mind. The only explanation for Grant's head wounds and his silence was that Sandra had knocked him unconscious with her flashlight.

Not only had he been making bad decisions, but it appeared he had put the airplane into a stall. Reports indicated opposing control forces. Anti-ice had been off. Sandra had fought to keep that plane aloft. But after all that, why would she fly it into the building? The wind conditions clearly could have blown her off course to the left of the runway. But why hadn't she corrected to miss the hotel?

Nothing made sense.

Grant had chosen to fly into deteriorating conditions. He'd descended too soon, and he stalled the aircraft. Stalling that plane was a hard thing to do in itself. If Sandra had knocked him unconscious, it had to have been in an attempt to save the flight.

But what happened on the final approach?

That's it! Kathryn climbed out of the tub. She quietly locked the door, dried her hands, and opened the file to the Regional transcript once more.

After her final words, the flaps had indicated movement. The grinding of gears had been nagging at her. They'd crashed with flaps up. The flaps had been raised on final approach and killed their lift—a death sentence.

Oh my God. This was anything but accidental.

Chapter 28

Kathryn stood in the bedroom doorway watching Bill, and his gaze didn't waver from the *Late Show*. His chest was bare, and the lower half of his body was buried under a comforter. She took a deep breath and approached. It was time they talked.

Her skin, misted with Estée Lauder's *Pleasures*, slid effortlessly between thousand-thread-count sheets. The security of the covers provided courage. She removed her silk robe. Her body, warm from the heat of the tub, trembled as she pushed the robe to the floor.

The boundless journey across a king size bed provided ample opportunity to stop, but she knew it was now or never. They would make love, celebrating his success, and then she would tell him about the investigation and they'd discuss her findings like they had when they'd first met.

Reaching her goal, she laid her cheek on his chest, and rested her hand over his heart. His cold skin felt good against her face. She smiled, and drew circles around a nipple with a single finger. Too much time had passed since they'd been alone, and that needed to change. Kids, work, schedules, and, most recently, the election, had consumed their lives.

His arms, once folded behind his neck, dropped lazily to her shoulders, and he slowly rubbed her back. He bent down and kissed the top of her head. Closing her eyes, she slid her hand down his abdomen.

His hand could have been a viper with the speed at which it grabbed her wrist.

"Sweetheart, I'm really tired."

Anger shot through her quicker than his hand had moved, but all she could say was, "You're hurting my arm." She pulled from his grip and sat up, then climbed out of bed and pulled her robe on, yanking the belt tight. Face red, she began to shake, but she forced herself to calm down.

She stood with her back to him, arms wrapped around her body, as she counted to ten. She fought a growing headache and tears. She wanted to talk to him. Discuss what she'd discovered. Talk about the election. Uncork a bottle of champagne and celebrate. He clearly wanted none of that.

When she turned to face him, his eyes flashed from her to the television, where they remained frozen. His expression—unreadable.

"We need to talk," she said. She moved from upset to pissed when the hint of smugness slipped across his face.

"Sweetheart, can't you give it a break for one night? We had a great evening together. I'm just tired. It's been a long day." His gaze, straight ahead, didn't shift.

"I don't care if you don't want to make love," she lied, "but I do need tell you something." He'd won the election, and there was no time like the present. "I met with John McAllister and accepted my old position."

He continued to stare at the television.

"Did you hear what I said?"

"You don't think I already know that was a bullshit story about lunch with a friend?"

Kathryn froze. She had no idea how to respond.

"You lied. You missed seeing the girls off on their camping trip.

This was a huge deal for them and you let them down. Now you think that a roll in the hay will make everything all right?"

"That's not what I was doing. I... I wanted to—"

"You don't know what you want," Bill said, cutting her off. "You're as crazy as your mother was."

Perhaps she was, but she did know what she wanted, and it wasn't to be a stay at home mom. She loved her girls, and their life together, but she needed more. She also needed her husband to love and trust her. Closing her eyes she willed herself strength to continue. "Bill—"

"Don't *Bill* me with your lies. I don't have time for it."

"Time? Our entire life has been built around you. I cook. Clean. Do your laundry. Run the kids around. I've catered to you. Our entire existence has been about you and your job. This damned election has consumed you. I need to do something worthwhile with my life, too. Besides, I'd planned on telling you, I just wanted to wait until after the election."

"Consumed? Do you know how important this election was?" He threw the covers back and jumped out of bed. She recoiled, creating space between them.

"I do know. That's why I didn't say anything before. I didn't want to add any more stress to your life."

"I know damn well you've told Darby and Jackie, and you've probably told Greg, too. Now I'm the fool for being the last to know about your sneaking around with McAllister."

"I wasn't sneaking around with him." Besides, who knew wasn't the issue. She was sick and tired of a life that revolved around Bill. Granted, she should have told him, but what was done was done. She drew in a breath of courage, stepped back, and folded her arms. "The point is they need me, and I want to do it."

"They *need you?* Jeez Kat, wake up and pull your head out of your ass. They don't need you. You've been gone for what, seven or eight years?"

"Ten." Ten years, seven months, and eleven days, to be exact.

"So you think after ten years you could fit into your old shoes?" He picked up the remote, killed the TV, and tossed it on the bed. "Do you really think you were that good the first time around?"

"I was the *best*! I was moving up until..." her voice cracked. She couldn't say, "until you got me pregnant, until I married you, until you prevented me from following my dreams."

"You and I know the only reason – or *reasons* – you got hired," he said, looking directly at her chest, "was because you're a woman."

Acid rose into her throat. "You bastard, *I* have a master's in criminal psychology. *I* was the person they came to when they couldn't solve an accident, and *I* traveled to accident sites worldwide to help them because I was good!"

He lowered his voice. "Babe, we both know that the only reason you were hired in the first place was because they needed to fill a quota. You can't deny that if a guy had the same qualifications as you, the job would have been yours regardless."

"You know, Bill, you're right. If I had the choice between an equally qualified man and woman, I'd choose the woman, too. I'd know that she would be working harder than the guy trying to prove herself. *And* that she wouldn't stay home with a cold like a sniveling baby. *And* I'd know that she could multi-task, think on her feet, follow through, and pick up her own damn clothes!" Her heart sped, and tears filled her eyes.

"So that's what this is all about?" he said, with a smirk. "You need a housekeeper. Is that it? I'm getting a significant raise with the union position, and we can get you all the help you need."

"This is not about a housekeeper. This is about me going back to work, and doing something I love."

Bill walked to the window, placed his hands on the ledge and stared into the darkness. Then he turned and said, "They actually offered you a job?"

"Yes. They did. They hired me as a consultant. I'll work directly for John and build my own schedule, which will be perfect because it won't take away from my time with the girls or the house—"

"Consultant? Oh, shit, Kat. Can't you see what he's doing? He's using you. Did you sleep with him?"

"Are you *kidding* me?"

"You spent the day in a hotel with him."

"Give me a break. This is nothing but professional." Heat rose in her face once again.

"You know, it's pretty shitty that you waited for two days to discuss this with me. Your job is here, in this home, to take care of the girls and me. You signed a marriage contract, in case you've forgotten." He placed his hands on his hips.

"It hasn't been two days. It was yesterday. And I didn't sign a contract to be your servant. It's called a marriage *license*, not a contract. The same license you signed."

She tapped her foot, searching for something to say, anything that would shift the path their conversation had taken.

"The girls are in school all day and you're busy with work. I need something more than cleaning this house. You're being a condescending ass." That may not have been a final winning statement, but fury overcame sense, and it felt good.

"This condescending ass says take an exercise class, or volunteer for something to keep yourself busy." He picked up a t-shirt off the floor and pulled it over his head. "Let's pretend for a minute that you had been an okay investigator ten years ago. There is no way you're that woman today. Why in the world would they pay someone like you to be a consultant when they have qualified people on staff?"

"You're right. They wouldn't," Kathryn yelled. She turned and strode into the bathroom, trying to maintain what little dignity she had remaining. She slammed, and locked, the door and leaned against it, then slid to the floor. When the bedroom door slammed from beyond she pulled her legs close, as her tears flowed.

In all the years she'd known him, he'd never spoken to her like that. *Did he really think those things?* Maybe she had been delusional about her abilities in the past, and did get hired because she was a woman. No, she knew the truth. But the truth didn't stop her tears from flowing. Clutching her abdomen, she crawled to her feet and made it to the toilet in time to empty her stomach. She rinsed her mouth out under the faucet then wiped it with a towel.

She dropped to the floor, rolled to her side and closed her eyes. John *had* called her, and he wouldn't have wasted his time. Bill was just angry for her lying to him. That's why he'd said those things. He wanted to hurt her, like she'd hurt him. Now that it was out, he'd think about it. They'd talk. Everything would work out. She couldn't quit now, not with what she knew.

She opened her eyes and had no idea how much time had passed. When she finally stood the blood returned to her legs. She stepped through an empty bedroom and peeked out the window. His car was still in the driveway. She tiptoed down the stairs, crept to his office and placed her ear to the door. He was talking to someone. The only thing she heard was, "flight eighty-five."

CHAPTER 29
SUNDAY

GREG GLANCED LEFT. His captain, Aaron Stephens, was staring out the window and smiling. Maybe Aaron was happy to be there, but he was the only one. Bill had said he'd be home in twelve hours and they probably wouldn't call him for rest of the month. Maybe. Still, Bill's midnight call had given him less than four hours of restless sleep, and those few hours were filled with nightmares and sweats. The he awoke to a screaming headache, and chills. Even so, there was no way in hell he'd allow Bill to fly this trip after all the wine he'd drunk hours before.

"Hey boys, ready to take me to Los Angeles?" Kristen said, stepping into the cockpit. She gave them their coffee. "So… How long's our flight today?"

"A little under three hours," Greg said.

"Good, the quicker we get in, the better," she snapped. She stepped out of the flight deck, then poked her head back in the door and added, "Everyone's seated."

Greg jumped when she spoke the second time. His nerves were on edge. Maybe it was the early hour. Maybe he was pissed that Bill had called him for the flight. He was supposed to have had two days off before he went back on call. He wanted to be lying next to Jackie's warm body, snuggled up, spooning her as he had done all night, fondling her breasts. He wasn't ready to fly. Physically or emotionally.

If he got furloughed, he'd have a hell of a lot of time to snuggle her, but their relationship would change. The stress of a furlough with the financial struggles would destroy his family. No, this would not be a good option for him, despite what he'd told Bill. The only way out was to work with Amir, hope he was good as his word on the job he'd offered, and pray to God that Jackie would forgive him. He warmed his hands on his cup of coffee.

AARON ACCEPTED his cup of coffee and said, "Thanks, darlin'." He was surprised to see Kristen on the flight. He couldn't figure out how Bill would pull it off on such short notice, but Aaron had never doubted Bill's ability. Kristen was supposed to go down on Bill's plane next month, but now that she was quitting early, she had left them no option. The only way to get action was hit the Director of Homeland where it hurt—family. But Greg's being there, that was a surprise.

When the time came, Aaron had no doubt Bill would make his final flight spectacular. He only wished that he could be there to see it and witness the results of their good work.

It amazed him how good he felt. *Acceptance.* He hadn't known if he'd chicken out until the moment he opened his eyes that morning. He was strong. There was a sense of freedom in making that final decision. Nobody had to put up with bullshit if they didn't want to, there was always an out, and Bill gave it to them.

No more bullshit for him. He'd be a national hero. They'd take down the bastards that destroyed Bill's dad, the same bastards that destroyed his career, killed his marriage, and stole his kids. Bill had thought this was all for him. But Aaron's personal reasons burned deeper than anyone could imagine.

He hadn't spoken to his children in years, except when they needed something. His son was doing hard drugs and was in and out of rehab centers that he couldn't afford. His daughter had two babies from two different fathers, neither of which she'd married. And his wife was sleeping around on him. All the same, how in the hell could he blame any of them? The demands of the job didn't allow him to be home long enough to take care of his family. He wouldn't even be able to support his wife when he retired. But none of that mattered now. There was one way he could help them financially, and that was with life insurance. An added benefit.

The airline also had insurance. But the bad PR, increased regulations, and higher premiums would cause them pain. In the process, the pilots would regain control and take back what was stolen. He and the guys were all part of something larger than life, something that needed to be done. Nobody had the guts to do anything but whine. Enough was enough. The airline execs picked the wrong people to do battle with. This was war. People died in war, something he'd experienced first hand. Had it not been for Bill, he would have been one of them. The casualties of war, while not personal, were an unfortunate necessity.

They would leave the world with no option but reform. A trail of smoke. Innocent bodies. Death. He'd seen it all in Nam. Now it was the executives' time to watch it all unfold in their own backyard. The corporate varmints were already scrambling like the rats that they were, with their food source in jeopardy. Two more crashes, and they'd be done. Besides, what did he have to live for, anyway? Nothing.

One detail remained. Bill promised he'd make sure Aaron's wife's lover would be on Bill's flight so the bastard could burn in hell. Bill always came through for him. He touched his thigh, and rubbed.

GREG SIPPED his coffee. He knew blaming an industry and the airline was an easy excuse. He could have purchased a more modest home and not made loser investments in the market, but he'd based his decisions on promises the company and union had made him. None-the-less, he'd embedded his family in harm's way with his bad decisions, and hoped the deal with Amir wasn't another in his long line of stupid choices. He refused to leave Jackie and Chris desolate.

He glanced out the window. With daybreak came the fog, but today's was thicker than it had been all week. He drew a deep breath, purged company thoughts from his mind, and looked left. "What the hell are you smiling about?" Greg asked.

"The sorry story I call my life," Aaron responded.

Greg understood that well.

The fog was now so thick that he could hardly make out the terminal twenty feet beyond. They waited for bags to be loaded and to receive a clearance. Greg had performed the obligatory walk-around to determine the airworthiness of the aircraft. The plane was fine; at least he hoped it was. He had walked halfway around, checking the wings, engines, and tires, and he realized upon standing at the tail that he hadn't remembered walking by any of it. He wasn't even sure how he'd got outside.

He contemplated another walk, but there wasn't time. On-time performance was more important. There was, however, ample time for a fuel truck, cargo loading, or catering to hit the aircraft and damage it, and they would never know until it was too late. The focus was to move planes. Time on the ground was money lost. He was nothing but an ant scurrying about creating an impression that he was important. It was all about image.

ATIS broadcasted the current weather. The visibility had dropped another thousand feet since he'd arrived at the airport. He sipped his coffee and closed his eyes. The FAA could mandate a better plan, but the FAA was nothing more than a fish on the end of the line held by airline management, and not until an accident occurred did they jump into the boat. *When did I become so damned cynical?* The visual of an ant hanging on the end of the fishing line for dear life flashed through his mind, and it was his turn to smile. But that smile faded quickly.

He opened his eyes and leaned his head back to see the overhead panel. Buttons—blue, green, and amber, the colors of performance and procedure—stared at him in a blur. He pushed those that needed to be turned on, and checked to see that the others were in the correct position, either armed or off. The interior preflight had once been the captain's responsibility, but Coastal changed procedures to give more responsibility to the first officer, which resulted in the expansion of his duties in an inverse proportion to his pay cut. He worked harder for less.

He glanced at Aaron. It wouldn't be long until he was cut back to a first officer and then he, too, would be in trouble. If Bill followed through, there'd be many people hurting.

Greg finished with the preflight and began digging through his bag.

"What do you need buddy?"

"Ibuprofen. I've got a killer headache."

"Here, take a couple of these, you'll be good as new." He handed Greg his bottle of Tylenol. When Greg tried to hand it back after taking a few pills, Aaron shook his head and replied, "Keep it."

"WHEN DID YOU get called for this trip?" Aaron asked, pulling the charts out of his book. He clipped them on the control yoke.

"Late last night."

"Does Bill know they called?"

"Bill called, not scheduling. I think he had some union stuff he needed to do. Said he wanted to do me a favor. That it would finish me up for the month and I'd be home when my son got back. Give me more time off."

"Bill's a good shit," Aaron said.

"The best."

Aaron confirmed the voice recorder was on. Show time. "Since the bastards took my pension, I'll have to work until I'm sixty-five, and I still won't make ends meet. None of this is worth it anymore. It's really screwing with my head."

"Well, if Bill can pull off his 'take it back' campaign, things might change. But it's going to take a long time and a lot of bloodletting."

"Blood might be what's needed. They're fully aware of the impact they have on safety when they screw with us. They just don't care. They think we're machines and can shut off our lives when we go to work. I'm surprised more planes aren't crashing. Who can keep their mind on the job when we're being stretched so thin? Hell, I busted my last check because of the stress."

"You ever think about been seeing Adams?

"Been there, done that." Bill had asked him to go when they finally decided to pull the trigger. He'd said it would paint a trail of emotional instability. Lend credence to the pending issues. They all visited him, and that trail had been paved in gold.

GREG WAS not surprised that Aaron was seeing the shrink, but the fact that he said anything about it shocked the hell out of him. Still, Adams was good. Thanks to him, Greg had finally found the strength and inclination to make love to his wife. Now all he wanted was to be in bed with her instead of—

"Hey, Captain, five minutes to push," the ground crew called over the flight deck speaker, interrupting his thoughts.

"Roger," Aaron responded.

Greg picked up the PA. "Uh…" He set the handset down. He'd forgotten what he was going to say.

Kristen poked her head into the cockpit and asked, "What was that all about?"

"The five minute call just came in," Aaron said.

"Huh. So, did you have dinner with Bill last night?" Kristen asked Greg. "I was told he was flying this trip today. What's up with that?"

Greg couldn't speak. He thought he was going to vomit, and just waved a hand. She responded by slamming the cockpit door.

He hadn't known about Bill and Kristen's relationship until yesterday. The situation had undoubtedly been the root of his nightmares and disjointed sleep.

Bill calling him to send Kathryn to the store for barbeque sauce so he could get Kristen out of Kathryn's bed was a shock. Greg hadn't known what to do, but he knew there were always two sides to every relationship. He'd talk to Bill when he returned, and give him a chance to do the right thing—either stop seeing Kristen, or tell Kathryn. If he did neither, Greg would have to tell Kathryn. As much as he loved and respected Bill, his alliance would always be with Kathryn.

"You okay buddy?"

Greg shook his head. His ears were buzzing and his skin crawled. He wasn't okay.

"Good," Aaron said and called for the preflight checklist. Greg read it the best he could and Aaron responded. There were large moments of time he couldn't account for, but Aaron didn't seem to notice. When he realized he was just holding the checklist, not speaking, Aaron would call for the next one.

The next few minutes passed in a redundant blur as they read and responded to each checklist. At least Greg had thought he'd read. He also thought he'd heard Aaron laugh. Aaron started the engines and Greg tried to read the after-start checklist, but the words bounced on the page.

Greg was on autopilot. Every word had been spoken many times in the choreographed play he called his life. He felt like shit. Maybe Aaron was right. What in the hell were they doing? He flew twelve-day trips and would go home exhausted, and he never completely got over his jet lag before he packed to leave again. He missed holidays, birthdays, and his son's first camping trip. *And for what?* He glanced at the load sheet.

One hundred and seventy-five passengers on board. He was responsible for all of their lives, yet he made less than the guy who picked up his garbage, and that bastard got to sleep in his own bed at night. He closed his eyes. His head pounded. "Aaron, I need to go—"

"Coastal Eight-Five, low visibility procedures are in effect, you're cleared to taxi to spot 2B, expect runway One-Six Left."

Greg picked up the microphone, but he didn't speak. Aaron took over and read back the clearance, and the aircraft began to move.

The fog hung low and Greg couldn't see anything beyond the flight deck, but that didn't matter. It wasn't his job to taxi. The low visibility chart sat in his lap. He located spot 2B. They'd passed over spot six, where the taxiway split between Alpha and Bravo, he thought. The numbers would descend as they proceeded toward the takeoff position, but the fog blanketed their visibility. He wanted to curl into a ball and close his eyes and make this day go away.

They crept along the taxiway, following the lights that were barely detectible from his perch. Twenty-six feet below the nose of their aircraft, the glowing points would guide them to spot 2B and then to the end of the runway, but to Greg everything blurred then lights floated his way. He shook his head, forcing them back to the taxiway.

Aaron continued to maneuver the aircraft with the steering tiller.

"Coastal Eight-Five, will you be ready at the end?" the ground controller asked.

"Tell them we will," Aaron said.

"Ah…firmative," Greg managed to say, but his tongue was thick.

He looked at the departure plate to review the procedure. He closed one eye so he could see it clearly, but it slithered across the page like a snake.

"Tell 'em we're approaching 2B," Aaron said, "and we're ready for takeoff."

"Coastal is ready for takeoff One-Six Left," Greg said, shivering. He felt worse than shit. Now he was dizzy and nauseous. Maybe he'd call in sick. That would throw the schedule off if they taxied back to the gate. Instead, he did what he always did and pressed on.

He stuffed his taxi chart back into the book and dropped it into his flight bag. He took the last swig of his coffee and tossed the cup toward the trash, but missed. He looked out the right window for traffic, but he wouldn't have seen it if it had been there. The fog was too dense.

They rolled onto the runway, but had they completed the final items on the takeoff checklist? He wasn't sure. They should've sat in position for that check.

Thank God they'd flown this departure so often that they could do it blindfolded. He took a deep breath. He just wanted to get in the air so he could go to the lav and puke.

"Coastal Eight-Five, you're cleared for takeoff runway One-Six Left. Winds calm. Altimeter two-niner, six-five, visibility six, six, and six."

The visibility had dropped to six hundred feet at the departure, mid, and end of the field—their minimums for takeoff. If they waited much longer, they wouldn't be legal to go. Greg repeated the clearance, his tongue thick, making enunciation difficult.

"Flight attendants prepare for takeoff," Greg announced over the P.A. *Or did he?* They were already on the runway, and it wouldn't have mattered if they were ready or not. He shook his head and licked his lips. His mouth was dry. And then he turned right and vomited into his flight bag.

Aaron aligned the airplane with the centerline lights and pushed the thrust levers forward and called, "TOGA." Greg faced forward, confused, and then wiped his mouth with the back of his hand. They were on the roll, and Greg had one task now—press the correct button.

He closed one eye to see the Takeoff and Go-Around button and then he pushed it, enabling the auto-throttles to engage and automatically apply takeoff power. When he pressed TOGA, the flight director command bars pitched up eight degrees providing their initial guidance, and he knew that he had made the correct selection. Their Boeing 767's autoflight system would engage after they were airborne. He thanked God that Aaron was the pilot flying.

The flight director indicated wings level, proving direction to maintain aircraft tracking on the runway, and would provide directional guidance when LNAV, the lateral navigation button, was selected at four hundred feet. Greg hoped he could find that button, too. Aaron kept his hand on the thrust levers, but the auto-throttles pulled them forward under their own power.

Centerline lights flashed below the flight deck, and Greg glanced outside, then back to the instruments. He checked the power, confirmed the flaps were set, and glanced at the initial altitude set in the mode control panel the best that he could.

Aaron initially maintained directional control with the tiller, but as the airspeed increased and the rudder became effective, he shifted control to steering with his feet providing input to the rudder.

The centerline lights continued to disappear underneath their aircraft as they accelerated down the runway. The lights were spaced every fifty feet, and at one hundred and fifteen knots and increasing, they flew by. Each light was sucked under the aircraft as the next followed. He watched them one by one until they, too, turned into a blur streaking by.

With three thousand feet of runway remaining, the lights would change from white to alternating red and white, and at one thousand feet they would illuminate all red. The aircraft was heavy today, but they still wouldn't see red and white. Their Boeing would be airborne far before the last three thousand feet.

They'd depart the twelve-thousand-foot runway in less than eight thousand feet and within seconds they'd be on top of the fog. Mount Rainier would stand proud at fourteen thousand feet at their eleven o'clock position, far above the weather, the city, and Greg's problems. He closed his eyes fighting off the urge to vomit again, counting the minutes until they'd break free of the weather.

When he opened his eyes, the lights were alternating red and white. They hadn't been on the runway that long. *Had they?* He looked at the airspeed, one hundred and twenty-five knots. They didn't have enough speed, and, yet, they were also too fast. He wanted to say something, but he didn't know what to say. Then all the lights turned red. He couldn't yell, "pull up," they didn't have the speed to fly. He couldn't yell, "abort," they didn't have enough runway to stop. They were going too fast and there was no time to say anything.

He finally yelled, "Aaron, do something!"

When Aaron didn't respond, Greg slowly pulled the yolk back. The plane was heavy. He didn't know if she'd fly. One glance told him that the speed had increased. Then they were airborne. Just barely clearing the end of the runway, but they didn't have enough speed to find altitude, and he leveled her off to accelerate.

Aaron laughed at Greg's response—*do* something. *Amazing.* Nothing surprised him more than Greg taking control, especially after puking his guts out. This should be fun. He decided to let Greg take the plane and crash her.

SeaTac Airport sat at four hundred feet, elevated above a golf course that lay directly to the south of the runway. They had wiggle room for a slight descent to gain speed. But there was no way he'd clear the trees. Aaron watched with amusement.

GREG HELD TIGHT. He focused. The trees in the near distance screamed that he needed altitude. With a little more speed on his side, he slowly pulled the controls back to climb the four hundred and fifty thousand pound aircraft, and prayed he could clear them. A quick glance left told Greg that Aaron's arms were folded as he watched. *Was he smiling?* They were slow and the aircraft shook, but they continued to fly and it looked like they may clear the tops.

The stall warning clacked intermittently, and the passengers screamed, but they were still flying. If he could just clear the trees…

THAT LITTLE SHIT'S going to make it. Aaron was impressed. But Greg's 'making it' wasn't in this script. He reached over and raised the flaps, killing their lift.

There wasn't enough speed to do anything. Greg no longer had the motor skills to move them back, even if he had had time. Instead, he pulled the nose up. He was touching the edge of the stall margin. Then Greg reached down and attempted to lower the flaps.

I'll be damned. Give the kid an A for effort.

But it was too late. There was nothing left but to kiss his ass goodbye as their plane descended into the heart of Des Moines and the traffic heading to Mt. Rainier High School.

CHAPTER 30

KATHRYN RAN in slow motion with a weight pressing deep in her chest. The thickness of the air made it difficult to move, and she used her arms to propel herself forward. She saw the closed door and ran toward it, but it was locked. No key was in sight. She began to pound, and then she awoke in a sweat.

It was 4:30 when she opened her eyes, just in time to hear Bill's car come to life. She padded to the window and watched him back out of the driveway. Then all she could see was her reflection. The image haunted her. She drifted to the bathroom, eyes red and swollen and lined with dark circles, she stared in the mirror.

Her brain felt like it had gone through the trash compactor. In all their years of marriage, Bill had never spoken to her as he had last night, and he'd never slept in the guest room before. Then again, she'd never spoken to him like she had, either. Or lied to him. What bothered her most were his loathsome words. She rehashed their argument and laughed. They clearly threw stones to inflict pain. *Did I really call him a condescending ass?*

The cold water she splashed on her face freshened her skin, but it didn't remove the pain and conflict she felt tightening her chest. Opening the closet she retrieved the bag that housed the files she'd hidden only a few short hours prior.

Kathryn carried the weight of all they represented to the kitchen, set the bag on the table, and then poured grounds into her coffee maker. She filled the machine with water and then walked silently into Bill's study. He'd never made it to the guest bedroom. He'd slept on the couch. The blanket lay on the floor as evidence.

She sat on the couch and ran her hand over the soft leather and wondered how time stole their lives and spat them into the future. She wrapped her arms around herself, leaned back, and closed her eyes fighting fresh tears. She shouldn't have lied to Bill or gone behind his back, but she couldn't undo that now. She also couldn't quit. Not with what she knew. Besides, Bill was hardly an innocent victim. He should have been supporting her.

The scent of coffee enticed her back to the kitchen. She poured herself a cup, but she didn't have the motivation to add the sweetness that she loved. She leaned against the counter, held the cup with both hands, and brought the brew to her lips.

The bag that lay on the table called to her, but all she wanted to do was throw it away. Instead, she picked up the home wrecker and returned to Bill's study and dropped it on the coffee table.

This was his place, a place that she didn't belong unless she had a dust cloth in hand. That, too, would change. For now, she only wanted to be close to him. She curled up on his couch and pulled the blanket close inhaling his scent. She'd apologize. But she would not give up the idea of working on these investigations. And yet, she wondered if any of it was worth the pain. Her family had to be more than fighting and sleeping apart. They'd have to figure it out. She wouldn't end her life like her mother had, no matter what. Last night's fight was her and Bill's slap in the face.

She sipped her coffee and looked at the bag. She thought about Sandra's thumbs and why she'd taken control of the plane. Then she thought about Linda and the loss of her husband. Objectivity would be a challenge.

She set her cup down and dumped the files out on the coffee table. She looked at them for a moment then opened a folder and began to read. She read the Regional file, then Global's, and cross-referenced them.

Kathryn stood then paced, theories bouncing in her mind.

With an empty cup in hand, she headed for the kitchen. She needed the warmth as much as the caffeine before she'd dig into the Skylark file again.

Dawn had arrived to another gray day. The fog grew heavy outside, silent and damp. She longed for the warmth of the sun. *The sun. The glare. Global's rudder.* "That's it!" How could she have missed the obvious? She realized what had bothered her, and powered up her laptop.

While her computer whirred to life, she ran into the office and retrieved the Global file, knocking the others on the floor in the process. When she got to the kitchen, she Googled the video of Global's crash and reviewed the live footage of the accident once again. She had concluded that the first officer was the pilot flying, since he'd been found with a broken ankle, and the captain had worked the radios.

She watched the aircraft fly the approach in a serious crab to the runway. In the final minutes the rudder moved to align the aircraft and the wing dipped to keep them from being blown off course. *All good.* But then the rudder had gone full right and the reaction had been a roll to the left that clipped the wing.

They assumed that the aircraft may have had a runaway rudder, but the centering mechanism had done its job after impact and neutralized the rudder. And yet, that didn't confirm that it hadn't been the rudder. 'Inconclusive' had been the final determination.

But the rudder had been deflected full right. The first officer was flying, and he had a broken *left* ankle. This could only mean that that he'd reacted and jammed his left foot into the rudder to correct the problem, to no avail. Then he rolled the wings left to avoid ground traffic. The captain also had a broken ankle. "Oh my God," she spoke quietly. His was the *right* ankle. The captain had been holding full right rudder on landing.

"I'll be damned," she said. *There it is.* The video showed that immediately after the rudder had moved full right, there was a negligible, but obvious, shift left, then it instantly locked full right. A runaway rudder would never come out "a little" after a runaway, but it would've taken itself to the limit without reprieve.

This hadn't been a runaway rudder, and it hadn't been the wind. The captain had done this intentionally, and it was the first officer who had attempted to counteract it. She noted the exact moment the fight began. The first officer took the battle to another level when he rolled the wings to the left to stop his plane from being a weapon of destruction that would've hit the aircraft waiting their turn for departure.

Kathryn shivered. The phone rang and she knocked her cup to the floor with her elbow. *"Shit!"* She opened her phone. "Bill?"

"No. It's me," Darby said, clearly shaken. "Turn on the TV. Any channel. Quick."

She ran to Bill's study and turned on his television. Fire was the first thing she saw, then the tail. It was a Coastal plane. "Darby. Oh my god. Wh…" She couldn't get the questions out. What happened? Who was the crew? Where was the accident? Her heart raced. *Bill.* He'd left early that morning, he could be…

"Greg was on that plane. I am heading to Jackie's. I'll be there in twenty minutes, meet me there. God, I hope she isn't watching this."

Kathryn closed the phone, and stared. Dropping to the couch, she watched in disbelief. She turned up the volume and couldn't pull herself away. Her body began to shake and fresh tears flowed. She was living the same nightmare all over again.

"We've experienced the fourth in a series of deadly plane crashes this year. This morning has brought this tragedy closer to home. A Coastal Airlines 767 has crashed during takeoff. Flight Eighty-Five. No word of survivors," the reporter said. "We have verification that this was a full flight, and out of respect for the families, the airline is not releasing any names. We don't know what caused this 767 to crash south of SeaTac airport during takeoff. We do know it was headed to Los Angeles and was unable to climb in the heavy fog. We cannot say if terrorism is to blame or not."

Kathryn rocked on the couch pulling the blanket close to her chest, shaking uncontrollably. "Oh Greg, no." She then dropped to her knees on the floor, on top of the files. Acid rose in her throat. Greg would be another file that ended up in a Wal-Mart bag.

Not Greg. No. It can't be. Darby has to be wrong.

Within no time she was in her room, throwing clothes on. Within minutes she was back downstairs, grabbing her phone, keys, and a jacket. She ran out the door, slamming it in her wake.

The car moved backwards down the driveway before she realized that she hadn't locked the door, and couldn't remember if she'd left the coffee pot on or not. "Screw it," she said, as she continued toward the street.

Seeing the road through the mixture of tears and fog was a challenge, and she drove too fast. Her heart was with Jackie. She needed to be by her side, but her mind was on the crash.

Kathryn wanted desperately to turn left and drive to the airport, to the site, as visions of the accident burned in her mind. That was where she belonged. They needed her. Greg needed her.

But there was nothing she could do for Greg now but take care of his family. She owed him that much. She wiped her eyes with the back of her hand and used her sleeve on her nose. Sirens roared in the distance, and the odor of burning fuel and death drifted near. She saw the red traffic light glowing in the fog, but the significance didn't register. She didn't slow down, and flew through the intersection. She didn't see the other car, but she heard it.

CHAPTER 31

KATHRYN HAD JUST missed slamming into another car. When brakes squealed, she had stepped on the gas pedal. She wasn't sure how the other car had missed her. Shaken, both she and Darby had arrived at Jackie's house within minutes of each other. Jackie had been awake making coffee when they'd arrived. She hadn't heard about the crash, but when she saw their faces, she knew that something bad had happened. The screams that came next were inhuman. They had helped Jackie to the couch, then sat with her and watched the progress on the television. There had been nothing they could do, and no place to go.

Jackie had sat between them and Kathryn held her hand, willing her strength. Darby's arm had been wrapped in Jackie's arm with her head resting on Jackie's shoulder.

Kathryn had called John just after she'd arrived at Jackie's. He'd been on site and had assured her that he would call with any news. That call came twenty-two minutes later with word that Greg was alive but severely burned, and he was being airlifted to Harborview. That was when they had headed to the hospital.

BLADES POUNDED the air as the helicopter hovered and then landed at Harborview, Seattle's trauma hospital. Kathryn watched the arrival in disbelief. The wind whipped her hair and stung her eyes. The helipad was located on top of the underground parking garage, but at street level, and 100 yards from where she had parked. The passenger would be Greg, the only survivor. At least when she'd spoken to John he was still alive.

Kathryn stood beside her car by the emergency entrance and Jackie sobbed in the passenger seat as they waited for Darby. When Darby pulled in behind them, Kathryn pointed to the helicopter and mouthed, "That's him." Darby nodded. Then Kathryn opened the door for Jackie, whose tears flowed as she heaved uncontrollably.

"Come on, honey, let's go inside," Kathryn said, extending a hand. She'd been trained for such reactions, but not with someone she loved.

"What if…" Jackie spoke between sobs. "What if he's already dead? I don't know what to do without him. How will I tell Chris?" Kathryn knelt beside the car and put her hands on Jackie's leg.

"There is nothing that I can say that will make this better. But right now, he is alive. And we'll take this one step at a time. Darby and I are here for you." She gently squeezed Jackie's leg. Darby's touch on her shoulder gave her strength. But Kathryn wanted to scream at the reality of it all. She wanted to run into the hospital and prove they were all mistaken.

"You're not alone and we'll always be here," Kathryn said. Strength she didn't feel spoke through her. "You can cry and scream and do anything you want. If you want to sit out here, we'll sit with you all day. Just know that we're here for you, and we always will be, no matter what."

She had told Jackie that Greg was severely burned. She wanted her friend to be prepared, but there was nothing Kathryn could say to prepare her for his deformed body. That vision would be etched in her mind for life. Jackie's dreams of the man she loved would be replaced with the disfigured man he'd become. It would be better for her not to see him at all.

Kathryn didn't want to see him herself. She needed to remember his eyes that sparkled with life when they'd played hide and seek as children. She needed the boy who'd been a man the day her mother died.

Darby walked around to the driver's side and climbed in the car. She put her hand on Jackie's back and rubbed, but she didn't speak. Kathryn knelt by Jackie's side on the cement. She and Darby exchanged glances while Jackie continued to sob.

Kathryn thought about their dinner the night before and how Greg had touched Jackie often. She had responded with smiles and laughter. She drank wine, and she glowed. She finally had her husband back, only for him to be ripped away. This time for good.

Then guilt filled her heart for the night that she and Bill had spent apart. Now all she wanted to do was hold him and apologize. Tell him how glad she was that he wasn't on that plane. What if their last night together had been spent in an argument?

THE PARKING LOT was full, but Kathryn had never felt more alone, despite sitting beside her friends. They'd long since taken Greg inside. She wanted to be inside with him, but she couldn't leave Jackie. And then Jackie's sobs slowed, and finally subsided.

"I think we should go in," Jackie finally said, breathing in jagged gulps of air. Darby handed her a tissue and gave her a hug. Kathryn stood and extended a hand. This time, Jackie took it and squeezed. The pain in Jackie's eyes broke Kathryn's heart. Jackie stood, and they embraced. Darby came around the car and wrapped her arms around them both. They would get Jackie through this.

They stopped at the main desk. "Greg Jameson," Kathryn said.

The woman glanced at Jackie and quickly typed the name into

her computer. "Intensive Care, Burn Unit, fourth floor. Elevator's down the hall to your left."

Kathryn held Jackie's hand and led her into the elevator, and Darby pressed the button for the fourth floor. They checked in at the front desk and were asked to stay in the waiting area. The doctors were attempting to stabilize him.

Jackie, Darby and Kathryn sat in the waiting room with three other people, all eyes glued to the television. On the screen they saw that the fog had lifted. High clouds remained. Smoke hung in the air from the wreckage. Trees and debris smoldered. The area had been evacuated, and First Avenue and Highway 99 were closed.

The media had a bird's-eye view from the general aviation ramp at SeaTac, on the far southeast corner of the field. They were also situated in the Lutheran churchyard on the corner of Fourth Avenue and 176th street. Families from the neighboring community filled the grounds and watched.

Kathryn knew that hill well. She had lived in that neighborhood as a child. Today her dad would stand in the churchyard, surrounded by many, but alone. There had been many times when they'd sat there together and talked as they watched planes depart. They had talked about everything until he left she and her mom. And after her mother died, all conversations eventually stopped. It took three years, until she had finally stopped returning his calls.

The cameras focused on the crash. She saw Bill on site now. He was visibly upset, and the camera crews were taking advantage of the footage. He waved his arms, obviously angry that he was not granted access to the secured area. They wouldn't allow him to get close so soon. They never did. His theatrics were normally for show, but she knew this time was different. Kathryn could see his pain. These accidents were always personal to him, but this one had occurred on his watch, with his airline, and his best friend was flying.

The lens zoomed in on Bill's face. Tears filled his eyes. The volume on the television was high so everyone could hear, but the visual created a sensory overload, and Kathryn doubted anyone was listening to the words. Horrific. Deadly. Unknown. And the question of terrorism was repeated often, in addition to the terms drama, suspense, mystery, and fear. They'd forgotten sorrow.

SeaTac Airport was closed. All planes were diverting to Boeing Field or sent east to Moses Lake. Nobody was allowed to depart. Kathryn watched Jackie stare into the television, and she picked up one of her hands. Ice cold. She held them in her own to warm them, and rubbed.

Jackie was in shock.

Kathryn scanned the room. Everyone watched the nightmare on television with horror. At least this was a distraction for those families waiting for their loved ones somewhere in the bowels of the hospital. Everyone except Jackie. Kathryn removed herself from the couch, opened a closet and found a blanket, and placed it over Jackie's shoulders. Darby pulled it around her front and draped it over her legs. Jackie didn't move or acknowledge the activity.

At the reception desk Kathryn asked if a doctor could prescribe something for Jackie. She was the first to see the white jacket move through the swinging doors.

The doctor's shoulders sagged. He looked at the ground. His pace was slow. Then he stopped, looked up, and returned her stare.

CHAPTER 32

THE DOCTOR was the first to break eye contact, and Kathryn's hope died. But he immediately returned his gaze to her. Dark circles that underlined his bloodshot eyes told a story of fatigue and sorrow. Hers were no different.

"Mrs. Jameson?"

"No, a close friend." With a head nod toward Jackie she said, "Jackie's his wife." She feared the worst. "Is he…?" She couldn't finish the sentence.

"He's alive. But I need to talk to his wife."

She looked at Jackie, then back at the doctor. "I think she's in shock. Can you give her something first?"

The doctor walked to the reception desk and spoke quietly. Returning to her side, he said, "Can you bring Mrs. Jameson to room 402?"

She nodded, and returned to Jackie and knelt in front of her. "Sweetie, Greg's alive." Fresh tears filled Jackie's eyes. "We need to go with the doctor now, he'll tell us everything."

Darby wrapped her arm through Jackie's arm and squeezed. "He's alive and he's going to be fine. I knew it."

Kathryn shot Darby a pained glance, and then guided them to room 402. The doctor stood at the window with his back to the door. He turned when they entered.

"Mrs. Jameson, I'm Doctor Green." He introduced himself in

an easy and comfortable manner. He shined his light into Jackie's eyes as he spoke of the damp weather. Easy conversation for the Seattle area. Then he took her pulse.

"Is Greg going to be okay?" Jackie finally asked. The doctor hesitated. Kathryn knew what he was thinking—Greg would never be *okay*. "It's too early to tell. He survived the first obstacle. He's alive. But he's in bad shape."

"Can I see him?"

"Not just yet. We need to move him to the burn unit, get him in an appropriate bed to redistribute his body weight. The next twenty-four hours will be the most critical. We'll need to reinstate his osmotic balance."

"Reinstate his assmatic what?" Darby asked.

Confusion in Darby's eyes mirrored the intensity and fear in Jackie's. Kathryn shifted her attention to the doctor.

Dr. Green pushed his hands into his pockets. "We need to hydrate him. He's suffered fourth degree burns, full thickness on his left arm, and fifth degree, or subdermal burns on both his legs." He paused, taking a deep breath, then continued. "He'll never walk. We need to remove both his legs as soon as possible. He's unconscious now and his vitals are weak, but we have every indication to believe he may come to."

"His legs? No!" Darby snapped. "He can't fly without his legs. You can't do that."

"And you are?"

Darby didn't answer, but instead she challenged him. "What in the hell are subdermal, and fourth and fifth degree burns anyway? I've never heard of such a thing." She sat by Jackie on the bed, and clutched her arm. Jackie stared at the doctor without reaction, or response, but her eyes pleaded for answers.

Kathryn placed a hand on Jackie's back, a silent sentinel to her friend. She knew all too well the severity of the burns, but she allowed the doctor to explain. She didn't have the heart.

"A fourth degree burn is through the full thickness of the skin. It's damage to the epidermis, and partial damage to subcutaneous fat. Subdermal burns are much deeper and include the complete destruction of the epidermis, dermis, subcutaneous fat and tissue." Speaking directly to Jackie, he added, "In your husband's case, his burns have severely damaged the fascia, muscles, and bones in both his legs. I'm very sorry."

Words of subdermal and subcutaneous flew over her friends' heads, their mouths hanging open, but she had a clear picture of the new Greg Jameson. Tears filled her eyes and she looked to the ceiling.

"When can I see him?" Jackie asked.

"Maybe by nightfall. We need to prep him for surgery to remove the legs. The sooner we take action, the quicker his body can focus on healing those parts of his body that will come back. We need your consent." When there was no immediate response, he continued. "There is absolutely nothing that can be done to save those legs. They're useless. He has no sensation in them and he'll never use them again. Unfortunately, attached to his body, they are draining his energy, and this could make the difference between life and death."

"He won't be able to fly. All he knows is being a pilot, that's his life. He won't want to live if he can't fly." Darby swallowed and blinked rapidly.

"He's not going to die!" Jackie snapped. "Bring whatever I need to sign."

Kathryn knew that Jackie envisioned the life of a man she once knew, not the man who'd emerge after surgery with a deformed upper body and nothing below. A man who'd hate himself, hate his life, and hate what he'd done to his family. She couldn't stand seeing him live the life he was about to embark upon, but she, too, wanted to do everything they could to save him.

Within minutes a nurse came in with a stack of papers for Jackie to sign.

"Are you girls family?" she asked, assisting Jackie with the pages that needed her signature.

"Yes," Kathryn said.

"Okay, sweetie, the doctor wanted me to give you a little something." The nurse rubbed her arm with an alcohol swab. "This will make you feel better." She gently pressed the needle into Jackie's arm. "You're all welcome to stay in this room if you'd like. I'll come get you when Mr. Jameson returns from surgery."

"Thank you," Kathryn said.

They propped pillows in the bed for Jackie to lean against, and it wasn't long until shoes were off and Jackie was lying in bed with Darby curled at her feet. Kathryn sat by Jackie's side and held her hand. They watched the television in silence.

When the medication finally took hold, Jackie dozed off. Kathryn stood and muted the television, and Darby unfolded her body and stretched. They both stepped outside the room.

"Could you stay with Jackie for a bit?" Kathryn asked. "I want to go to her house and get some things."

"It sounds like we're going to be here for a while, huh?"

"We are. I'll hit Starbucks on my way back. You up for a Venti?"

"That'd be great. But Kat..." Darby looked down, and when her eyes returned to Kathryn's they were moist. "They're cutting off his legs. What in the hell is he going to do? He'll never fly again." She folded her arms and rubbed them.

"He's going to live," Kathryn said. Darby didn't respond.

Kathryn leaned against the wall allowing a wave of nausea to pass. She understood Darby's fear. Flying was *Darby's* life, and if she couldn't fly, she believed *her* life would be over. Greg had a wife and son to live for. Darby couldn't see beyond the job. Despite that, Kathryn also knew Greg wouldn't want to live like this, either.

"He's never going to fly whether he has legs or not," Kathryn said. "He may not have use of his arms. Or he may live in a coma for years. We just don't know. But if he wakes up as nothing more than a charred body that can think, you and I both know he'll wish he were dead. He could even be blind. Which would be a blessing so he wouldn't see what he's become."

"Jeez, you think you could paint an uglier picture?" Darby pressed her fingers to her temples and closed her eyes.

The quicker they accepted the reality, the stronger they'd be for Jackie. She didn't want Jackie to see Greg in his current condition. She wanted Jackie to remember him as he was. She wanted to remember him like he was. But that was not in their reality.

"I'm not trying to be negative," Kathryn said, and Darby stared without comment. "Would you do me a favor? Walk down that hall, turn right and go through the double doors into the burn center. He'll be in one of the rooms. Ask them how much longer until we can bring Jackie down."

Darby raised an eyebrow, hesitated, and then headed down the hall. Kathryn waited while checking for bars on her phone. Jackie tossed and whimpered in her sleep. Her arms flinched, and she muttered something incoherent. Kathryn nodded at a family who walked by. Seconds later, Darby flew around the corner, pushing through the family, and ran into the bathroom across from the nurse's station. Kathryn followed.

When she entered the restroom, Darby was on her knees in an unlocked stall.

"You okay, Darb?"

"My God," she cried between heaves. "Why…" Then she puked again. Kathryn pulled towels from the canister and soaked them in cold water, then held Darby's hair back and pressed them against her forehead.

"Sweetie, you needed to know the truth so we can be strong for Jackie. We can't freak out when she sees him. We need to keep it together to pick her up when she falls apart." Kathryn wasn't sure how she'd hold it together. When it came down to it, she hoped she could be strong.

"He's just so…gross." Darby heaved again.

"Yeah, I know." She'd yet to see him, but she'd seen many burn victims that had been melted—hard, leather-like, with purple fluid oozing from everywhere. She closed her eyes and pushed Greg's face from that picture.

Darby stood and rinsed out her mouth, then splashed water on her face. "Maybe we can get them to wrap him up or something."

"I'm sure they will, so let's try to keep her out until that happens."

"God, Kat, I just can't believe this."

"Me either. I can't possibly imagine what could be worse."

CHAPTER 33

IT HAD BEEN seven hours since their nightmare began, and Kathryn was glad to get outside. She sucked in fresh air as her phone came to life. It chimed with five messages that had arrived throughout the day.

She removed a parking ticket from her windshield and stuffed it into her pocket. Within no time she merged onto I-5 heading south. With Bluetooth in her ear, she listened to her messages. Nothing from Bill, but she called him again and left another message. The first time she'd called, he'd been at the accident site. Now she had no idea where he was. She returned John's call and scheduled a meeting for the following morning. She dialed her dad's number, but couldn't bring herself to push the call button. He had called three times.

Kathryn had openly blamed him for her mother's death, but in the shadow of her heart she knew she was the only person to blame. The divorce wasn't his fault, nor was her mother's suicide. Filled with anger and resentment, she had kept his granddaughters from him. She hadn't even allowed him to walk her down the aisle. She'd cast him aside.

With Greg lying on his deathbed, the reality of how unexpectedly people could leave slapped her in the face once again. She'd been so stupid, and so unfair.

Her dad not only lost the woman he loved, but he'd lost his

family, too. He didn't lose his family—she'd stolen it. She'd hidden her involvement all these years and blamed him. Nobody knew the monster she'd been except for Greg and Bill, and yet they'd both forgiven her unconditionally. Her dad would, too.

Greg was the reason that she'd survived that day, and her dad had loved him as much as she did. How could she tell her dad what had happened to him? She took a deep breath and pressed call.

He answered on the first ring.

"Dad, it's me, Kat."

"Kathryn, baby. I saw the news. Is…"

"Daddy, Greg was flying that plane. He's the only survivor and they don't know if he'll make it."

"No," he gasped, and then fell apart. She could see the broken man all over again—face is hands, sobbing, as if it were yesterday. Her dad's open emotion turned on her tears, and they cried together. Greg had been a son to her dad, and the brother that she'd lost. They weren't just losing Greg; they were losing her brother all over again.

"Dad, I'm so sorry for everything. I'm sorry I blamed you for Mom's… accident. It was I. I made her do it."

"Honey, you didn't make Mom do anything, she was sick and couldn't get over the loss. Derek's plane wouldn't have crashed if I'd grounded it… his engine was way overdue. If anyone's to blame, it's me."

"You couldn't have stopped him from flying." Derek was exactly like Darby. There was no keeping a pilot from his passion. "And Mom never blamed you, she blamed me. I should've been in that plane, not Kevin."

"Katy, is that what you think? Oh, baby, no. She just didn't know how to say goodbye to them. Honey, are you okay?"

Tears blinded her, and she pulled off to the side of the road. She wasn't okay. It had been her turn to go with their uncle, but she'd let Kevin go because she'd had other plans. Nine-year-olds had their priorities, and hers wasn't with her uncle. She'd had a friend's birthday party to attend. His plane crashed. Uncle Derek and Kevin died. Her family fell apart and her mother eventually killed herself. Kathryn's drive from that day forward had been with a single-minded focus—figure out why planes crashed and stop it from happening.

And now Greg was on his deathbed, and Jackie and Chris faced a hell they'd call life. The casualties in an airplane crash weren't only those on the plane; the real life destruction came for those left behind to make sense of it all.

"Dad, you don't understand. Mom hated being a mother, and she hated me for being the one to live."

"Honey, that's not true. Your mother loved you. She just couldn't get over the loss. After the divorce when I pulled my head out of my butt, I got her help. She'd been seeing a psychiatrist for three years before she left us."

"But I told her I hated her." She choked on a sob. "I said I wished she'd been in that plane with Uncle Derek and Kevin so they could be the happy little family in heaven instead of her making my life hell. That was the last thing I'd said to her."

Her dad stayed on the phone with her until her sobs subsided. He told her things she'd never known about her mother's depression and memory lapses, and it scared her all the more. She was following down a similar path.

Emotionally drained, she merged back onto the freeway. She told her dad about the NTSB, and her suspicions about the accidents and her concerns about Greg taking the wrong runway. Her father had already done some snooping around on his own.

"They say the accident was due to the heavy fog, and the aircraft had departed not only off the wrong runway but at mid-intersection. They left five thousand feet of asphalt behind them." He sighed. "There is no way he could've got that plane flying in five thousand feet. She was just too heavy."

"But why'd they take the wrong runway? Was the low visibility system operational?"

"As far as they can tell. I suppose it could've had a momentary glitch, but it's working now, and worked fine for an Alaska flight that departed thirty minutes prior to the accident. I doubt that there was anything wrong with it."

"How could they've taken the wrong runway *and* intersection? Wouldn't the tower see them?"

"Not in a fog like that. It looks like they were cleared to follow the taxiway under low visibility procedures. The ground controller passed them to the tower, but when they came up on the tower frequency, Coastal said they were ready for takeoff. There was no way they could've taxied to the end in the short time it took them to transfer between controllers."

A mist began to cover Kathryn's windshield, and she turned on wipers that only muddied her view. She pulled the wiper fluid knob.

"It looks like they entered the runway, and crossed over Sixteen Left, via intersection Juliet, and then onto Kilo or maybe onto Hotel. Regardless, they lined up on runway Sixteen Center, not the left, which left only four to five thousand feet for departure. They needed at least six thousand feet."

"My god, how could they make a mistake like that? Greg was an excellent pilot."

"Not sure. But if anyone can figure it out, you can."

She wiped a tear from her cheek with the back of her hand. "Thanks Dad, I'll call you when I know more." A moment of silence elapsed and she added, "I love you."

"I love you too, sweetheart. Call me if you need anything. I'll be here."

GREG AND JACKIE'S driveway loomed in front of her before she expected, and she pulled into it. The scent of death slapped her in the face when she opened the car door. The accident had been less than five miles away. It amazed her that none of them had heard the impact.

She located the spare key to let herself in, but the door was unlocked. She was positive they'd locked it that morning as they left. She moved quickly to the bedroom. The thought that she could avoid the memories of dinner by refusing to look into the kitchen was short lived. Jackie and Greg's unmade bed undid that thought. She made it, and picked up his things off the floor. Coming into this room would be difficult enough for her.

Kathryn stuffed a pair of Jackie's sweat pants, a t-shirt, and a sweatshirt into a duffle bag, and then moved to the bathroom. She read the labels on the prescription bottles—a prescription for Greg and a bottle of Tylenol, but nothing for Jackie other than a pack of birth control pills. She left them in place. She dropped the toothbrush and toothpaste into the bag then slid the bottles of face wash and body lotion off the counter into the bag, too.

Walking quickly past Greg's office she noticed a light glowing under the door. She opened it, and the first thing she saw was that his desk drawers were opened, and the drawer that she'd helped Jackie put back was lying on the floor.

The house creaked, settling like many its age did. She stood for a moment, assessing the mess, and then quickly replaced the drawer to its home then stuffed the files inside it.

Kathryn stepped onto the front porch and closed the door quietly behind her, not sure who she was trying not to disturb. Perhaps ghosts of a life once lived.

She stood on the porch and tilted her face to the sky. Clouds had replaced the fog, and rain began to pour from the heavens crying tears for all. She knew there would be many more to come. But for her, she had to remain strong for her friends.

CHAPTER 34
MONDAY

THEY HAD TAKEN Greg into surgery when Kathryn returned with their coffee. Five drawn-out hours later, the surgeon told them he'd survived the operation. His vitals were strong, and he was stable. The long day slithered into an even longer night. She still hadn't reached Bill. Empty coffee cups, an unread paperback, and three empty packages of sugar free gum filled the windowsill.

It was shortly after 9:00 p.m. Sunday when they moved him to the I.C.U., his body covered with gauze like the mummy he'd become. Jackie made a nest at his bedside and hovered. Kathryn and Darby stood guard, propped up in chairs outside his room. Kathryn had bitten her nails to the nubs by midnight. A night of internal debate consumed her.

In the early hours of morning, darkness still blanketing the sky, Jackie had finally dozed off and Darby snuck home to shower and get a change of clothes. By the time she returned, it was Kathryn's turn to escape for her meeting with John.

They'd planned to meet in a little café about four blocks from Harborview, and she looked forward to stretching her legs. That was something she'd taken for granted all of her life until the moment they wheeled Greg into the room without his.

She exited the hospital on the second floor via the glassed hallway that crossed over Ninth Street to the Norm Maleng building. Startled by the large number of people gathered below, at the front exit, she stopped and stared. The media had camped outside all night, waiting until they could talk to the "only survivor" of the Coastal Airlines crash. Before anyone glanced up, she turned to avoid the crowd of vultures.

Once outside, the morning air, cool and moist, felt incredible. She drew in a deep breath. It tasted like life itself after the stagnant air in the hospital that held a mixture of death, pain, and sterilization.

Today Greg's accident wouldn't have happened, she thought glancing toward the sky. It had rained on and off throughout the night, and now a few isolated raindrops began to fall. Pulling her coat tight, she walked faster. She needed to speak to John about what she'd learned—pilots could actually be crashing their own planes. The thought ran a chill through her bones.

The sky grew dark. Clouds gathered before her eyes, and the wind picked up. She hurried and opened the café door, escaping Seattle's wrath.

John sat at a table in the far corner with two large cups in front of him. His brows were knit together, and his focus was on her as she approached.

Shadows across his face and red-stained eyes told her he'd gotten as little sleep as she had. This was the John from their field days during an investigation. The morning after, they'd suck down the coffee that would bring them back to life.

"What happened?" she asked when she sat. It was a rhetorical question, and she didn't expect an answer.

"They know what happened. The pilots departed using the wrong runway. What we don't know is why. The tower couldn't see them, and transmissions indicate they reported an incorrect position." John's words were sharp and cut to the point, but told her nothing she didn't already know.

She wrapped her hands around the warm mug and stared into its darkness. "This is a nightmare. The first officer's wife is one of my closest friends." She hesitated for a moment. "The first officer... He's the one who found me after my mom died." She glanced down. "He couldn't be more of a brother if we'd had the same parents."

John didn't respond. When she looked up, their eyes locked, and she knew exactly what he was thinking. She was too close to the investigation.

Holding her gaze, his eyes narrowed over the brim of his cup as he sipped. Reverberations of her words hung in the air.

"Interesting," he finally said. "I need to speak to him when he regains consciousness."

"*If* he regains consciousness. God only knows if he'll survive. He's stable, but he's in a coma. And... They amputated his legs last night." She looked away. When her eyes returned, a sigh escaped. "He's not going to have a life," she said, in a near whisper. "I just think that it would be better if he wou..." She stopped mid-sentence when the waitress approached.

The woman topped off John's cup and then left them alone. Kathryn continued. "He'll hate himself and wish he were dead for what he's done to his family, and for killing all those people."

The front door opened, and the cold wind created chaos among a stack of paper napkins. John caught one in his hand. He played with it for a minute, then crumpled it into a ball and dropped it onto the table. "He is the only person who can tell us what happened. We better hope he survives."

John was right, but her heart ached for Jackie and Chris, and the nightmare that would become their lives. Death would be a blessing. Either way, she'd lost a brother again.

Tears burned, and she looked towards the ceiling to regain her composure.

Grabbing one of the paper napkins from the table, she wiped under her eyes and sat up straight then told John about Greg and Jackie's financial status. He allowed her to ramble, listening intently. When she was done, he stared without comment. The clattering of dishes and chatting of customers filled the space. The café was filling with both noise and scent. Her stomach growled when she smelled homemade croissants.

"Have you got anywhere on the investigation?"

She nodded, glad to shift the focus. Debating how to tell him, she decided to build the case. "To begin with, the Regional crash, the first officer's thumbs were broken."

John raised an eyebrow.

"*Her* thumbs were broken and not the captain's. That meant her hands were on the control yoke and the thrust levers during impact, indicating that *she* was the pilot flying during the landing, not the captain." She hesitated allowing the information to settle in between them. "I think he gave up control long before the landing. We never heard him speak again after the stall."

"What if he was flying the plane and didn't have time to talk."

"I don't think so. He would've given her commands. There was too much silence. Think about it. The stall occurs and she calls him a bastard, followed by multiple thuds and then all communication stops until final approach."

"She could've been calling the plane a bastard when it stalled." John leaned back in his chair and folded his arms.

"I doubt it. Can you explain the thuds? I think she hit him with her flashlight. She called him a bastard because he put that airplane into a stall, and then she whacked him. Besides, his cranial damage is consistent with the size and shape of the flashlight found in the flight deck."

John raised a hand and rubbed his eyes.

She fiddled with her spoon, visualizing their approach. "They began their descent far too early. With a basic three-to-one gouge, I'm thinking they began their descent, maybe, forty miles too soon."

"Why would he do that?"

"To ice up the aircraft." The waitress interrupted them to ask if they needed anything else, and John ordered two chocolate croissants. After she was gone Kathryn continued, lowering her voice. "I think he entered the clouds, accumulated ice and pulled the nose up to induce a stall. That plane had wing anti-ice, but the reports indicated the switch was off. Sandra swore at him, hit him, knocked him unconscious, and flew the plane herself. I believe she was flying solo and couldn't pick up the radio."

John folded his arms and nodded for her to continue.

"The *only* words spoken were Sandra's. She told the tower they were landing and then said, 'what the fu…' It wasn't what she said, but how she said it. It was more of a question of surprise than a statement."

John leaned forward and lowered his voice. "So, for argument's sake, let's say that you're correct. What surprised her?"

"I think Grant came to and raised the flaps," Kathryn said, as the waitress approached with their food. Once she was out of earshot, she continued. "It wasn't only what Sandra said in her final breath, but you could hear the gears on the flaps move and they crashed as a clean airplane. Reports indicated they'd partially configured for the approach."

"What makes you think they weren't attempting a go-around?"

"Thrust was never increased. The power would have come first, then flaps."

"Raising the flaps that close to the ground, with speeds teetering in the stall margin in icing conditions, would do them in," John said, quietly.

"Yeah, I know."

"Do you have proof?"

"Proof flaps were up at impact? Proof they had been moved prior to impact? Proof the anti-ice was off? Yes. Of course."

She broke off a piece of her croissant and picked at the chocolate, thinking of Frankie. Then she proceeded to tell John her thoughts on the Global crash and how she believed that the captain had intentionally used the wrong rudder. She explained the glare on the video and how it coincided with the rudder direction and the captain's broken ankle, as well as how the first officer performed the landing and how she believed he rolled the aircraft away from the other aircraft in line awaiting takeoff, hitting the ground with his left wing, as he did.

The noise in the restaurant grew, but she lowered her voice and John leaned in closer.

"What about Skylark?"

She explained that the captain had known about the faulty radar flag and he'd ignored it. He'd also requested the first officer to call the tower six miles too soon, exactly at the moment the indicator would falter. The captain set the stage for something that should have been nothing more than a nuisance to crash his plane.

"The recordings and medical reports haven't been released. How do you know this?"

"It doesn't matter how I know." She knew that question would eventually arrive, and she navigated with stubbornness, just like he'd taught her to do. "The point is that all signs indicate that these captains are clearly flying their planes into the ground."

He tapped his spoon on the table, then the door burst open, again, and she glanced toward it. A group of young men entered, allowing the wind to whip through the restaurant. The breeze sent a chill through her body.

"Your job was only to interview the families, until I gave you anything else. I appreciate your efforts, but I'm not comfortable with you accessing confidential information on your own. The media could blow this up in our faces. If what you say is true, then we have something bigger than we expected. It's imperative that all our documentation and sources are perfect. Where did you get your information?"

She had no intention of telling him her source, and he should know that. He had taught her that the key to success was to never betray confidences. Besides, what she gathered on her own was nothing more than he was going to eventually give her anyway.

"I assure you nothing will blow up. Besides we're on the same team, remember? I know that three, now maybe four, accidents have occurred because of the captain."

"*Why?* Why in the hell would a captain crash his plane?"

"I don't know. But I know that Greg was an excellent pilot. They were having some financial trouble, but pretty much everyone in the industry is. He'd never allow this to happen on purpose."

John tapped his spoon and stared. She raised her cup to her lips without removing her eyes from his.

"Kathryn, I think that you might be—"

"Don't say it," she said, interrupting him. "I planned on telling you I couldn't do this. Greg's accident... It was too much. *I* thought I was too close, and feared I couldn't be objective. But last night as I listened to his machine beep, and watched the pain in Jackie's eyes, I imagined what if the next victim was Darby, or Bill.

"I have no choice but to continue. I have to figure this out." She spoke a little too loudly and heads turned their direction. "I have to do this for Greg."

John waited until the curious eyes turned away, and then quietly said, "*If* Greg was at fault, not only would the lawsuits wipe them out, but the impact of your friend killing hundreds of people would destroy his family. Are you willing to set the stage for that?"

He was right. She would destroy lives with the truth if Greg and the other pilots had done this on purpose. But if she were involved, she would also have an element of control and could prevent the truth from exploding into a lynching to boost the political career of someone in Homeland. "I don't believe Greg was directly to blame."

"Are you sure?" John asked. "What if these accidents are nothing but serial suicides? One pilot watches another family collect millions from insurance, and he sees that as a get out of jail free card."

"No. I can't believe that. They could've crashed their cars with the same financial result."

"Then why?"

She circled a finger around the brim of her cup and tapped her foot. She looked up and said, "*What if* terrorists located the pilots with the most to lose financially, then told them they'd kill their wives and children if they didn't take down the plane?

"Each captain had a family. I haven't had the ability to figure out the financial status of everyone, but I know how badly Greg and Jackie were hurting." Kathryn hesitated then took a sip of her coffee, then added, "Greg's an excellent pilot. I just can't imagine him making a mistake like taxiing via the wrong intersection."

"But he *did* make that kind of mistake."

"Exactly. So why?" Kathryn refused to think that he'd do something like this intentionally. And then there was Linda. Kathryn had seen her elegant home, but the cupboards were scarcely stocked. The yard was unmaintained unlike that of the neighbors. Paint chipping. Lines around the carpet where furniture had once been were all signs of financial distress—not collection of an insurance policy. No, she didn't think this was an insurance scam.

John leaned forward and rested his arms on the table and lowered his voice. "I need you to keep this quiet, all of it. Don't share your theories with anyone. I need time to think." He tapped his spoon on the table. "This information has definitely thrown a wrench in the gears."

She glanced at her watch. "I better get back." She stood.

"Has Bill been to the hospital yet?" John asked, helping her with her coat.

"No." She had no idea where he was. He hadn't returned her calls. In her last message to him she'd apologized and told him she was giving up on the idea of working. That was yesterday, and it felt a million miles away. Today she realized she had to see this through. He'd have to understand, because there was no way she was quitting.

John took both her hands in his. "You're good at what you do, and that's why I called you. Don't ever think otherwise. You are an amazing woman Kathryn, and there is nothing you can't do. Many lives are depending on you. Hell, I'm depending on you." He squeezed gently, and added, "I know you won't let anyone down, but don't let yourself down, either."

Choked up with emotion, she held firm to his hands silently thanking him. Just then, a flash caught her eye, and she glanced toward the window. The rain fell hard and she listened for the thunder that never came.

Outside, she tilted her face to the sky and allowed the cold rain to wash away the betrayal of her emotions as she headed toward the hospital. There was nothing that could stop her.

CHAPTER 35

JUST WHEN DARBY thought things couldn't get worse, Bill showed up.

"Hey, Bill," she said, when he walked into the hospital room and pushed past her like he owned the place. *God himself has arrived.*

"Where's Kathryn?"

"I made her go get something to eat and take a shower. We're taking turns." In Darby's world, when it came to Bill lies were fair.

Jackie adjusted a pillow under Greg's bandaged head. The previous hour had been filled with her wasted motion of touching, tucking, and hovering over his still body. Darby glanced at Bill. This was exactly why she'd never get married. Men weren't worth the pain. Well, all except one.

Bill stared at the spot on the bed where Greg's legs should have been. "So, what do the doctors think?"

"I don't know. They took his legs last night, what do you think?" Darby said.

Jackie pulled the sheet up to Greg's chin and adjusted his pillow "You know, guys, we probably shouldn't talk about that in here, just in case he's listening."

"You're right," Darby said. "Sorry."

Jackie speaking was progress. She'd gone into a quiet flutter mode since they'd brought Greg into the room. Calm and restrained, a Stepford wife. Maybe it was the drugs they'd given her. If that were the case, Darby wanted some. Still it was nice to hear her finally talk.

Bill pulled a hand through his hair. "At least he has insurance."

Darby sat on the floor by the door. "Jeez, Bill, can you give her a break?" She leaned against a wall and closed her eyes. Insurance would be worthless unless he died. Until then, he had good medical coverage, good enough to keep him in the hospital for a while, as long as Jackie could pay the twenty percent co-pay or until they maxed out their policy.

When the money ran out, they would kick him out because there would be nothing medically they could do for him. He'd end up in a long-term care facility. A facility Jackie wouldn't be able to afford. But Darby could. She'd be damned if he ended up a ward of the state.

"He can't hear anything," Bill said.

Darby scrambled to her feet. "You're wrong. They say that patients in comas can hear what's going on around them."

Bill rolled his eyes. "So where's the doctor?"

"I don't know." Despite Bill having major putz status, she kind of felt sorry for him. Greg was his friend. She went with empathy for a moment, knowing it would be short lived. She knew better.

Bill left the room as quickly as he'd entered, then yelled at the nurse to find the doctor. Greg's private room was across the hall from the nurse's station. One wall housed a large window that enabled twenty-four-hour surveillance.

Darby watched Bill behave like an ass. She made a couple air circles around her ear. The nurse grinned but continued to feign concentration on Bill's rant. He was oblivious to anything beyond himself. She returned her attention to Jackie.

"Are you hungry, sweetie?" Jackie hadn't touched her sandwich, or eaten anything else since they'd arrived at the hospital. "You're going to have to keep your strength up for Greg, and Chris when he gets home."

"I know. I will. I just… I'm not really hungry right now." She lightly stroked Greg's bandaged cheek with the back of her finger.

Darby glanced at Bill and his antics. The Woodland Park Zoo came to mind. Bill *was* under a lot of stress, his friend *was* close to death, and he *had* been somewhat civil to her when they'd all had dinner together the other night. Maybe she should give him a break. *Not.*

Attacking her on a personal level was one thing, but going after her skills as a pilot… That was too much. He had made her a fool when she was trying to prove herself. The worst, but also the best, followed—she and Kathryn became friends. She was tied to the ass for life, whether she wanted to be or not.

"Hey, ladies."

Startled, Darby jumped. This was the last place she'd expected to see Neil and her cheeks warmed. "Jackie, this is one of our pilots, Neil."

"It's nice to meet you," Jackie said smoothing the sheet below Greg's hips.

"I'm really sorry." Neil glanced at the bed, then immediately turned away.

Darby could see the pain in his bloodshot eyes. He, too, took this hard. They all had. All she wanted to do was hold him, tell him it was all right, but she knew that wasn't allowed. Then Neil changed the rules. He turned to her, opened his arms and she melted into them. He whispered, "I love you, Darby."

She fought the tears she'd buried the night before to be strong for Jackie. The fatigue combined with the warmth of his arms, and the magnitude of his words made the fight difficult. Then she smelled scotch seeping from his pores.

"Isn't this sweet?" Bill said from the doorway, his arms folded. Neil released her and stepped back. Bill pushed past them. "You can't find a friggin' doctor in this entire place."

"He'll be back," Jackie said. "He's really optimistic. He thinks Greg will wake up any time now."

"Really?" Bill asked.

Darby didn't comment. Reality was not as optimistic as Jackie's mind, but Darby wouldn't destroy what little hope her friend had.

"Well, it was nice to meet you, Jackie. I'm really sorry about Greg. He's a good man," Neil said. "Bill, can I talk to you?"

They walked out together and stood in view across the other side of the nurse's station. Darby looked away, pretending she was ignoring them. She couldn't understand what was spoken, despite their raised voices, but Neil stabbed the air with his finger, and Bill laughed.

She, too, needed to talk with Neil, but not now. Darby drifted toward the window and focused on the people below. Reporters, vans, cameras. She wished they would get the hell out of their lives.

"Hey guys, who's that arguing with Bill?" Kathryn asked, slipping into the room.

"Kat, thank God you're back. That's Neil."

"Oh wow. He's cute. But what's Bill's problem with him?"

"What's *not* Bill's problem? I told the ball and chain that you left to get food and take a shower because you stank."

"I still stink."

"No shit. I think we need another excuse."

"Stop!" Jackie yelled. Kathryn and Darby turned with mouths open. Then Jackie began to laugh, and soon Darby and Kat were laughing with her. Darby had no idea why they laughed, but it felt good, and contagious. Then Jackie sat on the floor and put her face in her hands and her laughter turned to tears. When she looked up, she said, "Thanks, guys."

She wiped her face on her sleeve, then looked from Darby to Kathryn and took a deep breath. "You're going to get me through this, aren't you?"

"We are," Kathryn said, kneeling beside her.

"Whatever it takes, Kiddo," Darby said. "But as much as I hate to ditch this party, I've got an appointment I need to keep. Will you be okay without me for a bit?"

"Go, we'll be fine," Kathryn said.

Darby darted out of the room and headed for the elevator, hoping that Neil and Bill wouldn't see her leave. She didn't want Neil to follow her. She avoided looking in their direction, pressed the elevator button, and tapped her foot. "Open. Open. Open," she whispered. When it did, she ducked inside and pressed 1. Just before the doors closed, a hand stopped them.

"Room for one more?"

She stepped back. "So what's up with you and Bill?"

Neil moved toward her and pulled her close. "Can we go have a drink?"

"I can't. I've got an appointment."

"Come on, babe, I need to talk to you."

"I'll be done in an hour."

"Just forget it." Neil dropped his hands and turned his back to her.

"Neil, don't be like this." She placed a hand on his back, and he pulled away from her.

When the elevator door opened, he said, "Never mind. It wasn't that big of a deal anyway." He walked out and waved a hand over his shoulder. He never looked back to see her mouth hanging open. Instead, he kicked the glass when the automatic doors didn't open quickly enough for him. Once outside, he stuffed his hands into his pockets and walked away.

CHAPTER 36

BILL WALKED into Greg's room and stared at Kathryn. "Where have you been?"

"You mean the night you walked out, or today?" She spoke a bit more sharply than she'd intended.

"I'm sorry." He sighed. "It's been a hell of a couple of days. Do you know what the prognosis is? I can't find his doctor and the nurses won't tell me a damn thing."

"The doctor said he's doing much better and he could wake up any time," Jackie said.

Kathryn doubted Dr. Green had said anything of the sort. Greg was stable, and all they could do was pray. "If you want to talk to him, he'll be back at three."

"I can't wait. I've got to be outside for the press conference, and then we've got the memorial tonight."

"What memorial?" Kathryn asked.

"The union is hosting a memorial for the employees and their families." He turned toward Jackie. "Do you think you can make it?"

When Jackie shook her head no, Kathryn said, "I'm going to skip it, and stay here with Jackie."

"No." Bill reached out and touched Kathryn's cheek. "I really need you with me. I'm not sure if I could make it through the night without you by my side."

Kathryn looked between Bill and Jackie, then at Greg.

"I think you should go," Jackie said, placing a hand on Greg's chest. "We'll be fine."

Kathryn didn't want to leave Jackie alone, but Bill was right—she should be there. If she wanted his support, then she needed to extend the same courtesy.

"I've got to get outside," Bill said, and gave Jackie a quick hug. He turned and took both of Kathryn's hands in his. "I'll be home by five and we can drive together." Then he pulled her close and held her tight. "I love you," he whispered. "There is nothing I wouldn't do for you."

After he left, Kathryn picked up the remote and turned on the television.

The press conference took precedence on all local channels. The camera crews had been waiting for Bill. Jackie pulled her chair close to Greg's bed and rested her head on the edge, watching intently.

Kathryn sat at the end of the bed and fought to keep her eyes open. The weight of fatigue tugged on her eyelids, and every molecule in her body ached. The last time she'd been horizontal was when she'd cried herself to sleep two nights ago. A memorial was the last thing she wanted to attend. But maybe she'd find out something about Greg's captain, and the night might not be a total waste.

"There's Bill. He's on TV," Jackie said.

He held a commanding presence and spoke of the industry, the problems with fatigue, and the pilots' long duty days. He spoke of stress and the resulting distraction. He presented a perfect package that anything was possible under the present conditions.

"All we know at this time is that the crew departed off the wrong intersection, and many lives were lost. We don't know why, but we do know that both these pilots were good men. Good pilots who didn't deserve this fate."

Bill glanced toward the hospital. "My best friend lies in a bed, unconscious, the only survivor. His legs have been amputated and the remainder of his body has been burned. The doctors say that his prognosis isn't good."

Kathryn looked at Jackie. Her expression didn't change with Bill's comment, but a line of pain slid across her face. Bill hung his head, and closed his eyes.

When he returned his gaze to the cameras, tears stained his cheeks. He brushed them away with the back of his hand and continued. "There's nobody more heartbroken than I, with what transpired at SeaTac yesterday morning. This is my airline. My best friend faces a fate worse than death, and the passengers on that aircraft were our friends and neighbors. I was supposed to be on that flight, but my best friend offered to fly it for me. And now he's…" Bill paused. "I will not let this slide to the back burner."

Kathryn and Jackie exchanged a glance, neither of them commented on the fact that Bill should have been on that flight and not Greg. They returned their focus to the television. Bill had called Greg to ask him to take the flight because he'd drunk too much. Flight Eighty-Five. *But why had Bill drunk so much if he was scheduled to fly?*

Bill's hands were balled into fists as he continued. "You think that our pilots can work day and night, across multiple time zones, with minimal rest? Do you think they can focus on their jobs, exhausted and worried about how they're going to pay their mortgages?

"Our union has accommodated and bent backward to help our company, as have most employees in this industry. We can't give anymore!" Bill yelled. "We won't!" Then he dropped the level of his voice and said, "Yesterday we gave blood."

He relaxed his fists. "Deregulation is the real villain. How can the airlines survive? Each flight means more money lost. We say we don't want government controlling our lives, but if the government doesn't do something, I assure you more accidents will occur. Who will be in control then?

"My friend hangs on for his life in this hospital. But he was hanging with a noose wrapped around his neck before the accident occurred, trying to make ends meet. If the government doesn't re-regulate the industry so that the airlines can survive, and the planes you travel on can maintain a high level of safety, then our employers will continue to strip away our work rules, our pay, and our time at home. At what cost?

"This morning I was notified that I've been elected the Airline Pilots Organization's president. As their president, I assure you that I will do everything in my power to make sure that another accident such as this never happens." Then he asked for questions.

A hand sprang up. "I understand that the first officer and you were dining together the night before the accident, and he'd been drinking. Was alcohol involved?"

"Not true. We did have dinner together, but, on my father's grave, I assure you he was drinking soda the entire night. Tests have confirmed that First Officer Jameson was sober."

"When will the airline release the final passenger list?"

"After all families have been notified." Bill nodded to a reporter from King Five news.

"Is it true that the aircraft had previous maintenance write-ups that showed the engines might seize on departure?"

"Not to my knowledge."

He scanned the crowd, and then nodded to a woman in front and said, "I'll take one more question."

"I understand that the Regional Director of Homeland Security's daughter was one of the victims on that flight, and that you and she had a personal relationship, can you confirm that?"

"I'm sorry, that will be all for today." Bill turned his back to the camera and walked away.

Lights flashed. The reporter was speaking, but Kathryn heard not a word after that final question.

CHAPTER 37

D R. ADAMS pointed the remote at the television and shut off the press conference.

Darby sat with her mouth open. "Jeez. I can't believe Bill didn't deny his affair on friggin' national television. If nothing else, to protect Kat from humiliation."

"How do you think she'll deal with this?"

"She'll be devastated. She has this unending trust of people." Darby crossed her legs and bounced her foot. "She'll think I knew."

"You did know." Adams poured himself a glass of water and Darby glared at him.

"Come on, how in the heck could I tell my best friend that I knew her husband was a sack of shit whoring around on her?" If it weren't for Kathryn, she'd have nothing to do with Bill. He was a gnat on the ass of life.

"You need to talk to her, sooner rather than later."

"I know." Darby played with the zipper on her jacket.

This was the first time he'd ever told her what to do. She knew he was right, but she also had no intention of ever telling Kathryn she'd known about Bill and Kristen. It had been going on too long. It would be the ultimate betrayal.

Bill had done some lousy things to Darby long before Kathryn was on the scene, and she'd planned to tell Kathryn all about them at the wedding. He'd threatened her. Again. Bill always made good on his threats. He'd made her life a total hell at the airline from the moment she wouldn't sleep with him. It took her over eleven years to prove herself. It was hard enough being a female pilot without Sky God bad mouthing her.

She did go to the wedding. She planned on ratting him out until she met Kathryn. Kat was the nicest, most genuine person she'd ever met, and she was obviously in love with Bill. God knew why. But then, everyone loved Bill. He was an excellent pilot, and Kathryn was right; he did have a brilliant mind. Something she would never openly admit.

Kathryn had told Darby she was carrying twins, a secret that only they had shared until after the wedding. Then Kathryn hugged her and told her they were destined to be best friends. Darby had never had a best girlfriend before.

"I suspect she'll ask if you knew."

"I can't tell her I knew, not after all this time."

Adams leaned back in his chair and folded his arms. They played the stare-down game. Darby was getting really good at it, but she was still the first to look away.

"How are things with Neil?"

She slumped in her chair, tilted her head back and closed her eyes. "That damn wedding," she said softly, and rolled her head from side to side. She'd met Neil in a drunken stupor, but at the time he'd been married. Ten years later he was single, back in her life, and she was in love with him. She opened her eyes. "The last time we were together in Tampa, sober, he said he loved me. But he still won't make us a couple. Said he's not ready yet. Then today, at the hospital, he freaked when I couldn't go have a drink with him."

"It appears you both love each other. Why do *you* think he doesn't want a commitment?"

She sat up a little straighter and picked at a fingernail. Chips of red flaked off. "The ex-wife did a number on him. Until he trusts me, he's keeping me at bay." Tears filled her eyes.

Adams raised an eyebrow and handed her a box of tissue. "Have you been to his home and discussed this with him?"

"No. I'm not going to throw myself at him. Besides, he's got the kids half the time, and it just hasn't worked out." She pulled another tissue and blew her nose. Changing the subject, she said, "I can't get the visual of Greg out of my mind. It was so gross. I puked for an hour."

"How's he doing?"

"They cut off his legs last night, and his body... It's melted. He'd be better off dead."

"What do you think about the accident?"

"What do *I* think? I think it sucks. I think that I could've been on that flight, and I think that if I had been, maybe nobody would be dead right now. Or maybe I'd be the one in the hospital without my friggin' legs." Tears slid down her cheeks. "It's just so unfair that this happened to Greg. He deserved better."

Adams nudged the box of tissues toward her, and she pulled multiple sheets out and blew her nose, then wiped under her eyes with a finger. She had never lost it in a session before, though Adams had probably wanted her to break down for a long time before now.

"Where'd those tears come from?"

"I don't know. Greg's burnt body. Bill's betrayal of Kathryn. The thought of losing Kathryn's friendship. Falling in love with Neil. Take your pick." She blew her nose hard. "Life just sucks right now. My friends think I have it great, but I don't have shit. I'm alone, and always will be."

Dr. Adams stood, walked around the desk, and pulled a chair close to her.

"We all make choices in our lives, and if you don't like yours, change it. Only you have that power."

She wiped her cheek. She'd known all this for a very long time. But knowing and doing were two different animals.

CHAPTER 38

THEY DROVE in silence to the memorial. Kathryn decided to hold her head high, and keep up pretenses that she and Bill were still together. He parked the car at the end of the cul-de-sac closest to the building.

The prospect that Bill was having an affair numbed her, and defied everything she believed. When Bill arrived home at 4:45 she'd asked him if he knew Kristen Walker, and he'd said, "Of course, everyone knew Kristen." She'd cried, asked questions, and threatened that she wouldn't attend the memorial with him unless he told her the truth. He'd said, "I love you. I love the girls, and the family we've created. We're not doing this now. Help me get through this night and we'll talk."

She'd agreed—but only for her daughters.

Now stunned by the colossal crowd, she dug deep and willed herself to get out of the car. He jumped out and ran around to her side, and opened the door.

Hundreds of people attended the memorial. It was supposed to have been a private reception for the families and friends of employees only, but as it turned out, there had been many employees traveling to Los Angeles, more than she'd realized. And with the crash of a plane, the entire airline and all employees were impacted.

Bill held her hand and helped her out of the car. They walked together into the community center. Everyone looked, whispered, and smiled pityingly at her while they greeted Bill, but she held her head high.

A table covered with hundreds of white candles sat beside an open bar. The candles would be lit at nightfall, outside on the field, with the landscape of Puget Sound as a backdrop. Off to the right stretched a buffet of fruit, vegetables, and cheese.

A microphone had been placed in a corner area for anyone who wanted to speak. Left of that stage, a fire crackled and warmed the room. Outside in the center of the field, a second fire burned in an open pit, and people gathered around. They cried and held each other.

Bill kissed her on the cheek and whispered, "I'll be right back." He waved at someone, and left Kathryn alone. She wanted nothing more than to be in the safety of the hospital. Since that wasn't an option, she moved to the bar and selected a glass of wine—dangerous with so little sleep. At the moment, she didn't care. The glass just touched her lips when Darby entered the room.

"Darby," she yelled, and waved. Darby gave a quick wave back, and joined her. They embraced, and then she, too, selected a glass of merlot then they moved closer to the fire.

"I saw the conference today. Kat, I'm so sorry."

"You and everyone else. *Please* tell me it's my imagination and nobody is staring, and talking about me."

"No, you're not wrong. They're definitely looking. They could be talking about someone else, but I doubt it."

"Oh, that helps," Kathryn said. It was just like Darby to speak the bitter truth, no matter how painful. But somehow she always made the truth easier to swallow.

"If they are talking about you, it's only to avoid the pain in their own sorry-ass lives."

"I still can't believe it's true. There's no way I wouldn't have known. But still, he wouldn't even deny it. He just said, 'we'll talk later.' But in light of everything," Kathryn said, glancing around the room, "it makes my situation nothing in comparison. At least my husband's alive so I can kill him on my own, a slow and painful death."

Darby laughed and then her attention turned to the front door.

"Look who's here, and he's heading directly toward Bill. We should move closer so we can witness the attack first hand."

Kathryn turned. Regional Director of Homeland, Walker, was headed Bill's way, with fists held tight at his sides. She knew him well and how much Bill hated him. This was going to be anything but good.

"How could Bill be hooked up with *his* daughter?" Kathryn asked. "You go. I'll wait here."

She didn't want to know. Not now. Ignorance at this point gave her a reprieve from having to do something, and destroying her daughters' illusion of family. Instead she watched Darby casually slink towards Bill and Walker.

Bill excused himself from the group he'd been talking to and walked out the door to the patio. Walker followed. Once outside, Bill stopped and turned.

They both stood beyond the sliding glass doors, outside of earshot, and Walker's red face was close to Bill's. Bill was tall, but Walker stared at him at eye level, and Bill didn't retreat. Instead, Bill placed his hands on his hips, a stance Kathryn knew well.

Darby never made it close enough to eavesdrop. Someone stopped her for a hug, and she mouthed "sorry" over the man's shoulder.

"Men are such assholes," a woman slurred as she stumbled

into Kathryn, splashing wine on the floor.

"Excuse me?"

"Our biggest mistake is we're so damn naïve." She gulped her wine then stared into the empty glass as if wondering what happened to the contents. She looked up, eyes bloodshot. "Bill's a cheating sack of shit, honey. I'm sorry." Then she took Kathryn's glass and drank from it.

Kathryn glanced over her shoulder at Bill and then looked back at the woman. "You can't believe everything you hear on the news."

"Don't count on that. Maybe you should ask Bradshaw. Those asshole pilots know everything. Sweetheart, we're always the last to know." She turned and stumbled away.

Kathryn returned her gaze to the patio in time to see the Director push Bill, but she didn't care. Her heart moved to her throat. Tears filled her eyes and blurred everything, and she began to shake. A hand touched her arm, and she jumped.

"Are you okay?" Darby asked.

"Some woman just told me you knew about Bill and Kristen."

Darby looked stricken and her face flushed, and Kathryn pulled her arm from Darby's touch. "You knew! It's true, and you didn't say anything!"

"Kat, please. Let me explain."

"I can't believe you lied to me. I thought we were friends."

"We are friends, we—"

"You are not my friend. You're a damned liar!" Tears burning, she turned and stormed away, bumping the wine table and knocking numerous glasses to the floor.

CHAPTER 39

BILL OPENED the front door and walked into the house, and Kathryn remained in the car. She never should've allowed him to drive home, again. He'd had too much to drink. Despite what she'd said, she did care. She cared too much, if that were possible.

Exhaustion created illusions. She knew she'd overreacted, and hundreds of people witnessed that reaction. She should have kept her cool. They'd all think she was nuts. But that didn't matter, now she needed to face the noise of her life and deal with Bill and his infidelity. He didn't deny the affair because he wouldn't lie to her. And then there was Darby. She had known.

Kathryn pulled herself from the car. She took a deep breath, climbed the front steps, and closed the front door behind her. She found Bill sitting on the love seat in the living room with a cocktail in hand.

"You *were* having an affair. Darby confirmed it." She had no tears left to cry. They, like her marriage, were done. She wasn't sure which was a greater betrayal—her husband cheating, or her best friend knowing. She sat heavily on the couch.

"Why do you think it took so long for her to tell you?" Bill asked.

Kathryn stared without response.

He moved to the ottoman across from her. "Why do you think that she and I never got along? When she found out about Kristen, she gave me an open invitation anytime I wanted. She said she'd tell you about me if I didn't sleep with her. Darby's nothing but a whore. Has she told you about the pilot she's been screwing, and that he's married? If I were you, I'd pick my friends a little bit better."

Darby's boyfriend was divorced, and Kathryn highly doubted Darby would want anything to do with Bill. There was also no way she'd allow Bill to derail this conversation into anything other than what it was—*his* infidelity. "Have you slept with anyone else?" Not that it mattered now, but she needed to know.

"Of course not."

"But you don't deny you slept with Kristen Walker?"

He stood, and walked to the window. He didn't speak, but when he turned, tears filled his eyes. "I don't deny that." Bill lifted his drink to his lips and emptied the glass, leaving only ice. "I loved her."

His words knocked the wind out of her. "You loved her?" She could barely choke the words out.

"It had nothing to do with you."

"It has everything to do with me, you bastard."

Bill shook his head as he went to the bar, and refilled his glass with Scotch. She fought to maintain control. She wanted to throw something at him. Anything. She glanced at the lamp. But that wouldn't change the fact that the man she'd loved and had given her life to was in love with another woman. A dead woman, no less.

"How long?"

"A couple, maybe three years. Babe, I'm sorry. I really am. Neither one of us saw this coming. It had nothing to do with you, it just happened." Then he added, "I love you."

"You love me? You don't know the meaning of love." She looked away. Clinking ice echoed, and a chill clawed up her back. *Three years? Oh my God, I've been such a fool.* "Walker knew about you and his daughter."

"Yes. He blames me for her death." He set his glass down on the coffee table, and pressed his palms to his eyes. "I blame myself, too. If she hadn't come to Seattle to see me, she wouldn't have been on that flight."

"I'm supposed to feel sorry for you?"

He dropped his hands and faced her. "I'm not asking you to feel sorry for me. I'm asking you to understand and *forgive* me. I want another chance. I've never stopped loving you. Never."

"Forgive you? After three years of screwing another woman?"

"For the girls, and for us. This was our wake-up call." He moved to the couch and sat beside her. He ran a finger down the side of her face and under her chin. "I'm sorry."

His touch made her cringe, and she pulled her face from him and stood. "Right now, I hate you. I think you should sleep down here tonight."

"Yes, of course. We can talk tomorrow. I love you, Kat. I know you love me too. We can still make our marriage work." Eyes filled with grief, he added, "I'd actually told her I couldn't do this anymore. I'd told her to go home and it was over. That's why I called Greg to take the flight, so we could spend the day together—you and I. I had planned on telling you, and asking your forgiveness."

She stared for a moment then turned without response. Walking to the stairs she glanced over her shoulder. He was staring into his glass, jiggling it and splashing gold fluid over the ice. He was deep in thought, and for just a second she could have sworn she saw a smile. She turned, then climbed the stairs in disbelief.

Sitting on her bed, she opened her cell phone and dialed the hospital. The phone rang multiple times. *Please let everything be all right*, she prayed, while she waited for Jackie to answer.

"Kat. How are you?" Jackie asked, more emphatically than she should have, when she finally picked up.

"Darby called you."

"She did. Are you all right?"

"Did you know?"

"I had absolutely no idea. But if I did, I don't know if I could've said anything either. That's a tough one."

"Apparently Darby gave Bill an open invitation."

"Bullshit. That lying sack of scumbag shit bastard...Darby never did. And never would." The words were so out of character for Jackie that Kathryn had to laugh.

Jackie was right. Darby never would. Bill had cheated and who knew was not the issue. "Thanks. I needed to hear that. How are you and Linda getting along?"

"She's wonderful. I can't thank you enough for introducing us. She's spending the night."

Asking Linda to stay with Jackie had been an inspiration, and Linda had been happy to do it. Kathryn closed her eyes. "How's Greg. Any change?"

"His vitals are stronger." She sighed then added, "Kat, what happens when he actually wakes up?"

"We'll figure that out when the time comes." Unfortunately, that was another question that Kathryn didn't have an answer to.

CHAPTER 40
TUESDAY

JOHN PACED Walker's office. "Dammit, Dick, if you were behind this photo being published, I swear—"

"Don't you threaten me!" Walker yelled. "I have people crawling all over my ass. This investigation is no longer your responsibility, and as of this moment, I'm taking over."

At 6:00 that morning John had held the *Seattle Times* and furiously dialed Walker's number. John and Kathryn's faces were on the front page. There was no way in hell anyone would have known who she was without a tip from someone. *Walker.* When he didn't answer his phone, John drove to his office and waited for an hour for him to arrive.

"I don't need to threaten you," John yelled. "Can't you see what has happened by exposing Kathryn's connection to us with Bill on his rampage? What in the hell were you thinking?"

"I had nothing to do with this," Walker said. "But that doesn't matter now."

This accident would be the most publicized of all. With Jacobs beating his chest and pointing fingers at the industry, the FAA, and God only knew whom else, Walker would need the fight to be his. Walker and Bill had a history that reached back twenty some years. Neither understood that they were working for the same cause—aviation safety. John had watched them, for years, position for power and notoriety as they fought at accident sites—Walker blamed the pilots, and Bill defended them. But Walker's current anxiety had nothing to do with Bill.

John knew Walker's fixation on controlling his daughter had been his life. He'd obsessed over Kristen's every move since the day she was born, and twenty-four years later, his attempt to protect her didn't stop her from being in the wrong place at the wrong time. His fury was not from his boss asking him about Kathryn Jacobs, but the fact that his daughter had died and he'd been helpless to stop it.

"It's a photo. It's nothing but two old friends having coffee. Besides, she thinks that she's undercover. Nobody knows she's working for us. She'll stick to our story."

"Bill knows. She's out," Walker said. "It should've been over before it ever got started when she turned you down. You have no clue what you did. I hold you fully responsible for this fiasco." Walker slammed a fist on his desk. Then he lowered his voice and said, "If the media gets wind that your employees are giving out secure information, we're both screwed."

"Nobody will get wind of anything. Your problem is not with Kathryn; it's with Bill. And there isn't a damn thing we can do about him now."

Bugging the Jacobs' home to spy on Walker's daughter was not the most brilliant of ideas, but John had gone along with it. Walker had been sure that Bill was using his daughter for his political gain, and he would've done anything to protect his only child. The excuse that Bill was holding meetings in his home and harboring information vital to the investigations was a joke.

Now she was dead. John knew Walker would do anything to find her killer and end the bastard's life. If terrorists were involved, the war on terrorism would escalate beyond belief.

Walker and McAllister had worked together for years, but this was the first time they'd used government resources for personal reasons. Walker's obsession had grown to an uncontrollable level. John suspected Kristen knew exactly what she was doing, and had driven her father insane on purpose, a game she'd enjoyed over the years.

"Bill Jacobs is not my problem," Walker growled, glaring. "Kathryn Jacobs and your employee that violated protocol are my problems now."

"We can't go there," John said, exasperated.

He couldn't lose Samantha, especially with the Coastal crash lying on his desk. Walker may have taken his case, but that didn't remove his department's responsibility for the grunt work.

"Bullshit. I can go anywhere I damn well please."

John stood, placed his hands on Walker's desk and leaned in. "We're only in this because of you and your damned obsessive behavior." Their eyes locked. "You ordered me to hire Kathryn Jacobs, and we need her."

Walker looked away. "This thing has blown up in my face. That bastard killed her. He was supposed to be on that flight, not her. She picked up that trip because of him. She should never have been on that plane. He's alive, and now she's dead."

"Jacobs may be a bastard, a womanizer, and an asshole, but that's all he's guilty of. You can't convict a guy for adultery, and he wasn't flying the airplane. Besides, he's on our side."

"On our side? You've got to be kidding. Have you been listening to his outbursts in the media? He's never been on our side. Jacobs is all about Jacobs and his asshole pilots. He's been protecting those bastards for years. You know damn well that he seduced my baby, and if he hadn't told her he was flying that flight, she'd be alive."

Bill was one of the most brilliant men John had ever met, and his passion was nothing but dedication to the safety of the industry. Every time he opened his mouth, his power and popularity grew. Jacobs was becoming a household name, and Walker despised him for it—something he wouldn't mention at the moment.

John also couldn't tell Walker that he knew Kristen had come to Seattle to tell daddy that she'd decided to quit her job, for some plan that she and Bill had concocted. They had listened to the same recording, but Walker had no idea that there'd been another set of ears—his. Walker was correct, Kristen only took that flight to return to Los Angeles to be with Bill, and he never showed up.

"We need to focus. We need to find out why in the hell these airplanes are crashing. When we find the answer to that, then we'll know why Kristen died," John said.

Walker pushed his chair away from his desk and stood. He walked to the window. When he turned he said, "I want Kathryn Jacobs off this case. She doesn't work for the department, and she never did. Do you hear what I'm saying? You *will* make a public statement to that effect. I want that Schafer woman to be held accountable for sending out secure information, and I don't give a shit if they *were* friends. I want—"

"We can't touch Schafer. Not without the department knowing how we knew she provided information to Kathryn."

"The hell we can't. We don't have to know where she sent it, just that she did. At least taping that asshole's house wasn't a total waste, we found a security breach."

"This wasn't a security breach."

"She violated procedure."

Procedure? They bugged a man's home with company resources and without a warrant for Walker's personal interest, and he was worried about procedure? John stared at Walker for a moment then said, "We need to keep Kathryn on the investigation. Her access to the files was positive."

"No! There'll be no ties to that family, and I want you to personally pull that equipment out of their house today. I'm done with them both."

"She's put together an interesting theory, and I think—"

"Dammit, John. I don't care what you think. I want every bit of our equipment out of that house, and I want no trace that we were ever there."

CHAPTER 41

KATHRYN AWOKE to a screaming headache and the smell of coffee. She swallowed two Tylenol then pulled on her sweats. In spite of everything, she didn't want to destroy her family. When her parents divorced, her family had fallen apart. Then she'd run away from her dad. This time, she would stay and work things out, if at all possible, for her daughters. It may not end with happily ever after, but she owed it to the twins to try. She closed her eyes and shook her head.

She wouldn't subject her kids to a broken home if she didn't have to. She had to give them a chance. Didn't she? She would put the anger behind her and deal with facts.

Working things out sounded good in theory, but she wasn't sure how to make that happen. She would never trust him again. Maybe she'd go see the psychiatrist after all. For now, she would listen and see where the wind blew.

Socks and shoes on, her hair in a ponytail, she was prepared to face her husband. Then she thought about Darby.

She'd suspected there had been something more with Darby and Bill the day she met her at the wedding, but as soon as they'd become friends, she'd pushed everything else from her mind. She wouldn't forgive Darby that easily for not saying anything about Bill's cheating, but she'd give her a chance to explain. Life lost color without Darby.

Kathryn called the hospital and checked on Greg, then picked up her iPhone and headed down the stairs. She'd slept nine hours, and she had needed every minute.

"Good morning," she said flatly, when she walked into the kitchen. Bill was reading the newspaper and didn't respond. She poured herself a cup of coffee and sat at the table across from him.

He folded the paper and set it on the table, then slid it in front of her. His gaze burned through her as she read the headline. Her picture stared at her from the front page of the Seattle Times, as John McAllister held both her hands. The *café*. Bill's photo from the press conference paled in both quality and size in comparison.

She read the headline. *"Is Kathryn Martin Jacobs, Former NTSB Investigator, Back on the Job?"* Ignoring Bill, she continued to read. *"Kathryn Jacobs was seen meeting with NTSB Director John McAllister Monday morning, the day after Seattle's fatal crash. Kathryn's husband, Captain Bill Jacobs, the recently elected Airline Pilot Organization's union president, gives a press conference on the steps nearby..."*

The article spoke of Greg's condition, paraphrased Bill's press conference, and mentioned his alleged affair with Walker's daughter. She set it down. "Well?"

"Well? You lied to me, again. You met with McAllister behind my back, and *after* you told me you were quitting. Your picture is plastered on the front of the *Times*."

"I changed my mind. We need to know what happened to Greg."

"Don't use Greg as your reason to lie." Bill leaned back and folded his arms. "This is exactly why I had to find a relationship outside our marriage."

"Are you kidding me?"

Bill stood then walked to the counter, and poured himself a cup of coffee. "I'm sorry. That was uncalled for," he said, then turned toward her, and leaned against the countertop. "But I want you to call McAllister and tell him you'll quit," he said softly. "For our family."

"I can't do that."

"You need to make a choice between that job and our marriage."

"So you have an affair and we get over it, but if I work you'll throw our marriage away?"

"No. *I'm* not throwing our marriage away. I made a mistake. But you need to decide whether you want to be a wife and a mother. If you want to lose your family for that job, then that's your choice."

"I don't have to choose between work and family."

"I won't have my wife working for the enemy."

"The NTSB is not the enemy. Besides, you didn't have a problem with it when we met."

"Well, you quit, didn't you? Things are different now. I had an election to contend with, and this is a huge conflict of interest."

"The election is over. You won, and they can't take that away from you."

He set his coffee cup on the counter then turned toward her. "But what about the kids and the house?"

"We'll hire that housekeeper." She wrapped her arms around herself to fight off a wave of nausea, and then added, "women can work and take care of their kids."

Bill moved to the table and sat beside her, and stared out the window. He drummed his fingers on the table then turned. "Yes, they can. And you probably better than anyone."

This was the Bill she'd fallen in love with, it was a shame he'd gone and destroyed the life they'd created. No, she wouldn't quit, despite what he'd said, but his acceptance would make life easier.

Kathryn glanced at the newspaper. She'd been on the fast track, moving up in the department. Truth be told, she'd been scared. She knew better than getting pregnant. Maybe that, too, was an out. Never again would she allow life to control her, she was in the drivers seat.

CHAPTER 42

BILL WAS IN his den on the phone when Kathryn finished cleaning the breakfast dishes, and she listened at his door. "See you soon. Thanks, Doc," Bill said. *He's seeing a doctor?* There were so many things she didn't know about him.

She climbed the stairs to her bedroom and sat heavily on their bed. She removed her sweatshirt, stuck her fingers through the hole and wiggled them, then stuffed it in the garbage can. Darby would call this justifiable homicide. She'd been trying to get Kathryn to toss that shirt for years, and it was finally time.

"To new beginnings, Darby," she said. She and Darby needed to talk. She took a deep breath and stood up quickly, then became lightheaded. She closed her eyes and leaned on the dresser as her skin began to perspire, and her heart raced.

She went into the bathroom and closed and locked the door, then turned on the shower. Her stomach rolled violently and she turned and threw up in the toilet. The room spun. She made it to the sink and rinsed her mouth out with cold water, holding tight to the counter. She turned to face the tub.

The room was now swaying and she dropped to her knees so she wouldn't fall, but as the water fell into the tub, she began to shake violently.

Dark red flowers bloomed in the water. She didn't understand why it was so dark, why it was so red against the white porcelain.

She raised her hands and covered her ears. She watched the water spill diluted pink onto the floor.

SHE RETURNED HOME to apologize, but her mom wouldn't talk. She pounded on the bathroom door, calling to her, crying for a response, but there was none. The water kept running, and when it trickled under the door, she grabbed a screwdriver and popped the lock. Her mother lay submerged in red up to her neck, her arm draining the last of her life force over the edge of the tub in trickling rivers that matched Kathryn's tears.

"Mom, why?"

But she knew why.

The next thing she remembered was Greg's hand on her shoulder, and his voice telling her that everything would be okay.

"KATHRYN, OPEN THE DOOR," Bill yelled, pounding on it. She gasped. She was kneeling at the edge of the tub. The shower's full force sprayed down, and clear water circled down the drain.

How long had she been like this?

This was the first time she'd had *that* nightmare in almost a year. The darkness of her past wormed its way into each day with more clarity the closer they came to the anniversary of her mother's death. *Please, not again*, she thought. Her heart pounded in her ears and her knees weakened. She thought about the psychiatrist's number that Dr. Anne had given her. It *was* time.

Bill pounded loudly.

"I'm in the shower," she called. "I'll be out in a few minutes." She stood and opened the medicine cabinet and located a bottle of Tylenol. She couldn't remember how many she'd taken, but didn't care. She needed the headache to stop so she popped two into her mouth, then leaned over the counter and drank out of the faucet.

She stripped, and stepped into the spray. Hot water poured over her, while Bill played with the lock.

Memories of her mother's death swirled through her mind. She had to stop blaming herself. Logically that made sense. But logic and reality didn't always mesh. Maybe it hadn't been her fault. But she'd been so cruel.

"Baby, I'm worried about you," Bill yelled. Then the door popped open, and he stepped into the bathroom with a screwdriver in hand.

"I'm fine." Her head ached, and her heart pounded hard against the cavity of her chest. She dumped shampoo into her hand and rubbed it into her hair. She took slow, deliberate cleansing breaths.

"You were crying out. Are you sure you're okay?"

She was far from okay.

"Maybe we could get you to talk to someone," Bill said. "I know the perfect person."

She tilted her head back and rinsed the shampoo. Forcing herself to move through the motions of her shower, she hoped Bill didn't notice her uncontrollable shaking. He was right, she needed help, but she wouldn't tell him that.

Bill stood, leaning against the counter, rotating the end of the screwdriver on the tip of a finger. She turned from him, pointing her face to the hot water, but he didn't move. He just stood in position and then he began to tap the screwdriver on the counter. Slow, and rhythmic—Tap. Tap. Tap.

CHAPTER 43

WHEN SHE FINALLY climbed out of the shower, Bill's car was no longer parked in the driveway. Had he told her he was leaving? She wasn't sure.

Sitting on the end of her bed she rubbed her temples trying to remember the last twenty minutes of her shower. Then her mind shifted to the case. She'd left the files in Bill's office the day of Greg's accident. She had set them to the side of the couch and thrown the blanket over the top, but Bill had never mentioned them. She hurried downstairs.

The blanket was where she'd left it, but no files underneath. Her heart pounded while panic swept over her. What could she have done with them? Had he found them he would have said something. She looked under pillows, and on both ends of the couch. Had Bill taken them? Then she noticed the top drawer to his desk was open and a corner of the plastic bag stuck out.

All the folders were accounted for. When she removed the bag from the drawer, she saw Bill's planner. He never went far without it. Curious about his doctor's appointment, she turned the page. Today, *2:00 p.m. Doctor A.* Another appointment had been penciled in with the same doctor at 8:00 for tomorrow morning.

She contemplated putting the planner back in the drawer, but Darby's voice echoed—it's the wife's job to snoop. Job or not, she had to know and she turned the pages.

Bill had been seeing this doctor for over a year. Her initial instinct was to worry, and then she wondered why he hadn't told her. Then again she hadn't told him about her doctor visits, either. Neither of them had shared the personal details of their lives for a very long time. Not wanting to worry the other was an excuse—they had drifted apart.

Worry shifted to anger when she found the initials, K.W. The only other consistent meetings in his planner were those with Kristen Walker. A rope tightened around her heart, but curiosity got the better of her.

Flipping through the pages she counted the number of times K.W. had been written on the calendar. She'd been stupid for far too long.

He'd said they'd been seeing each other for three years and that they were in love, but Kathryn couldn't find Kristen's initials prior to six months earlier. Her name coincided with his Los Angeles flights, and those had started six months ago, too. She'd thought he was flying turns to be home with her and the girls every night. She'd been so wrong about too many things.

Kathryn scanned the pages and found nothing other than union meetings, scheduled trips, and a few more initials that meant nothing to her. She'd been such a fool, but the past was behind her. It was time to move forward. She turned the page to the coming month.

"Tell K" was written three weeks from today. *Tell Kristen or tell Kathryn?* Was he going to tell her that he was leaving her for Kristen? Or had he planned on telling Kristen it was over, like he'd said? Either way, it didn't matter. The pain in her heart grew, radiating throughout her soul. She jumped when her cell phone rang. With a hand on her chest, she opened it.

"I need to talk to you," John said.

"I'm about to leave for the hospital. Is noon okay?"

"I need to see you now. My office."

"Give me forty minutes."

She closed her phone and returned the planner to his desk. She also returned her files to where she had found them. They would be safe there until her return.

CHAPTER 44

KATHRYN WALKED into John's office, and he stood and took both her hands in his and squeezed. It had been a long time since she'd been in his office, and the memories overwhelmed her, as did John's reassuring welcome.

"Sit. Please." He extended his hand to a chair opposite of his desk. There was a moment of awkward silence after they sat, until he asked, "How is everything this morning?"

"Fine." Something was wrong, but she waited.

John drummed his fingers on the desk then he finally spoke. "Kathryn, we have to sever this relationship. I'm sorry."

"I don't—"

John raised a hand interrupting her. "When your face appeared on the *Seattle Times* it brought in quite a few phone calls."

"And?" She tried to push the "sever" part of his statement from her mind, but panic simmered. *He's firing me.*

"When you went undercover, we didn't put you on the books. That was a problem."

"So put me on now."

"Walker denied your involvement. Now that he's made a statement, we can't go back. Anything that you discover under false pretenses can't be used. And if something were to happen to you while you're working undercover for the department, well... let's just say that we've exposed ourselves to a huge liability. Legal tape has tied our hands. This situation is beyond my control."

"Just say you hired me now, after the article came out."

"Can't do it. Everything's changed." John closed his eyes for a moment and slowly shook his head, then met her eyes with concern in his own. "I care about you. I appreciate your effort and commitment, and I assure you you'll be compensated for your time. However, the Seattle crash has taken precedence over everything else. The Department of Homeland Security is up to its neck in this one." His stare burned like fire. She looked away. "Walker has..." and then he stopped.

"Walker has what? Is this about his daughter and my husband? I'm sure you've heard the rumors. Well, let me assure you, they're all true. But that's no reason to—"

"I'm sorry." John spoke softly. "For everything."

She didn't know if she should laugh or cry. Her head ached and she thought she was going to puke. Perspiration beaded on her brow, and she wiped a hand across her forehead.

"I opened this door for you, and I am the one slamming it in your face." He walked around his desk, stood in front of her, and leaned against the edge. "Causing you pain was the last thing I wanted to do."

She believed him, but his words didn't change reality. "But—"

"I'm sorry."

She allowed silence to choke the room, and her mind ran through the previous four days with rampant speed. Her life had been nothing for a very long time, but John had been the catalyst to change that. He'd given her a voice and an opportunity to do something good again. Maybe this was better because she *was* too close, and she could focus on her family and friends.

She was lying to herself—this was not better. John might as

well have stuck his hand down her throat and ripped out her heart, as fire her.

The pilots had crashed their planes on purpose, but what could she do now? Nobody would believe her. Bill might. Maybe she could tell him what she'd figured out, and together they could—

"You've pulled more together in these cases than our active investigators have, and I'll personally run down your leads. Now may not be the time, but I assure you that if you want to return, I will do my best to make that happen. It may be a year or two, but don't give up on me." John folded his arms across his chest. "Your career path would've put you in D.C. in one of the top positions today, had you stuck with us. You were that good."

She stared at him without comment. Her career path. She'd be in D.C., but without her daughters. With what she knew now, that wouldn't have been a life option for her. Still, having a taste of her old life she realized that she needed it back more than ever. She could have done it all, kids and work. With what she knew now, there was no going back. But this time it wasn't her choice, she was being thrown out.

"Do you need to get to the hospital?" John asked, politely ending their conversation.

Kathryn stood and John opened the door, and she left without saying good-bye.

Walking quickly to the elevator, she didn't make eye contact with anyone. She didn't want the staff to see the humiliation she carried out the door.

They had all watched her enter with head held high, and now she exited with a record for the shortest career ever. She prayed the elevator wouldn't stop until it reached the bottom floor. At least that prayer was answered.

Stepping out into the lobby, she turned left and exited through the back door, the one designed for the staff. She'd parked there as if she belonged.

Across the parking lot, she saw Sam walking toward her car, carrying a box. Kathryn yelled to her, but Sam continued to walk quickly. Sam tossed the box into the front of her car, climbed in, and closed the door. Kathryn ran toward her, running between cars.

"Sam! Stop!" she yelled.

Sam didn't stop. Instead, she backed out of her parking spot and drove in the opposite direction, the long way out of the lot, glancing into her rear view mirror for only a moment.

CHAPTER 45

KATHRYN STEPPED OFF the elevator on the fourth floor, and her heart skipped a beat when she saw Jackie and Linda standing in the hallway. She rushed toward them, but panic was replaced with relief when Jackie turned with a smile on her face.

"What are you guys doing out here?"

"The doctor's with Greg," Jackie said, and hugged Kathryn. When she pulled back, Jackie's eyes were moist.

"What happened?"

"He can hear us. He squeezed my hand when I told him I loved him." Jackie grabbed Kathryn's hands and held tight.

Tears filled Kathryn's eyes, too. "That's incredible."

"He really *can* hear and respond," Linda said. "This is nothing short of a miracle. I never really thought he'd…" Linda didn't finish her sentence, but she didn't have to. Kathryn never really thought he'd come to either.

Kathryn debated whether or not she should call John. She opted for not. Right now, she needed her friends, and she wanted to hold Greg's hand and tell him that she loved him. There was only one person missing.

"Have you guys seen Darby?"

"No, I tried to call her. She didn't answer," Jackie said. "But Bill's here. He's in the lounge, on his phone."

"The doctor kicked him out," Linda added.

"I bet that went over well." Kathryn glanced over her shoulder. She didn't have the nerve to tell Bill she'd been fired. She also wouldn't forgive the affair. Not yet. She wasn't even sure if she still loved him. "Can we go downstairs for a few minutes, until the doctor's done?"

Jackie told the nurse they'd be in the cafeteria. The nurse promised to page them as soon as the doctor was finished with the tests.

IN THE COFFEE BAR, they ordered three hot chocolates and sat at a table close to the door.

"So, what happened this morning?" Linda asked. "Do they have any more information?"

Kathryn looked from Linda to Jackie. Linda had become one of the girls overnight. Living in the hospital at someone's deathbed brought an intimacy like no other.

"John fired me. 'Severing our relationship' were his exact words. I'm no longer involved."

"No way." Jackie's mouth dropped open. "Why?"

"A picture in the *Seattle Times* started an avalanche, and something about his boss seeing it, and his denial that I worked for him. He thinks if I discover anything and I'm not working for them officially, I'll be more of a liability. Really, I think that newspaper was just an excuse. I'd have thought it would have opened the door for more." Kathryn sipped her hot chocolate. "Oh, and Bill was not only having an affair with Kristen Walker, but he said he loved her." She set her cup down and added, "More or less, that's it."

"Jeez, Kat, I can't believe this." Jackie touched her hand.

"Are you okay?" Linda asked.

Kathryn shrugged. She wasn't sure if she was okay. Nothing

was right in her world except for Greg coming to, and she wasn't even sure if that was right. But if he talked, they would know what happened. Mostly, she wanted to tell him how much she loved him.

"I think I've cried enough tears for a lifetime. But as bad as my life is, I keep thinking of Greg, and that keeps me grounded. His accident put life in perspective. Besides, without working, I'll have more time to help you with Greg and Chris." She had worked on that rationale all the way from McAllister's office.

"Bill's in love with that woman?" Linda asked. "Is he leaving you to be with her?"

"Now, that might be an option," Kathryn said with a slow smile. "She's dead. She was on Greg's flight."

"Oh, my God. I didn't know."

"That's okay. It actually saves me the trouble," Kathryn said. "But the funny thing is, I don't blame her, I don't even blame Bill."

"Dammit Kat, you have to blame someone," Jackie said loudly.

Yeah, myself for letting Bill control me. It was time she took responsibility for her own life. Attempting to change the subject, she said, "When Greg wakes up, we'll call John so he can question him, and we'll find out what happened."

"No!" Jackie snapped. "You'll do the questioning."

"They didn't do shit with Grant's investigation," Linda said. "You can't quit."

"Didn't you guys hear what I said? I'm not giving up. I was fired. They don't want me. It's over."

"Don't you hear what we're saying? *We* want you." Jackie took her hand and squeezed. "It's not over."

"They'll blame Greg for this accident just like they blamed Grant," Linda said. "The media may have ripped that first officer apart, but Grant should have been in control of the flight. The NTSB said as much, and I need to know what really happened."

"Don't let them do this to you," Jackie added. "Or to us. I know you'll find the truth."

Dammit. Dammit. Dammit. She tapped her finger and stared at the faces pleading for help. Searching for hope. They sat in silence, waiting. What could she say to them? That their husbands may have intentionally killed hundreds of people?

"There's nothing I can do," Kathryn finally said. "There's just…"

"Just what?" Jackie asked.

Kathryn drew in a deep breath, and then she told them about the recordings. She explained what she'd heard on the transcripts. She told them what her dad had said about Greg screwing up his location when they were cleared for takeoff. Leaning in close, she whispered her greatest fear. "I think they crashed their planes on purpose." And then she waited for them to walk out of her life.

"Holy shit," Linda said. "If Grant did this on purpose, that would explain our huge insurance policy. But I just can't believe he'd kill all those people."

"You had a large insurance policy? But your house…"

"A little over two million. I've only touched what was needed for the mortgage. I haven't used it for anything else, yet. I feel like I'm cheating on him. Like it's blood money. But I may not have a choice much longer. I can only sell so much."

Tears filled Jackie's eyes. "Kat, I need to tell you something. The day after our party, I did a little more snooping and found a bankbook for a savings account. Greg opened it the day before his accident with a $350,000 deposit."

Kathryn couldn't believe what she'd heard. Not as much about the large sums of money as the fact they didn't walk out when she'd told them that their husbands might have crashed on purpose.

"Do you have any idea where Greg got that money?"

Jackie shook her head. "I hoped from a friend, but we really don't have friends with that kind of money. Truth is, I didn't want to know. I thought he might have done something illegal. I was just so mad he'd spent so much, and I had to go back to work while he had that much in the bank."

"Okay, let's put that aside for a minute. Do you have life insurance?" Kathryn asked Jackie. She wanted her friend to be financially protected, but that could provide motive.

"I don't think so. I think those payments were the first to go."

"Do you care if I go to the house and look through Greg's office to see if I can find anything?"

"No. Look, please."

"I can't believe Grant would take his life for insurance. But then, there are things I never thought he'd do. We were going to lose the house. Lose everything. I had no idea until after he died. He lied to me about it all. And then the..." Linda glanced at the table and spoke quietly. "He had an affair a few years back. Not in a million years would I have believed it. I thought we had the perfect life." She blinked a tear back. "So, yeah, nothing surprises me these days. It turns out that Francine had found out about it. She'd told her dad that she hated him. They hadn't spoken for months."

"I'm so sorry, Linda," Kathryn said.

"Maybe I could find out if the other wives had policies as large as ours."

"Other wives?" She had forgotten about Francine's comment of the 'dead wives club.'

"Oh, yeah, from the last three crashes. The list keeps growing." Linda touched Jackie's arm. "We've formed a support group. I could invite them over and put brandy in their tea and find out anything you want to know."

They quietly sipped their cocoa, each lost in their own thoughts.

"Was there anyone new in the guys lives before their accidents?" Kathryn asked.

Jackie shook her head no, but Kathryn would have known if Greg had. Or would she? They hadn't really talked for a long time.

"The only new person in Grant's life, since I'd found out about his affair, was a counselor. He'd been seeing him for almost a year. He'd kept it secret for a couple months, and I actually thought he was seeing someone again. When I confronted him, he told me what he was doing."

"I thought Greg was having an affair, too," Jackie said. "Do you think he could've been seeing a counselor?"

"I'll bet that's exactly what he was doing. I just discovered Bill's seeing a doctor. Maybe—"

"What I don't understand," Linda said, interrupting her. "Is that if they killed themselves for insurance, why take out an entire planeload of people? Grant may have been a bastard, but it takes a real sicko to do something like that. Grant still had nightmares from Vietnam. He was many things, but a mass murderer? I don't think so."

"And Greg would never do anything like that no matter how bad things got," Jackie added.

"What if they didn't do this on their own?" Kathryn hesitated. "*What if* terrorists forced them to crash? What if terrorists located pilots that were worth more dead than alive and told them that they'd kill their families if they didn't crash their planes? Would they do it? Instead of living to watch their wives and children slaughtered, would they kill themselves and a planeload of people, while leaving their families alive, and financially better off?"

Jackie and Linda looked at each other, then back to Kathryn. Speechless. Exactly what Kathryn had thought—they might.

Kathryn looked at her watch and asked, "Do you guys mind if I leave for a bit? Darby won't answer her phone, and I really need to talk to her. Besides, I don't want to deal with Bill right now."

"Go. We'll call you if Greg talks," Jackie said.

She hugged Jackie. "I feel so bad ditching you like this."

"Don't be crazy. Go," Jackie said.

She hugged Linda as well, and said goodbye to them at the elevator, then ducked into the bathroom.

When she was leaving the restroom, she ran into a doctor and stumbled. Not any doctor, but one that could have been directly out of Grey's Anatomy. She flushed.

"I'm so sorry," she said, righting herself.

He steadied her, nodded, and continued down the hall and out the door.

Be still my heart. She placed a hand on her chest and then her phone rang. The call was from the hospital.

CHAPTER 46

DARBY AWOKE feeling like she had fallen off of a ten-story building and landed on her head, but one look in the mirror told her she'd landed on her face. She turned and leaned with her butt against her dresser and closed her eyes.

She'd been awake most of the night, but that was due to her failed self-medicating technique with a fifth of Jack Daniels. There hadn't been much remaining in the bottle, but mixed with the wine from the memorial, it was just enough for her to find religion, and she'd been praying to the porcelain god all morning.

Her day of reckoning, when Kathryn would discover the truth, had haunted her for months. She should've listened to Adams.

Opening her eyes she scanned her room and spied her pink fuzzy robe. She turned it inside out and slipped into it, then pulled the belt tight. She wished situations like this had come up when she was younger, a time when she held her alcohol better.

Kat had the right to be mad. If the tables had been turned, Darby would have been pissed too. All the excuses in the world didn't change the fact that you don't lie to your friends. Okay, little lies like her duck-butt haircut looks good, but for the important things like who's sleeping with her husband, you had to tell her the truth. Take the medicine quick and hope to hell she was a good enough friend to believe you. Usually the husband stayed and the friend was toast, but she should have had more faith in Kathryn.

She slid her feet into her pig slippers, leaned forward against her dresser and stuck her tongue out at the mirror. Definitely sick. Her tongue was covered with white and yellow gunk. Tongue sweaters screamed toxins—nothing that coffee couldn't fix. Or was that lemon water? The thought of lemons rolled her stomach.

"Where in the heck is my phone?" she said, dumping the contents of her purse on the floor. She searched through her jeans pockets. Nothing. She hoped she hadn't lost it at the memorial. That was the last thing she needed.

She sat on her bed and rubbed her aching head with her palms. She must have one hell of a dried up and dehydrated brain for how badly it hurt.

The night was a fog that drifted back to her in pieces. After Kathryn swore at her and told her they were no longer friends, she cleaned up the mess that Kathryn had made, and tried to minimize collateral damage. Then she'd sat on the floor and drunk wine. She'd listened to everyone talk, and watched the candles burn down.

Darby remembered seeing Neil with his ex-wife. He'd said she'd lost friends on the plane too, and he needed to support her, and couldn't talk. That was when she traded in her glass of wine for the bottle. Nobody noticed her, except for Bill, who finally asked her what she'd done to Kathryn, and she'd told him how much she hated his sorry ass. He'd laughed at her.

She bent over and picked up Bear. "How did I get home?" He stared without response and she tossed him on the bed then made her way to the window.

Her car was halfway in the driveway. There was something to be said for plastic garbage cans, and she hoped hers would bounce back. Now officially in the "never say never" club, she'd driven drunk, and she thanked God she'd made it home alive without killing anyone.

In the kitchen she poured coffee grounds into her machine, dumped water in, and pushed the button. The thought of coffee also rolled her stomach. There was a first time for everything. She opened the fridge and located a diet RockStar energy drink. On the shelf above, her cell phone lay beside the empty Jack Daniels bottle.

She carried her phone into the bedroom and plugged it into the charger, then popped four ibuprofen.

It was almost noon, and if she didn't feel better by midnight, she'd call in sick for her flight the next day. That actually sounded pretty good right now. She'd tell scheduling she had eye trouble and couldn't *see* going to work. Ha. Ha. Darby thought she was funny, even if the schedulers might not. There were probably a lot of memorial-induced sick calls today.

She was lying on her back with her head hanging over the edge of her bed when her phone came to life. She rolled to the floor, grabbed it, and returned to her hanging position. She hoped that between the drugs, the energy drink, and the extra blood flow to her brain that she would accelerate her recovery period. So far, this strategy wasn't working.

Three missed calls. Two were from Kathryn, and the other was from Neil. She listened to Kathryn's messages first. Kat needed to talk to her and she'd said that she loved her. Kathryn had already forgiven her. Darby smiled.

Then she listened to Neil's message. His call had come in at eleven-thirty that morning and he was already drunk. Maybe still drunk. He was on his way over. She thought about brushing her hair, and maybe her teeth, and that was as far as she got before he was pounding on her door.

She dropped her phone to the floor, rolled off the bed, and landed on her hands and knees. "I'm coming," she yelled, as she pushed herself to her feet.

When Neil stepped into the entryway, he wrapped his arms around her and held her tight. He pulled back, took her face in his hands and kissed her closed mouth. Hoping she'd brushed her teeth sometime between prayer sessions, she parted her lips. He tasted like scotch, and she thought of puking. But he soon moved his lips to her eyes, and then the tip of her nose. He lifted her, and despite his stagger, he managed to carry her into her bedroom and laid her on the bed.

Neil removed his clothes and Darby watched. Bear stared in disapproval. She rolled her eyes and stuffed him under the pillow.

He untied her belt and opened her robe.

Neil kissed her breasts, and she moaned in pleasure. This was exactly what she needed to take her mind off of the world, and for a rapid recovery. He relieved all the tension in her body, and his mouth and hands rediscovered every inch of her skin. Her headache vanished. Sex *was* the best cure.

He touched her like it was their first time. But it always felt like the first time with Neil. He slid his fingers down her abdomen, and then traced her bikini line with his tongue. He held her hips with both hands, pressed his face deep between her legs, and explored, licked, and sucked until she couldn't stand it anymore, and cried out as she came hard.

Neil climbed on top of her and then began to cry. Something was desperately wrong. He was reacting to the crash as if one of his—

"Did something happen to one of your kids?" she whispered, holding him tight.

"No." He wiped his eyes. "I'm just *so* sorry for everything," he said, sitting up.

"*Sorry?* Sorry for what?" Darby asked, pulling a pillow close.

"What in the hell is going on?"

"It's just… Greg lying in the hospital. I can't do this anymore. I love you too much."

"Do *what?*"

"Be married to another woman. It kills me to know that it's not you I wake up with."

"What the *hell?* You're divorced."

"I love you. I want you to be my wife, but I have to tell you—"

"Your wife?" Darby said, stunned. She jumped up and pulled her robe on, and yanked the belt tight. "Get dressed."

Neil was divorced. He had to be. She stormed into her living room and paced until he joined her. He sat on the couch, and she stood by the fireplace, foot tapping. She waited with arms folded. The truth was never a good start to any conversation. *Married?* Her face flushed with a fire burning uncontrollably below. She had to have heard him wrong.

He couldn't be married.

"Bill and Kathryn's wedding, the night we met… It wasn't by accident. Bill was afraid that you were going to ruin the wedding. At least, that's what he'd told me. He gave me five hundred bucks to buy you a drink. He wanted me to get your attention away from him and Kathryn. So I did. You were cute and funny, and I didn't mind. Hell, I would've done it for free. But at the time, well, with the third baby on the way, every little bit helped and—"

"He paid you to buy me a drink? What in the hell? How much did he pay you to sleep with me?"

"Nothing. I swear. But when you didn't remember anything the next morning, and I couldn't remember the half of it, I realized he must've put something in our drinks. He'd given me the key to a hotel room and said you'd been drinking too much, and it would be a good place to let you sleep it off. So I did. And—"

"Don't you, for one second, find something odd about this?"

"Well, now I do. But at the time I didn't. Hell, Darby, Bill's like God at the airline, and his shit doesn't stink. I was on probation and he could have cost me my job. One bad write up from him and my career would've been over."

"He paid you to buy me a drink? He bought you a hotel room? He drugged me so I'd have sex with you?" She couldn't believe her ears. "Did he pay you to hook up with me again last year, too?"

"Not exactly." Neil lowered his voice. "He blackmailed me."

"He what?" Her blood now officially boiled, and she fought the urge to scream to relieve the pressure. Her foot tapped faster.

"He had the hotel room taped that first night and said that if I didn't start seeing you again that he'd show the tape to my wife. If you knew I was married, you never would've dated me. What was I supposed to do? I had to lie."

"You son of a bitch! Our entire relationship was a fake? Sex because Bill was making you? Why in the hell would he care, or give a damn about me?" She began to pace. "Oh my God, Bill watched us have sex!" *Shit! Shit! Shit!* Then reality shouted—*I slept with a married man!*

"Sweetie, he said that he had his reasons. But I was really seeing you because I'd fallen in love with you."

"And when was that, exactly? Before or after you went home to your wife?"

"I don't know. I think I fell in love with you the moment we met. But that's not the point. After Bill won the election I congratulated him, and he took me aside and asked if you ever mentioned anything about Kathryn. I never told him anything you said about his wife."

"What is this, the friggin' fifth grade?"

"He also asked me if you'd been seeing Doc Adams. He said that he was worried about you. I told him that you were going, but I didn't know how often. He said that I'd 'better know' if I didn't want my wife to find out about us."

"So, you're telling me all this now because..."

"Because I love you. I don't care if my wife finds out and I don't know what in the hell Jacobs thinks you're going to tell me, or why. I don't even care if you're seeing a shrink. I just don't want to be part of his game, whatever in the hell it is. I told him that. And I've decided to leave my wife for you."

"You lying sack of drunken shit. You think that you can come in here and tell me that I was unknowingly prostituted by Bill friggen Jacobs, and now you're my hero and are leaving your wife for me, when I didn't even know you had a wife?"

Her heart rate shifted from hangover sludge to a Starbucks triple shot. She no longer shook from the wine flu, she shook from humiliation and rage, and no longer could she contain the explosion that brewed deep inside.

"Come on, Darb..."

"Don't you *Darb* me. I want you out of my house. Now. I don't give a shit if you leave your wife or jump off the goddamned Space Needle. I will never, as long as I live, waste another breath on your lying, cheating, ass!"

"Stop it, Darby. Please stop. I love you. You know that I do." He stood and pulled her into his arms.

She attempted to break free, but he held her tight. "You bastard let me go." She kneed him in the crotch and pulled free from his grip. "Get the hell out of my house. Now!"

While he bent over holding his manhood, whining like a baby, she walked stoically to the door and opened it, then said,

"Get the hell out."

He apologized for everything and said he wanted to talk, and he loved her. But Darby stood her ground. There were some betrayals that even love couldn't fix. Then she thought of Kathryn.

Chapter 47

The doors opened on the fourth floor to the sound of Jackie's wails. They pierced Kathryn's ears and her heart, breaking it further if that was humanly possible. Animal cries, so primal, echoed through the hallway. Doctors and nurses ran in and out of Greg's room. A defibrillator sat on a cart outside the door. Jackie was on her knees, and Linda knelt beside her. Linda was rubbing Jackie's back and glanced up as Kathryn approached.

"What happened?"

"Greg had a massive heart attack." Linda shook her head and dropped her eyes.

Kathryn knew he was gone. But how could he be dead? How could she not have been with him? The surgery had been a success. He'd been gaining strength, and he had acknowledged them when they spoke to him. The doctors hadn't worried about his heart. She couldn't understand this turn of events and knelt by Jackie's side. "I'm so sorry," she said, fighting to be strong for Jackie.

Linda spoke quietly to Jackie, and a nurse attempted to calm her, but Kathryn doubted that Jackie heard any of them.

"Can you please find a doctor?" Kathryn asked.

Linda wrapped her arms around Jackie and rocked her. She quietly repeated, "It's going to be okay. Everything will be okay."

Kathryn slipped into Greg's room. His body was still there. She wanted to pull the sheet back and prove to them they were all wrong. If she didn't know better, the lump under the sheet could've been a pile of pillows. But she did know better.

Bill stood with his back to her and stared out the window. He and Greg had been good friends and despite his faults, he'd just lost someone he loved. She stepped toward him, reached her hand out and touched his shoulder. He turned, pulled her close, and held her. They cried together.

When he pulled away, he wiped his eyes with the back of his hand. And she touched the end of Greg's bed and said a silent prayer for him. The words came naturally. Tears stained her cheeks when she returned to Jackie's side.

"Come on, sweetie, we need to go say goodbye to him." Kathryn and Linda helped Jackie to her feet, her sobs now under control, and walked her into the room. The hospital staff arrived to take his body, but Kathryn asked for a few moments.

Jackie stood by his bed, catching her breath, and said, "Can I have a minute alone?"

"We'll be right outside," Linda told her.

"Bill, can we give Jackie some privacy?" Kathryn asked when he didn't move.

He nodded and walked out of the room behind them. "Kat, I'm… I'm just so sorry for everything."

"I know. Me too. But now's not the time," Kathryn said, flatly. "Jackie needs me. I'm going to take her home, to our house. You can stay at her place. We're all going to need some time."

Kathryn watched Jackie through the glass. Linda told her that Greg had gone into cardiac arrest just as she and Jackie returned to the floor, and they weren't allowed in the room. Jackie watched her husband take his final breath through this window. His eyes had been opened and he had stared her way.

Jackie no longer cried but instead spoke quietly to him. She pulled back the sheet and stroked his bandaged face and kissed where his lips should have been. How would she tell Chris his dad was gone? Kathryn couldn't imagine.

Kathryn walked to the end of the hall in search of reception for her phone. Standing by a window she'd found bars and dialed Darby once again.

CHAPTER 48

WHEN KATHRYN RETURNED to Greg's room, Jackie sat on an empty bed, deflated. The hope of Greg's survival had kept her going. Now that he was gone, fatigue and emotional exhaustion had taken over. The dam broke, and Jackie raised her hands to the sides of her head, covered her ears, and began to cry again. This time, Kathryn folded her friend in her arms.

"How can I live without him?" She asked between sobs. "How am I going to tell Chris?"

"We'll figure it out," Kathryn said, rocking her while she cried. When Jackie's tears finally subsided, Kathryn said, "Let's get out of here."

"He was getting better. Dr. Green said so. How could he have had a heart attack?" Jackie begged for answers that Kathryn didn't have.

"I don't know, sweetie, but we'll find out."

Jackie wiped her face with the palms of her hands and straightened.

They signed the necessary papers at the nurse's station. A woman handed Jackie a plastic bag, and gave her condolences. Greg's gold chain lay curled at the bottom of the bag, as well as what was left of his wallet. His wedding ring, dark with soot, was whole. Jackie took the bag and clutched it close to her chest.

Bill approached, but Kathryn shook her head no. She needed

to be with Jackie. He opened his mouth, then closed it, then turned and walked down the hall. She hated him for what he'd done, and yet, despite everything, she still felt compassion for his loss. Marriage was a thing people took for granted until it was ripped away. They had a lot of work to do, but it would be worth the effort for the girls.

Jackie was packing her bag when Dr. Green arrived. He asked Jackie how she was doing, and she said, "fine." But 'fine' would take a great deal of time. Then Kathryn asked him if she could speak to him for a few minutes, and they stepped down the hall.

"What happened?" she asked.

"He had a cardiac arrest, which is common in patients like this. His heart was working overtime, and with the added stress, it just gave out."

"Had his heart shown any signs of stress or rhythmic problems that would lead you to believe he'd be at risk for heart failure?"

"None, but I can't—"

"Was he actually responsive to questions?"

"I understand you're a close friend, but I'm sorry, I can't discuss this with—"

"Yes, you can," Jackie said, as she approached. "I give you permission to tell Kathryn anything."

Dr. Green looked between the two women. He sighed and shook his head. "Yes, he was responsive. He acknowledged voices and responded to questions with right and left hand answers. While he couldn't squeeze with his left hand, the movement in the arm indicated the effort. He heard us, and he understood what we were saying. This cardiac arrest surprised me, too."

Green stuck both hands in his pockets and shifted his weight. "He was actually doing quite well, far beyond expectation. The tests we performed, literally minutes before he passed, indicated positively that he was conscious. His vitals were strong. His heart was strong. I was gone not for more than five minutes, and when I returned he was in arrest."

"So you don't know what prompted the heart attack?" Kathryn asked, with hands on her hips.

"I suppose the testing and his excitement level as he came to created a level of stress. Or perhaps he had an anxiety attack."

"Anxiety? With the drugs that were pumped into his body for pain relief?"

She locked eyes with Green, and he looked away. "No, I don't think it was anxiety."

Kathryn folded her arms, "You know what I think? I think we need an autopsy."

Chapter 49

"It's horrible that Greg died, but it's better than being a living corpse," Bill said to Doctor Adams. Bill had been prepared to take out Greg if he'd woken up. He loved him like a brother, but there couldn't be any loose strings. But then he up and died on his own. Heart failure. Once again the hand of God, with the help of his father's intervention helped Bill toward the fulfillment of his destiny.

"It's a terrible shame. He was a good man." Adams twisted a pen between his fingers.

Bill returned his attention to Ryan Bolt's file and continued to read. Ryan had been seeing Adams for three months. He didn't fit the profile, but that wouldn't be a problem, not this time. He'd touched Adams's office, and that's all that mattered. He closed the file, set it on the desk, and watched Adams closely.

Adams poured a glass of water, spilling some on his desk. His hands shook, and his shirt, stained from sweat, clung to his body. He leaned back in his chair and closed his eyes.

"Are you okay, buddy?" Bill asked.

"I'm fine." Adams opened his eyes and stared at him. Silence filled the room, and Bill waited. Sometimes he wondered who the doctor was. Then Adams finally spoke, "I can't do this anymore."

"Can't do what?" Bill asked, but he already knew the answer to that. The fortunate thing was, he wouldn't have to much longer. "I can't do this," Adams said, spreading his hands and waving his arms wide over his desk. "I can't do any of this anymore. My patients are dying. They're coming to me searching for answers, and I can't do a damn thing to help them."

"I know, Mike," Bill said with compassion. "Not until the FAA gets off their ass and forces the airlines to increase training, instead of allowing them to cut it, will we see change. Don't get me started on work rules."

"Greg Jameson was a good man," Adams said.

"Yes, he was. It kills me that scheduling snagged him for my trip. It should have been me," Bill said, lowering his voice. "I should have been in that plane, not him."

Bill had never seen this side of Adams in all the years they had known each other, and that had been most of their lives. They'd been brought together through unfortunate circumstances—depending upon perspective. Five years older than Adams, Bill had been his big brother, and Adams was a sponge. The airline industry had torn them both apart and had devastated their lives.

When Bill first learned the truth about his father's termination, he wanted to kill the person responsible. But that person turned out to be five-year-old Adams. Years later Bill decided a better course of action. He knew Adams would become useful one day, and he'd been right.

"Most of these guys need to be grounded. Hell, you've read their files and know their flight records better than I do. So why in the hell are they still in the sky?" Adams rubbed a hand over his face.

"You've got to take the good with the bad." Bill leaned forward resting his arms on his legs, and added, "Unfortunately, ninety percent of our resources, both time and money, go to that one percent of the problems."

"What money? I don't see one penny going to these guys. They come in here looking for answers that I can't give because they're pulled out to fly before we can do anything. How in the hell am I supposed to help them like that? I can't." Adams pushed away from his desk, and stood.

"Mike—"

"They're not only depressed," Adams said, "but their training records are ridiculous!" He picked up a file and tossed it at his desk. "Where's the extra training? Where's the compassion? Hell, Jameson couldn't even take the time off that he desperately needed, and don't get me started on Aaron Stephens. He was the worst of all with his damn instability." Adams put his hands on his hips and added, "You're the president. Change it."

"I plan on it, Mike." This reaction was something that Bill had not expected from Adams, but he welcomed the rage. Emotional instability was something that always came in handy.

"I hope you do before someone else dies," Adams said. After moments of silence he returned to his seat. "I'm sorry."

Bill leaned back in his chair and crossed his legs. "No need to be sorry. I feel exactly as you do. Besides, change is coming sooner than you think." He'd change it all right, but unfortunately Dr. Michael Adams wouldn't be here to see it. But something else was bothering Adams, and Bill decided to push a few buttons to find out what was really going on.

"Despite everything, Walt and Grant had been excellent pilots. Both highly respected training captains who—"

"Who had too much baggage to be flying," Adams said. "They were emotional messes, both of them."

"Maybe so, but—"

"I'm also not comfortable with you reading the pilot's files any longer," Adams interrupted Bill, again. Bill allowed the disrespect for one reason only—Adams's days were numbered.

"Don't go there, Mike. Not after all I've done for you. Besides, there's nothing in here that I don't already know." Bill set the folder on the desk. "I'm sorry, you're right. I shouldn't have put you in that position. But I do need a favor."

"Anything, you know that."

"Kathryn's been depressed, and I'm worried about her." Bill closed his eyes for a moment, and when he opened them, they were moist. "She hasn't been interested in me physically for a very long time. That's no excuse for my…" He hesitated then said, "But with Greg's accident, his death, and my affair, I'm afraid she's going down the path that her mother took, and might hurt herself. I've wanted to get her some help, to talk to someone, but she refuses to go."

"Will she come in to see me?"

"Maybe. Would you talk to her? Maybe prescribe something to help her sleep." Bill stood and paced. "Hell, I don't know what to do, Mike, I just love her so damn much."

Bill returned to his seat then put his face in his hands.

"Don't worry. I can squeeze you both in tomorrow afternoon."

Bill looked up and said, "Thank you." Wiping a tear from under his eye he asked, "could we do it tomorrow morning instead? I'm taking the early L.A. flight."

Adams opened his calendar and glanced at his schedule. "Could you bring her in at seven-thirty?"

"That would be perfect, buddy." Bill opened his briefcase and set a manila file on the desk. "I took the liberty of writing up what's been going on."

"Thank you," Adams said, reaching for the folder.

Bill placed his hand on top of the file to prevent Adams from opening it. "Later. Tell me what's going on with you. We've lost pilots before. Look at you, you're a mess."

Adams opened his mouth but no words came out. He closed his eyes and slowly shook his head. When he opened them again, anguish blanketed his face. Sweat gathered on his forehead and he wiped it with a handkerchief. Then tears filled his eyes. He drew a deep breath and said, "I killed Greg Jameson."

"You what?" Bill couldn't believe what he'd just heard.

"He wouldn't have had a life. *Hell* would have been better than the pain and mental anguish he would've gone through. His existence would have destroyed the family that he loved so dearly. He would've wanted to be dead."

So true. You did the right thing, buddy. "But how?" Bill asked.

CHAPTER 50

A HOT SHOWER, a cup of herbal tea, and two prescription sleeping pills later, Jackie slept. Kathryn pulled the covers up to her neck then closed the curtains to block what remained of the day from her bedroom. She quietly closed the door and returned to the living room to sit with Darby.

Darby proceeded to tell her everything about her past with Bill. A huge nothing. He'd hit on her when she'd first arrived at the airline. She'd turned him down. He didn't like it and had made Darby's life hell. Darby had planned on destroying their wedding to get even until she'd met Kathryn. Obviously Bill *didn't* get everything Bill wanted.

There was no way Kathryn could stay angry. She wasn't sure if she would have done anything different herself. The fact that Bill paid Neil, and he was married, infuriated her. She felt sorry for Darby. But the visual of Neil flying off the porch after a kick in the ass made her laugh. Then she thought of Greg. She still couldn't believe he was gone. She'd felt loss like this before, but this time was different, and she was angry for so many reasons.

"I don't know what we'll do without Greg." Kathryn wiped a fresh tear from her cheek.

"I loved him too."

Everyone loved Greg. They sat quietly for a moment, each in their own thoughts then Kathryn said, "When Bill said you'd been hitting on him, I knew he was lying."

"I know he's your husband, and he cares about the pilots and safety, but he's an ass."

"He wants to make it work." Kathryn allowed the words to settle in between them. "I know how hard this is for you to understand, but if it's possible, I have to try for the girls. I'm not sure if I can forgive him for cheating, I don't even know if I still love him, but I want to try to make our family whole.

"After Greg died… I don't know. I just thought that all this cheating and lying crap is stupid. You don't throw a marriage away if there is something of substance to build from. We'd been growing apart for a very long time and I'd blamed our schedules. Maybe that was part of it, and I'm not excusing him, but the kids deserve a chance to live in a home with both a mom and dad, if it's at all possible. It may not be, but I have to try."

"I guess I can understand that. But Kat, marriage kind of needs you to love your husband."

"I know. Deep down I'm sure I do, it's just… I feel so betrayed." Kathryn hugged herself and said, "Besides, he actually changed his mind about my working for the NTSB, that's baby-steps in the right direction."

"Oh, God, I forgot about your job."

"I got fired."

Darby eyes widened. "Are you kidding me?"

"I had a lemonade stand that lasted longer than this job." She handed Darby the bowl of potato chips, then told her what had happened with John.

"So Greg dies, and we're no closer, than before I started, to stop this from happening again," Kathryn said.

"I flew with Greg, he was a great pilot. I can't see him taking the wrong runway. Stephens, though, that's another story. Hard to believe they ever allowed him to upgrade. He always had something going on in his life with the family. Major drama. The guy was an emotional mess."

Kathryn slid closer to Darby and whispered, "You know how Jackie told us they were broke? She found a bank account with $350,000 cash."

"Holy shit. What's up with that?"

Kathryn opened a bottle of water and took a drink, then told Darby everything she'd learned from the tapes and her suspicions that the pilots intentionally crashed their planes, as well as her terrorist theory.

Darby raised an eyebrow. "If terrorists wanted to crash planes, they could down more by threatening air traffic controllers to vector planes into each other."

"True, but the controllers aren't in financial trouble like most pilots. There's leverage with pilots. They're depressed, stressed, and possibly already searching for an out."

"Most *are* worth more dead than alive." Darby stood, and paced. "My God, if this is true, then everybody who steps on a plane is playing Russian roulette." She placed her hands on her hips and tapped her red fingernails on her jeans. "Unless they're on my plane, of course."

Kathryn smiled. It wasn't often that she saw Darby's ego surface.

"*What?*" Darby said. Kathryn raised an eyebrow in response, then Darby added, "Oh, you know what I mean. I don't have kids. They'd have no leverage on me."

"I didn't say anything," Kathryn said, tucking a strand of hair behind an ear.

Darby threw a potato chip at her. "If they did anything to

you or the girls, I'd hunt their sorry asses and… Well, let's just say they'd *want* to be dead. But take out a planeload of people? I don't think so. Besides, how would I know they didn't kill you after I was gone? I wouldn't. Nope, I'm not buying it. I don't think the pilots would do it."

"I just can't see any other explanation. Unless… What *if* the pilots were unable fly with the loss of automation like that Airbus? All of them appeared to have done something to intentionally take down their planes. What if their mistakes were not intentional at all? Maybe they just screwed up because they couldn't fly without the magic?" *A fate worse than pilots crashing on purpose.*

"That's definitely a concern, and, unfortunately, exactly where we're headed." Darby sat heavily on the couch. "What was it you wanted to ask me the other day?"

CHAPTER 51

"C'MON," KATHRYN SAID, "I'll show you." Kathryn and Darby entered Bill's office, but the charts were no longer on his desk, and his flight bag was closed and locked. Darby had once told her that a flight bag is as sacred to a pilot as a purse is to a woman. You just didn't go there. But now she dropped to her knees and played with his lock. Kathryn looked on with interest. She heard a click, followed by a "yes" and his flight bag locks popped open. Her best friend had skills she'd never imagined.

"How'd you do that?"

"Lucky numbers, birth dates, the airplane he flies. Bill's on the Boeing 767, and it's a dual type rating with the 757, so 7576. Easy." Darby snapped her fingers.

Darby opened Bill's New York area chart and followed Kathryn's finger on the path of Regional's arrival.

"Well… Based on what you've said, they definitely began their descent forty-five miles too soon. And into the heart of a storm… Hmm. Pretty lame. But bad decisions don't mean intentional. Maybe his mind was elsewhere."

Darby folded the chart and returned it to Bill's bag, then began to dig through the pockets inside.

"What are you doing?"

"Snooping." Within seconds, Darby held an envelope. She opened it. "Holy shit," she said, looking through a stack of pictures, before handing them to Kathryn.

Kristen Walker. Nude. Behind that picture were additional photos of different women. Kathryn looked through them, her face flushed. The pictures all showed varied levels of nakedness of eight different women, and Bill's reflection hung on the wall in the background of each, holding a camera.

There was a photo with Kathryn, and Princess, with the girls as newborns, a couple black and white shots of his mom and dad, and one of his military squad. But her attention returned to the women.

"Oh God, there wasn't just Kristen, there were many." She handed the photos back to Darby, all except one. "This is the woman who told me about Bill last night."

Darby pulled it from her. "Simone. No wonder the bitch was pissed, he was cheating with her, too. I had no idea Kat, I swear."

"And to think I was willing to stick by him for the girls." Kathryn's heart ached knowing that she was about to destroy her daughters' worlds.

"Battle is on baby, and we're nailing his sorry ass! Let's find what else he's stuffed away and confiscate it all."

"I have proof that he was cheating with Kristen, and with these photos, what more do I need?"

"If you want to take his cheating ass to the cleaners, you're going to need ammunition, and lots of it."

She had no intention of taking Bill 'to the cleaners,' she just wanted custody of her girls. He'd said he wanted to make it work, but he'd been lying about everything. She fought the urge to scream, and she was too shocked to cry.

Kathryn sat at the desk and opened the top drawer. Her files were still there, but his planner was gone. He'd been home. She closed the drawer and attempted to open the drawers to the left, but they were locked. She opened the top drawer, again, and searched, but no key. The drawers to the right were equally unsuccessful in her search.

She leaned on the desk and wondered where he'd hide a key. That's when she noticed the desk lamp was tilted. Lifting it, she found a key lying below. It fit. She turned and released the lock.

A stack of financial ledgers filled the drawer. She opened the first. There were entries for jewelry she'd never received, a car purchased two years earlier that she'd never driven. "Oh my God, I've been so dumb."

Darby rushed to her side and pulled the ledger from her and scanned the pages before handing it back. "You're not dumb. You loved and trusted the rat bastard. We'll make copies." She stood beside Kathryn and logged onto Bill's computer.

Kathryn continued to look through Bill's ledgers, fighting the urge to break everything in his office in the process. She no longer had any idea who her husband was, other than a man of multiple secrets and affairs, affairs that had been going on for a very long time.

January 2008, $4500 Princess Cruise Lines. She'd never taken a cruise in her life. *September 2006, $190,000 M.B.A.* He'd told her he had a M.B.A. before they were married, but now she doubted everything he'd said. Then she'd discovered that he'd received two paychecks per month. She'd thought there had been only one.

She had scrimped and saved their entire marriage, and did everything on a tight budget to make ends meet. Bill had said he'd purchased the Porsche at a third of the price from a pilot, to help him out. At the time she had thought that was too good to be true, and she'd been right.

There were so many secrets, far too many lies, and she cringed at the reality of her sharing a life with a man she'd never known.

She wouldn't bother making copies. She'd take the actual proof.

"Bingo!" Darby cried.

Kathryn closed the ledger and turned her attention to the computer screen.

"Simone Blake. She's been working for Coastal for one year. She lives in town, and she'd been scheduled to fly the Los Angeles trip two days ago. She trip-traded with Kristen Walker. Holy shit, she should have been on the flight that crashed."

"Is there any way to see if there's any connection between Simone and the other flights that crashed?"

"Maybe H.R. would have a record of where she worked before. Not that they'd give it to me."

Darby stuffed the photos of the naked women into her purse and placed the envelope with the others back into his bag. "There's no way Mr. Bill is destroying this evidence. I'm taking these for safekeeping." She closed and locked his flight bag. "I hate to leave, but I've got an early flight, and I'm seeing Adams before I fly."

"Your union counselor?"

"Yeah. He'll probably piss his pants when he hears that Neil was married, unless he knew. That would really piss me off."

"I'm thinking Bill's been seeing him, too. Dr. A. was written in his planner multiple times, and I overheard him on the phone the other night. Maybe we should hire this guy for a group session. He could do all of us at the same time."

"That'd be him, Dr. Michael Adams. But I'll pass on the threesome. We do need to get you on Adams' list, though. You definitely need someone doing you," Darby said, shutting down Bill's computer. "Besides, he's hot and single, and you're going to be available soon."

"Ha. Ha. I would never see that guy. I can only imagine what he and Bill have discussed. Besides, he obviously knew Bill was cheating on me."

"Don't worry about that. I'm sure there is no love lost there." Darby took one look around the room then pushed Bill's flight bag against the wall where she'd found it. "If nothing else, you could trade him sex for information about the other pilots."

"Or maybe you could break into his office and just steal his files." She clutched her ammunition tightly to her chest and turned off the light.

Darby followed Kathryn into the living room and pulled on her coat. "I'm not surprised Bill's seeing Adams, especially since he's the one who hired him."

"Bill hired Adams?"

"Sort of. He knew how bad things would get with the industry so he convinced the union to hire him." Darby picked up her purse and walked toward the front door. "Bill's an ass, but he really does care about the pilots. At least the male version."

"Or maybe he planned on sleeping with everyone at the airline and knew they'd all need help after he was done."

"At least you haven't lost your sense of humor."

"It's definitely being tested," Kathryn said.

Darby paused at the door, and turned toward Kathryn. "Bill knew pilots would be hurting financially and emotionally after deregulation. He saw the writing was on the wall, and didn't want the history of his family's demise to repeat itself. Bill can be very persuasive. APO jumped at the opportunity to hire Adams. He's the best of the best."

"You make Bill sound like a nice, caring guy," Kathryn said, opening the door.

"We know better, and don't *you* forget it. Bill may love the airline industry, and his heart might be in the right place as far as that goes, but Bill is still all about Bill. His hiring Adams goes far deeper than caring about the pilots. I just haven't figured out what his deal is, yet."

CHAPTER 52
WEDNESDAY

KATHRYN'S HOUSE was dark, apart from the glow from the streetlights that cast luminous shadows across the living room floor. Jackie was asleep, yet there was an audible creak of footsteps. Then they stopped. Kathryn dialed 911 on her cell phone and positioned her thumb over the send button, then crept quietly toward the noise. She walked through the dining room, and a board creaked, but this time it moved under her foot. She froze.

"Is someone there?" a quiet voice called from the kitchen.

"Jackie?" Kathryn continued into the kitchen and turned on the light. "What are you doing in the dark?"

"I didn't want to wake you."

"Don't ever worry about that." Jackie's sunken eyes were swollen, and filled with grief. More than anything, she needed sleep. "How about a cup of chamomile tea?"

Kathryn filled the teapot and removed two cups from the cupboard. Jackie moved to the kitchen table and sat. Tears began to flow all over again.

"Baby, it's going to be all right," Kathryn said, wrapping her arms around Jackie. Tears filled her eyes for her friend and their loss, and for her stupidity with Bill. She, too, doubted anything would ever be right again.

She finally managed to get Jackie calmed down enough to sip

some tea, then tucked her back into bed and she curled up on top of the covers beside her. Unfortunately, she couldn't turn off her mind. *Why did Greg take the wrong intersection? Why did Linda's husband crash his plane? How did the crew miss the auto-throttle reduction? How many pilots were seeing a counselor?*

Bill had hired their counselor, Michael Adams. Her mind moved in a circular, fast-forward spiral. There was a connection; she just couldn't see it.

"Oh my God," she whispered.

Jackie snored quietly.

She climbed out of bed and went downstairs, turned on her computer then picked up the phone and dialed.

"Linda, I'm so sorry to call you at this hour, but what was Grant's counselor's name?"

"Michael Adams. Why?"

"No reason. Go back to sleep. I'll call you later."

Kathryn tapped her foot impatiently, waiting for her computer to boot up. Grant had been seeing Michael Adams and he didn't work for Coastal. When Darby said Bill's union had hired Adams, Kathryn had assumed it was for Coastal Airlines. She'd forgotten that the Airline Pilots Organization was a national organization, a combination of many different airlines.

She typed "Doctor Michael Adams," and multiple links popped up. Optometry, hematology, allergy, immunology, and hundreds more. She scrolled through them. Nothing fit.

And then there it was. Dr. Michael Bernard Adams, Ph.D. Clinical Psychologist. That link directed her to the Airline Pilots Organization's Dr. Adams. Not only was he the counselor for Coastal Airline's union, but he was also the counselor for all the APO affiliated airlines.

She crept into Bill's office and retrieved the files. When she returned to her kitchen, she laid the folders on the table, and began to read.

Skylark, Global, Regional, and now Coastal.

Each airline involved in an accident all belonged to the same union—the Airline Pilots Organization. It was the largest pilots' union worldwide. *A coincidence? Perhaps.* But all the pilots involved also lived relatively locally. If they'd been seeing anyone, it would have been Adams.

Both Grant and Greg had been seeing him, and Bill. She flipped through Skylark's file, located the medical information, and saw that there were two lines blacked out on the captains' records. She checked Global and Regional. Medical information had been blacked out in their records as well.

It was 4:30 a.m., and she paced. When she looked at the time again, it was 4:31. "Oh, hell," she said, and dialed the number.

It rang six times before a sleepy voice answered.

"Sam, it's me Kat. I'm sorry for calling so early, but I have to know something."

"Kathryn. Haven't you done enough damage? Now you're killing perfectly good dreams."

"What are you talking about?"

"I got my ass on suspension, pending investigation, because you couldn't keep your mouth shut about me giving you the files."

"Sam, I never—I told no one. I promised you and I kept my word. Is that why you drove off?" Silence followed, and she'd thought Sam had hung up.

"Jeez, Kat. What is it? What do you want?"

"I need to know why there are lines blacked out under the medical portion of the reports."

"Confidential."

"Sam, I promise I said nothing. This is important."

"No, Kathryn, it's crossed out because it's confidential. They were seeing a shrink about something or other, but it couldn't become part of their record. The union saw to that."

"You didn't happen to see who they were seeing, did you?"

"Nope. And Kat…" Sam hesitated. "I'm sorry about that jerk you're married to, but I always told you that he wasn't worth the trouble. Now don't call me again. I'm on sabbatical and have a lot of sleep I need to be catching up on, and if you find whoever ratted me out, take care of him for me."

Kathryn returned to her computer. She'd deal with the rat infestation later.

There were many articles on Adams's outstanding achievements and his work with the union. She cross-referenced his name with airline accidents. He'd done considerable work with Posttraumatic Stress Syndrome Disorder, and had been very successful with hypnosis in treating his patients.

She was surprised at how many people with the name of Adams continued to pop up that had also touched an airline accident. She carefully read each title as she continued to scroll through multiple stories. Then an article dated February 3, 1964 caught her eye, and she opened the link.

A horrifying event occurred yesterday when passenger Michael Adams created a disturbance on Universal Airlines' inaugural flight of their Boeing 727 aircraft.

Adams's allegedly attacked another passenger while his five-year-old son's cries brought passengers to the rescue. Passengers' inability to control Adams's violent rage brought the captain into the cabin, at which time restraints were utilized to control him. Adams was dead upon arrival.

Universal Airlines apologizes for their passengers' inconvenience. Medical professionals are looking into Adams' strange behavior. Captain William Jacobs was unwilling to comment, but he is being held fully responsible. Executive E. H. Cummings, Director-General of Universal Airlines, will be looking into this further and has extended condolences to the family.

Captain William Jacobs, Universal Airlines—Bill's dad. Her fingers moved rapidly, and she quickly located the obituaries of 1964. Michael Bernard Adams, Senior. Deceased. Complications due to an epileptic attack. Surviving family members, Marian K. Adams and Michael Bernard, Junior. She stared at the screen without blinking. People were ignorant about epilepsy in the sixties, and most would have assumed he was crazy, even if they did believe he was afflicted. Could Adams be reaping revenge on the passengers?

She closed her eyes and tried to imagine the trauma a young child would experience if his father died in front of him and nobody helped, how that could manifest in later years. And Bill had hired him. Did Bill know that he had a past with his father? Bill's dad was responsible for Adam's father's death. That's why he'd been fired. Adams could be destroying the life that Bill loved. One plane at a time.

Then realization slapped her in the face. The M.B.A. in Bill's ledger wasn't money for a master's degree in business, Bill had paid Michael Bernard Adams $190,000. *But why?* She stood and paced, running the possibilities through her mind. She glanced at the wall, at the framed painting of her daughters' handprints at five years old. They'd made them in kindergarten for Mother's Day. What if Adams came after her children?

"I wonder." She typed Marian K. Adams into her computer.

"Wonder what?" Jackie said from the doorway.

"Oh my God," Kathryn said, when she startled. "You scared me."

Jackie pulled a chair up beside her. Kathryn told her everything she'd discovered while she looked for data on Marian Adams.

Dr. Adams's mother was not only alive, but she lived in a very expensive nursing home. An exclusive high-care nursing home. Bill was paying Adams to make amends. He'd given him a job and money for what his father had done to the doctor's family—but it wasn't enough. Bill was now paying with blood.

"What if Dr. Adams used Bill and the union office to access the pilots and then hypnotize them to crash the planes?" Jackie said. "Maybe he drugged them, too."

"Hypnosis sounds a little far-fetched. I'm not sure what he's doing, but there is definitely a connection," Kathryn said, tapping her pen on the table beside the computer.

"This is all so weird," Jackie whispered.

"Oh my God!" Kathryn cried. "Darby's scheduled to see Adams this morning before her flight." It was 4:57. Darby would be having coffee now, 'getting primed' for the flight.

Kathryn dialed her number. No answer. Maybe she was in the shower. She dialed again. And again. The phone rang and then went to voice mail. On her third attempt, it went directly to voice mail. Her phone had been turned off.

"I've got to go," Kathryn said, then ran upstairs, and Jackie followed. She pulled on her jeans and sweatshirt, then found her tennis shoes. "I've got to stop Darby from going to Adams this morning," she said, as she tied her shoes. "She's not answering her phone, and she's supposed to see him before her flight. I'll call you as soon as I talk to her. Don't worry, I'm sure everything will be fine."

Kathryn ran down the stairs, and grabbed her purse and jacket.

Jackie stood at the top of the stairs, holding the railing, saying nothing, with tears flowing.

"Call Linda. Have her and Frankie come and stay with you," Kathryn yelled. "There's really nothing to worry about."

CHAPTER 53

DARBY GLANCED at the clock on her nightstand. 4:35 a.m. She'd been awake since 3:00 a.m. opening mail, paying bills, and caffeine loading. The morning was still dark, but she'd slept like a bear for seven hours. She had literally crashed the moment she'd returned from Kathryn's, and she didn't move until nature called. Then she was unable to fall back to sleep, an occupational hazard. Thank God Los Angeles was a short flight. Still, the eleven days after would be hell.

The thought that Bill had paid Neil to spy on her assaulted her on far too many levels. She completely understood his asking Neil to get her away from the wedding. She'd been drunk. Of course he wouldn't want her to tell Kathryn he was a sexist ass on his wedding night. But to pay someone and then film them? Bill Jacobs was a freakoid, and Neil was a bastard. She needed new men in her life. Or perhaps none.

She closed her laptop and placed it on her bed beside her open suitcase. Packing for an eleven day trip presented more of a challenge than flying the plane sometimes. She folded her uniform shirts and stacked them inside her suitcase. Mild in Los Angeles, cold in New York, and then the heat of Bangkok. She needed something for all seasons. Her bag would be heavy.

"I'm such an idiot. Bill is such an ass. Neil is a prick with a capital P," she told bear. She was probably a laughingstock among the pilots. Their saying that women gossiped was the joke. Hell, she'd heard more gossip from the guys than any of her girlfriends since she'd been flying.

Men were the worst, except for Neil, or so she had thought. "I will never believe a pilot again. I will never date a pilot again," she chanted. She'd loved him, but now she hated him with every cell in her body. How quickly he'd changed with that one little transgression. Little, that was a joke. He may have once been a Mazerati—beautiful, sleek, fast—but he just hit a wall at one hundred miles per hour and was totaled, and worthless, as far as she was concerned.

When she finished packing, she walked into her bathroom and turned on the shower. Her cell phone was ringing, but she had no desire to answer it. Who'd be calling her at this hour anyway? Scheduling? They could hang tight for fifteen minutes. Neil? He could hang his sorry ass until he choked.

She returned to her bedroom, turned on her stereo, and removed her robe, then tossed it onto the bed. She still couldn't imagine that Bill would pay someone to sleep with her, or whatever in the hell Neil said he'd been paid for.

Darby was sure Neil loved her, and maybe he really did want to make it work between them. She'd never seen him that upset. But how does he rebuild trust after lying about being married? He doesn't. He was just like her dad—a lying, cheating bastard. Which she figured counted at least ten points against him. Besides, he had three kids, and she couldn't handle kids. Another three points against him. She loved Kat's girls, but that was different, she didn't have to parent them. She could bring them junk from her trips and go home to a quiet, clean house. It was kind of like being a grandma.

She pulled off her t-shirt, tossed it into the hamper, and stepped into the shower. She turned her face into the spray. Three points for kids, another six for not telling her she was bought and paid for, and ten for being married. He was dangerously close to twenty points. One more and he'd lose her forever.

She soaked her hair and leaned against the wall, allowing the water to cascade down her body. She rubbed vanilla scented oil over her chest and massaged her breasts, thinking about her yoga teacher telling her to massage her breasts in circles twenty times per day to clear her lymph nodes. There was also a correlation to the direction and size, and she quickly changed directions, just in case. She slid her hand down her abdomen, and one leg then the other. Her hands moved between her legs and she thought about Neil, and wished he were with her now. Everyone was allowed at least one weakness, she mused. But he was married, a weakness she would never allow.

But the way he shampooed her hair, with fingers sliding through the strands, and tips firmly massaging her scalp… She could never quite duplicate his shampooing technique by herself. Then he'd slowly relocate his hands over her back, washing, massaging, kneading, and they always continued south. She liked that a lot. The thought of him aroused her.

But she would never forgive him. If Kat could be strong, so could she.

She couldn't believe that he actually wanted to leave his wife for her, and that bothered her. Maybe after she sufficiently punished him, they'd talk. If he left his wife because he wanted to leave his wife, then that was one thing. But it couldn't be for her. If he agreed under those conditions, maybe she'd contemplate a relationship. But, and it was a big but, he'd have to be single for at least a year. If, and only if, he was single, then she might get back with him.

Who am I kidding? Of course I will never get back with him.

She loved him. But she knew that if he cheated on his wife, he'd cheat on her too. He would pay for his lies.

"Shit," she said when her stereo increased a few decibels. She was going to have to get that thing fixed sooner than later or the neighbors would vote her off the island. Begrudgingly, she opened the curtain and...

"What in the hell?"

"Shhh," he said, placing a finger to his lips.

CHAPTER 54

DARBY PULLED the shower curtain close to cover her body. "What in the hell are you doing here?"

"Canceling your flight."

"You're a freaking lunatic. Get the hell out of my house."

She instantly knew that she was in big friggin' trouble here, and she glanced toward the doorway.

"Run. You'll only make it as far as the bed. But then, I think you'd like that."

Her mind flew through her options of escaping. It was a short list—there were none. And then she saw the syringe.

She screamed when he lunged forward, and her feet slipped out from under her. She fell backward, holding the shower curtain as she did, and the bar fell down and hit him on the head.

"Dammit." He attempted to throw it aside, but she hung tight to the curtain. Then he hit her with the bar and ripped the curtain from her arms and tossed it aside. He stood and stared at her naked body. All she wanted to do was disappear. She scrambled backwards in a sitting position; pulling her legs close she wrapped her arms around them.

She was trapped. And he was clearly aroused.

Moving like a python, he knelt, grabbed her ankles, and pulled. She fell back and hit her head on the tub, and her ears began ringing.

"I wish we had time for a quickie," he said, holding her head down under the flow of water.

She gasped, trying to breathe, but the water flowed directly onto her face. She flung her legs wildly and kicked him with all her strength.

"Calm down. It'll be easier that way."

He placed a washrag over her throat and pressed hard. She couldn't breathe. She twisted and kicked, but he was too strong. Blackness closed in. She closed her eyes. Playing dead would be a better game, and if she were lucky, he'd quit. But she knew better.

And then she heard pounding at the front door, and she opened her eyes. At the same time he cocked his head and looked away, and she seized the opportunity and kicked him one more time.

But it wasn't hard enough.

"Shit," he said, and pressed harder on her throat again.

She saw stars but continued to twist and scream. Then she watched as he plunged the needle between her legs.

"At least it's good for one last thing," he said.

She grabbed herself where the needle had entered and cried out.

He stood, soaked from the shower, and threw the syringe at her, laughing.

Her heart raced, and her chest grew tighter with every beat. She could no longer yell. Tears filled her eyes as she realized she was going to die smelling of vanilla.

CHAPTER 55

THE SCREAM from deep within the house shot fear through Kathryn's veins as she attempted to open Darby's locked door, but it was the ensuing silence that frightened her the most. She pounded on the door and yelled. She reached above the frame for her spare key, but it was gone. She ran to the side of the house as she dialed 911 on her cell.

The side door was equally as unrewarding as her attempt to explain that something might be wrong to the emergency operator—neither worked. She checked two windows then rushed to the backyard. That door was locked too. She frantically looked around locating the biggest rock she could find. She set her phone down then heaved the rock through the glass. She reached her hand inside and unlocked the door, picked up her phone and yelled, "There's been a break-in. Somebody's been hurt!"

Kathryn grabbed a poker and ran up the stairs two at a time to Darby's room. The shower was running, and she hoped that Neil wasn't there. But that scream had not been one of pleasure.

"Darby?" she called. Still no response. She ran toward the bathroom, calling to her friend with the poker held high overhead. But she dropped it when she saw Darby's lifeless body sprawled in the tub.

The water was red, and the shower curtain was lying on the floor. She fell to her knees. "No." For a moment she saw her mother. "Get an ambulance now!" she yelled into the phone before dropping it on the floor. She shut off the shower.

"Oh my God, Darby, what happened?" she whispered. She reached down and pressed her fingers to Darby's neck. Her pulse was faint and raced erratically. It felt like a hum, but at least she had one. Kathryn grabbed a towel and knelt on the floor beside the tub. On her knees, she was leaning forward when a piercing weight crashed down upon her skull.

CHAPTER 56

KATHRYN AWOKE to a paramedic kneeling in front of her. Her head ached and she instinctively moved her hand to touch the sticky lump. The room moved in waves. The ringing in her ears was almost as unbearable as the nausea. Closing her eyes for a moment she took slow, deep, breaths.

"Aren't you the lucky one?" the paramedic said. "The tub took the brunt of the broom handle. Had it been that poker laying there, you'd be dead."

"I don't feel very lucky." Kathryn opened her eyes and then panic took hold. "Where's my friend? Where's Darby?"

"She's on her way to Harborview. A second ambulance will be here in a few minutes for you. The police are going to need a statement. How ya feelin?"

"Like a brick landed on my head." She stood, and wobbled. "I need to get to the hospital." Statements could come later.

"Hang tight until the ambulance arrives. They'll take you."

Hang tight? Are you kidding me? Why hadn't she been put in the ambulance with Darby? She leaned against her dresser so she wouldn't fall. When the paramedic and the officers turned their heads, she picked up her phone and headed for the door.

Her body shook uncontrollably and despite her determination being stronger than her legs—they held. An ambulance's siren increased in volume, approaching quickly. She ran down the stairs and out the front door. Placing her hands on her thighs, she vomited into Darby's rhododendron.

She climbed into her car, backed out of the driveway, and drove onto the street, passing the ambulance as it pulled into the driveway.

An aching head wasn't her problem. It was the blurred street. She closed one eye and managed to keep the car on her side of the road.

Twenty minutes of concerted effort later, she pulled into the hospital parking lot. Leaving her keys in the ignition and her car running, she ran into the main entrance and gave the clerk Darby's name. She was directed to the emergency room entrance.

Turning, she promptly slammed into John. He caught her and stopped her from falling. "Kathryn. What are you doing here? What happened?"

"Darby. Somebody broke into her house and hurt her. She's in emergency."

"Looks like you got in the middle of that fight. Come on, I'll take you." He held her elbow and guided her toward the emergency room entrance.

When they arrived, he asked to see Darby Bradshaw. The nurse looked from John to her, and back to John again, then nodded and made a call. The doctor would be out as soon as he could. They sat on the couch and waited. She told John about Greg and everything she'd learned about Adams.

The seconds ticked by slowly. She tried not to watch the clock. Instead, she fidgeted, and picked at a thread on her sweatshirt while they waited. A drop of blood trickled down her forehead.

"We need to get you admitted," John said as he raised his handkerchief and gently wiped.

"Not until I know that Darby's okay."

The medics who'd been at the house walked in the door, and

she leaned back to hide behind John. Then her phone rang.

Kathryn lied to Jackie and said everything was fine, as John stood and stepped toward the counter.

He opened his cell phone, dialed, and spoke quietly. Glancing over his shoulder at her, he nodded when their eyes met. Kathryn looked away and focused on Jackie.

Clearly relieved that Darby was okay, Jackie said, "I just found a letter for you, and it said 'open immediately.' It was lying on the floor beside your nightstand. I probably knocked it off last night. I'm sorry, but I thought I should let you know."

"What does it say?"

"I don't know. I didn't open it."

Of course you didn't. She closed her eyes and squeezed the bridge of her nose. Patience. Unfortunately her head hurt, and she had none. She counted to three and asked, "Can you read it to me now?" She waited for what seemed like forever.

"My dearest Kathryn. I'm so sorry about my infidelity. There's far more going on than you know, but that doesn't excuse anything. I love you with all my heart, and I'm willing to get the help we need, if you are. The girls and I love you. We need you. The girls need us together. Meet me at Dr. Adams's tomorrow at 0800, and we'll start working things out. Love, Bill."

Jackie read her the address, but Kathryn knew the building.

"That's in twenty minutes. You're going, aren't you? You have to go."

"Yes. I'm going. I'll call you later." She hung up and called Bill's cell phone. It went directly to voicemail, as the doctor and John walked toward her.

"I'm sorry," the doctor said. "There was nothing we could do,"

"What do you mean?"

"She's gone."

What? She couldn't be hearing him correctly. No. You're wrong. Kathryn lifted her hands and covered her mouth. She looked up at the doctor in disbelief. Darby could not be dead.

"We need to check you in," John said. He extended his hand to her, but she pulled away.

"That's a nasty cut." The doctor knelt in front of her and slid her sleeve up, exposing her arm.

When she realized he was about to stick a needle in her, she pulled her arm free and jumped to her feet, knocking into the doctor. He lost his balance and fell backward.

She backed up, moving closer to the door, keeping her eyes on both John and the man in white. She had to get out of there. She had to find Bill and warn him. There was no way Darby was dead. They had to be wrong.

"Where are you going?" John asked as he helped the doctor to his feet.

"I don't know," Kathryn spat, turning toward the door.

"You're not working on this case," John yelled.

She turned and faced him. "*Exactly.* You're right! I'm not working on anything, and you have no authority to stop me from doing it."

Kathryn steadied herself as she walked out the door, and then she ran.

CHAPTER 57

KATHRYN FLEW through southbound traffic on I-5, and prayed she'd make it in time. In time for what? She had no idea. She was thankful that her car was still parked out front, and the doctor hadn't stuck the needle into her arm. She was already dizzy and focusing was enough of a challenge. Now only three things crossed her mind—Adams, Darby, and Bill.

If Doc Adams had been involved in the accidents, why would he attack Darby? He wouldn't. Then who? Neil? He had been pissed, but pissed enough to come back and hurt her? Maybe it was an accident. And then she thought of the syringe in Darby's tub. *Adams.* It had to be him.

"Darby, you can't be dead!" she yelled. She pressed speed dial to call Bill for the third time. For the third time it went to voicemail, and she slammed her phone shut.

"Dammit."

Blood trickled into her eye and she wiped it with her shirtsleeve. Then her phone rang, and she opened it.

"Slow down!" John yelled. "You're going to kill someone."

She glanced at her speedometer. 75. "John? Hello? Can you hear me?" she said, just before she hung up. The great thing about cell phones was that they were so damned unreliable. She wasn't going to listen to him. Who was he to tell her to slow down or anything else? She was tired of everyone telling her what to do.

If Adams were a psychopathic killer, she'd stop him. She had no idea how, but she would. Maybe she could get into his files. She only wished that she could talk to Bill first. Adams was getting sloppy, which could only mean one thing—he didn't care who knew any longer. Bill was in trouble.

If she hadn't been so damned emotional, and derailed by John and Bill, she might have seen things more clearly sooner, and Darby would be with her now.

She pulled into the parking lot, climbed out of her car, and ran into the Airline Pilots Organization's building. She read the directory board then stabbed the button multiple times for the elevator door to open. When it did, she pressed ten. She thought she was going to vomit, and leaned against the back wall taking a deep breath.

The elevator carried her directly to her floor, and when the door opened, she was in the hallway. Adams's office was the first door on the right, and it was unlocked. She stepped into an empty reception area.

Standing in front of Adams's closed office door, she listened. She hesitated for a moment then quietly knocked. There was no answer, but there was movement inside. She opened the door and a man stood in front of her. Her heart pounded in her throat. She knew instantly where she'd seen him.

"You must be Mrs. Jacobs. I'm glad you decided to come."

"Where's Bill?"

"He's been here and gone, but he suggested we talk."

"About what?"

"He's concerned about you. Please, come in. Sit down." When she didn't move, he said, "You're bleeding."

"I'm fine."

He opened his mouth, but hesitated. He didn't remove his eyes from her wound. "You've gone through a lot lately. Bill's concerned." He took one step toward her, and she moved back. He hesitated, then retreated and sat behind his desk. She took a cautious step and entered the room.

"You were at the hospital the day Greg died." The doctor she'd almost run down was the union psychiatrist.

"Yes, I was. I went to pay Mr. Jameson and his family my respects. It was a tragic accident. But right now, my concern is for you." He leaned back in his chair and steepled his fingers. "Bill tells me that your mother had an untimely death and you've never been able to get over it. Maybe we should start there.

"What does my mother's suicide have to do with anything?" She asked. "Bill said I was coming here to work things out between he and I." The thought of her mother ached deep within her heart— tomorrow would be the twenty-seventh anniversary of her death. She'd found her in the tub, just as she'd found Darby. The nightmare continued. She touched the goose egg on the side of her head.

"That's a nasty bump. Would you like something for pain?"

She shook her head no, and that's when she noticed the diploma on the wall. "You went to Stanford?"

"Yes," he said, leaning back in his chair glancing at the wall. "A fine university." He folded his hands on his chest and smiled. The smile was definitely forced.

The same college Bill had gone to. "Dr. Adams…"

"Mike, please," he said, smiling warmly, now. His eyes were the color of caramel and melted when he spoke. His teeth were straight and white, and the touch of gray at his temples spoke of wisdom. He dripped of sincerity, and she hated him. But his voice was kind and gentle, and she wanted to tell him everything.

Instead, she pressed voice memo on her iPhone, inside her pocket, hoping to record something useful.

"My mother's death was tragic, just as your father's was. I'm sorry about what happened to him." Adams' composure changed just for a millisecond. The smiling eyes hardened. His shoulders tensed ever so slightly. "That must have been really difficult for you."

When he didn't respond, she continued. "And all those people, not understanding epilepsy. Did they hold him down?" Her words hung in the room without a response. She shook her head slowly and continued. "Did he die on the aircraft? Did you have to sit by him after he passed? The captain didn't help, did he?" Adams's eyes narrowed.

"You've done your homework."

"Did you know that Bill's dad was the captain?"

"He told me years later."

Adams father had had a seizure, and Adams, as a small boy had tried to tell the passengers, but nobody would listen to him. The captain had come out, Bill's dad, and he should have helped, but he didn't. Bill's dad had put Adams's father in handcuffs and his father had died before his eyes. The reason Bill's dad had been fired, and ultimately killed himself.

"I'm sorry." Bill's dad had killed him with his ignorance. She sat patiently and waited for Adams to continue. She hoped it would be soon, as a weight tugged at her eyelids. If she sat here much longer, she would pass out and then really be in trouble.

"That was a long time ago, but we're not here to talk about me. We're here for you."

"I'm only here because Bill asked me to come so we could work things out."

"I supposed he did." He glanced toward her head, and she

instinctively touched her wound again. "What happened?"

"Don't you think it's strange that all the pilots who've crashed were your patients?" Kathryn asked, ignoring his question.

"Concerned, yes. Surprised, not really."

Her suspicions had been correct. They had been his patients. "People are dying, and you're the one connecting factor. What I can't figure out is how you managed to get them to crash their planes."

An eyebrow raised, but he didn't comment.

He opened a folder and began reading. His brow furrowed, and then he asked, "How long have been thinking about taking your life?"

"Taking my life? You've got to be kidding." This was ridiculous. What in the hell was he doing? "Where is my husband?"

He didn't respond, but continued to silently read.

"Why did Bill give you $190,000? Was it blood money for his dad killing yours? Maybe he just felt sorry for you." This time he didn't smile.

"That is quite enough, Mrs. Jacobs. You have no idea of what you're talking about. His dad would've helped had he known my father was sick. He was equally a victim of circumstance. Bill assisted me financially because we're friends. Brothers. We want the same thing—to make sure that airline travel is safe for everyone."

"I don't doubt that was Bill's intent, but was it yours? I'm just wondering how much longer you planned on continuing to blackmail my husband."

"That's enough." He pulled a pad of paper from his desk drawer, and put a pen to it.

"What are you doing?"

"Taking notes. You're hysterical. We need to get you some

help," Adams said, as he wrote.

Kathryn watched him, wondering what to do next, when she noticed the syringe laying on the credenza behind him.

"It *was* you. You killed Darby."

"Please, dear, calm down." Adams stood quickly and was around his desk within seconds. She pushed her chair backward with her feet, creating distance between them. He stopped advancing.

"Where is Bill? What did you do with him?"

"Bill is on his flight. You need to relax. Darby is not dead. She cancelled her appointment this morning. You're just having another hallucination."

"You're a liar. You killed Greg, and Darby."

"Your imagination's working overtime. Please settle down. This behavior is uncalled for," Adams said, reaching for her. "You're going to hurt yourself."

She kicked her legs hard against the desk to slide her chair further backward, out of his reach. But the chair tipped, and hit the wall. "Get away from me you murderer!" She screamed and rolled out of the chair to the floor then scrambled backward like a crab. The only problem was that her back was now against the wall, and there were no rocks for her to crawl under.

He knelt at her side, and reached for her, touching her arm. She kicked and yelled attempting to pull it away. Just then, the door flew open.

Adams jumped to his feet. "Excuse me. This is a private session."

CHAPTER 58

THE NOISE was so loud that Kathryn thought her eardrums had shattered, and she instinctively covered her ears, but she was a second too late. Bone fragments, blood, and brains hit her first, and then a two hundred pound body fell on top of her.

She fought to push him off, but his weight and the angle made it difficult. Panic washed over her, but she managed to slide out from underneath him. Then she checked his pulse. But a beating heart would do nothing for a man with a hole in his head. He lay on the floor face down with the exit hole staring her in the face—the bullet that exited Adams's head lodged in the wall.

John gently touched her arm and helped her up. He pulled his phone out of his pocket and dialed, then asked for an ambulance. Walker stood nearby, holding the gun that killed Dr. Adams.

"Why'd you shoot him? He could've provided information. Now we'll never know why he did this." She leaned against the desk to balance herself.

"That murdering bastard killed my daughter. He was about to hurt you. We know everything we need to."

"Walker, enough," John said steadily.

Her body shook violently as she dialed Bill's number. Still no answer. *Where in the hell is he?* "I have to find Bill."

"We need to get you to the hospital. Bill will be just fine," John said, touching her shoulder.

"No. Something's not right. Bill was here this morning. I think he might be in trouble." She dialed crew scheduling—they'd know how to find him. And they did. Bill had been called out for the Los Angeles flight because Captain Bradshaw had been a no-show.

"We have to stop that flight. When does it depart?" she asked.

"It's scheduled out at 8:40," the scheduler said. "You'll have to talk to dispatch, I'll patch you through." It was 8:35.

The phone patch rang through, and she was connected.

"For crew scheduling, press one. For dispatch, press..." She pressed two. "Please enter your employee number and press pound." She typed in his employee number, then his password. But he'd changed it. She tried multiple numbers but none worked.

Dammit. She closed the phone. "I'm going to the airport. I have to stop that plane." She ran out the door.

The elevator came quickly. Once outside she ran down the stairs, taking two at a time. She tripped, stumbled, righted herself, and then ran to the car. She drove through a red light, directly across the highway, and onto the airport property.

Bill's flight had already pushed back, and now only the tower controllers could stop its departure. She pulled up in front of the tower and jumped out of her car. She ran to the door and pounded. The door was locked, and nobody sat at the desk. She repeatedly pressed the intercom, and beat on the glass. "Please! Someone open this door!"

Someone finally responded. "May I help you?"

"Stop the Coastal Airlines L.A. flight from departing!"

"What?"

"Jesus Christ! Just stop flight Seven from departing. Please. It's going to crash."

"Excuse me?"

"My name is Kathryn Jacobs. My husband is the captain on that flight," she yelled. "You have to stop that plane!"

It wasn't minutes before black-and-whites filled the parking lot and guns were raised. She saw movement inside the building, but no faces, and nobody would open the door.

"Raise your arms and put your hands on the door," an officer shouted from behind.

She complied. "I work for the NTSB she yelled over her shoulder. "We need to stop a flight!" she yelled. "My husband is the captain and he's sick."

"Can I see your I.D.?" The officer asked.

"I don't have I.D., but if you call…" And she stopped speaking. The reflection in the glass frightened even her. Adams's body matter was splattered over her clothes and face. Her head had an open wound, and fresh clotted blood clung to her hair. She was telling them a flight was going to crash. She was the lunatic Adams had spoken of.

The officer pressed her against the glass doors with force. He held an arm across her back and used the other hand to cuff her. He flattened her face against the cold glass. She could see the clock on the wall. 8:45.

It was too late. His flight had pushed back and there was nothing she could do but pray that he and the people on his flight wouldn't fall victim to the hands of a psychopath on a revenge mission. She dropped to her knees and gagged, but there was nothing left in her stomach.

CHAPTER 59

"Do you think we're going to get any service on this flight?" Ryan asked. "I need coffee. I need it black, and I need it strong."

"If I were king, we'd have our own flight attendants, and we'd be serviced the entire flight," Bill said pulling charts out of his bag.

"I thought you were the king."

"Oh, yeah," Bill laughed. "I forgot. In case you're wondering, it is good to be the king." Ryan managed a couple of chuckles as he flipped through his charts.

When Bill had been a first officer, he too had played the "suck up and yes sir" game with the captains, and laughed at all their stupid jokes. Not until he had become a captain did he realize that all praise was appreciated, even the false sentiment.

He looked at his watch. Kathryn should've been at the office by now, but he doubted she'd made it after being knocked unconscious. That didn't matter, Adams would create all the documentation he needed to confirm she was unstable and suicidal. If Bill had done his job well, she'd eventually find the trail he'd left for her—photos of the women, the ledger with Adams's initials, and the recordings. He knew once she had the opportunity to review the transcripts, she'd figure out the pilots were crashing their planes. She'd soon lead Walker to Adams, and everything would fall into place.

It had been a moment of inspiration, years prior, to give Walker ammunition against his pilots—from that time forward Bill owned him. Bill's payback was Walker giving his wife a job, when the time was right, so she would have access to everything she needed to put the pieces together, and wrap Adams up in a nice little package.

He smiled.

The lead flight attendant poked her head into the flight deck. "Can I get you guys anything before we start boarding?"

"We'd love some coffee, but let me get it. I need to stretch my legs." Bill slid his seat back and crawled out of their tight quarters, and winked at Ryan.

"Are you sure?" she asked, not hiding her surprise.

"Of course. You gals work too hard. Besides, we need to get this baby out on time and it's going to be a full flight. I have no problem helping myself, if you don't mind me in your kitchen… Rebecca," he said glancing at her nametag. "I'm pretty good there." He grinned and stared into her eyes, at the same time he touched her elbow.

Blushing, Rebecca returned to the boarding door and spoke to the agent. Bill pulled two Styrofoam cups out of the cabinet and filled them both with coffee. At least it was strong enough to kill the bacteria and hide the taste of drugs. He dumped equivalent of ten Tylenol capsules full of drugs into one of the cups.

"Here ya go, buddy." Bill handed a cup to his first officer.

They finished their respective preflights, and performed their checklists. He glanced at his watch. Fifteen minutes to departure. He called to the back of the aircraft to see how the flight attendants were doing, and then he checked on cargo loading. Everything was on schedule.

"You got a hot date in L.A.?" Ryan asked. "Oh, I'm sorry…"

"It's okay. The crash impacted us all, in one way or another."

"Yeah, it did," Ryan said. "When did they call you? I thought I was flying with Bradshaw today."

"She no-showed. They called this morning." He'd miss Darby. It was a shame that Kathryn had shown up when she did. He'd planned on having a little fun with her before he left. But sacrifice was the key to his success. He also hoped that when he'd hit Kathryn that it hadn't been too hard. He needed to keep her alive through the grand finale. Her showing up when she did was a surprise. But it had meant she was ahead of schedule—a good thing.

"I'm glad we've got a chance to fly together," Ryan said, tossing his cup in the garbage bag. "I wanted to thank you for all you're doing for the pilots."

"Of course. We're all in this together," Bill said.

Ryan stifled a yawn. "I'm going to get some more java."

"Sit." Bill pushed he seat back. "I'll get it for you." He stepped into the cabin and poked his head out the aircraft door. The jetway was empty, but many people still stood in the aisles.

"Can I get you something?" Rebecca asked, again.

"Just getting more coffee for Ryan. He's really sucking it down. You guys almost done back here?"

"Everyone's on board, but finding their seats is another story. We've got a special needs group today. They're taking a bunch of kids to Disneyland. It's so sweet."

"Yes, it is," he said." He got Ryan's coffee, fixed it up with double what he'd added the first time, and returned to the flight deck.

Bill folded himself back into his seat and then called for their departure clearance. "Here, take a couple of these. They'll give you a pick-me-up. Vitamin B." *They'll pick you up so far that when you fall, you'll never get up again.* He'd already loaded his second cup of coffee, but he couldn't be too careful.

Within minutes, the doors were closed. Three minutes early. Good. The ground crew pushed the aircraft away from the gate, and Bill took control. Then he looked at the overhead panel and pulled the cockpit voice recorder circuit breaker.

"Call ground and tell them we're ready to taxi," he said.

Ryan picked up the radio and stared at it. Then said, "Ground control...uh...flight Sev..."

Bill laughed, and picked up his microphone. "Coastal Airlines Seven is ready to taxi, runway Three-Four Left."

"Cleared to taxi to Three-Four Left, Coastal Seven."

Ryan stared at him, his eyes glazed. His lips moved, but no words came out. Bill ignored him and continued taxiing their Boeing 757 towards their departure point, while Ryan began swatting the air.

"You still want to make the takeoff, buddy?" Bill asked. Then he laughed.

"Coastal Airlines, contact the tower on 119.9," the ground controller said.

"Roger, Coastal Seven going to tower." Bill switched the radio to the tower frequency. "Seattle tower, Coastal Seven is with you. Ready for takeoff on the left."

"Coastal Seven is cleared for takeoff Three-Four Left. Mountain five departure. Departure control on 119.2. Have a good flight."

"You ready to go, buddy?" Bill said. He reached over and buckled Ryan in tight.

He advanced the thrust levers toward takeoff power, and then pressed the auto-thrust selector. The thrust levers took control as they increased automatically under their own power, providing takeoff thrust. Bill ignored all the normal callouts.

He was cleared to contact departure once airborne, but he

didn't. He stayed with the tower and listened. He also continued to climb. He passed through one thousand feet and increased his rate of climb. He was supposed to turn right to a heading of 070 degrees at four thousand feet. Instead, as he passed through two thousand feet he made a slight left turn.

He was supposed to be flying the Seattle 341 degree radial, but flew a course of 330 degrees—directly toward the Space Needle, that was now only fifteen hundred feet below their altitude.

"Coastal Seven confirm you're on a three-four-one course. Coastal, state your intentions!" ATC demanded.

Bill didn't respond. Instead he continued to climb. Then he reached down and positioned a fuel control lever to cut-off, shutting down the left engine. Bells rang and lights flashed in the cockpit. And then he pulled the right fuel control lever and shut down the right engine.

With both engines shut down, his 230,000-pound airplane was suddenly a glider. The backup generator, the RAT, came to life providing hydraulic power to his flight controls.

"Show on," he said, pressing in the cockpit voice circuit breaker.

Had he wanted to, he could have restarted the engines. He had enough altitude. But that wasn't in the plan. Instead, he pulled both the fire switches and simultaneously fired their bottles, releasing extinguishing agent into the respective engines, preventing them from being restarted. There was no backing out now.

He was directly over the city of Seattle without any power. His airspeed bled back to minimum maneuvering, and he no longer could maintain altitude. Adrenaline fueled his smile and gave him limitless power.

CHAPTER 60

KATHRYN'S TEARS didn't flow from the pain of her arm being jammed into her back, her face pressed against the door, or the wood stick that had smashed into her skull hours before. She cried because of her helplessness. Because she was unable to reach Bill and stop his flight, and because of her inability to get to Darby in time. She cried for Greg and Jackie. All she wanted to do was hold her girls and tell them how much she loved them.

The handcuffs clicked tight behind her back, and she was on her knees on the blacktop. She'd lost. There was nothing she could do now.

"Remove those cuffs," John yelled.

She glanced up. Walker flashed his I.D. "This woman is working for us."

"We'll take full responsibility for her," John said. "Remove these cuffs," he yelled a second time when the officer didn't respond. "Now!"

"Open those goddamn doors," Walker yelled.

Everything from that point moved quickly. The officer removed her handcuffs, and John helped her to her feet. She rubbed her wrists as they hurried her inside. They poured into the elevator and rode to the top, toward the control center—the heart of the control tower. John handed her a handkerchief and she wiped her face.

"You were right," Walker said. "We found drugs in Adams's

office, and Bill had been on his schedule multiple times, as were all the captains involved in the accidents. There were clippings of the accidents stapled to his files. ATC is unable to make contact with Bill's plane, and he's not following his clearance." The elevator doors opened.

"My God," Kathryn said as they rushed into the operations room. "Adams is also an expert in hypnosis and mind control."

"We need you to talk to Bill. Our only hope is that you can talk him out of crashing that plane. We've no idea what mental state he's in, but he's unresponsive to the controllers." John handed her a headset with an attached microphone then looked at her head. He pulled the headset back and threw it on the table, and gave her a handheld microphone instead. He turned up the audio on a speaker.

The large screen glowed in front of them, as air traffic controllers vectored flights away from the area. The lead controller showed them which blip was Bill's.

His plane was descending into the city. This would be the Twin Towers all over again if she couldn't do something. He'd take out half the city with the fireball he'd create.

"Bill. I don't know if you can hear me, but please say something. Wake up!" she yelled, pressing the talk button. Then she waited. Walker nodded for her to continue.

"I went to the office to meet you this morning. Bill. You have to do something, please talk to us!" She hesitated, waiting for a reply, but when there was none, she continued. "The girls need you. They're on your plane," she lied. "Bill, bring them home. They love you. The union needs you. The pilots need you. You're going to make a difference in the world. Bill, talk to me God Dammit!" This time when she paused, the radio came to life.

"Kat... Dr. Adams..." Bill's voice was weak, and then the radio went quiet.

Kathryn yelled over the silence. "He's dead. He won't hurt anyone ever again. You have to land that plane. Over."

Bill's voice broadcasted again, this time stronger. "Seattle Tower, Coastal Seven. We've lost both our engines and turning left to a heading of 160 degrees. I'm returning to SeaTac airport."

They watched as the blip of his aircraft changed directions, but it turned slow and wide as the aircraft lost altitude with every degree of change.

"There is no way in hell they're going to make it," a voice said.

"Get emergency equipment out to the runway. Get hold of the Coast Guard. Get everyone standing by," someone else yelled.

John put his hand on her shoulder. Now all they could do was wait. There was no time to evacuate the city. All binoculars in the control tower were on the plane. During the turn the 757 rapidly lost altitude. They were too low to make it back to the runway.

An emergency broadcast aired on all radios. SeaTac, Boeing, Renton, and Tacoma Narrows Airports were all closed for departing and arriving aircraft. McChord Air Force base was also notified. But Bill didn't have enough altitude to make any of those fields.

Chapter 61

Bill shook his head and grinned. Kathryn continued to surprise him. He hadn't expected to hear her voice, or for her to figure out that Adams was their man, so quickly. Especially today. He had no doubt that if Adams was dead the blood was on Walker's hands—just as he'd anticipated. Once given the right information, Walker would've taken care of anyone responsible for killing his baby girl. Kathryn had been the breadcrumb for Walker to follow on the trail to Adams. Still, he hadn't expected her to be the homing pigeon.

Now she pleaded for him to wake up. *Sweet.* He reached up and started the APU as he continued his turn toward SeaTac Airport. He'd need the electricity from his auxiliary power unit to extend the flaps when the time came.

He had planned on dead-sticking his 757 into Paine Field, but the winds were off and the plane was heavier than he had anticipated. He looked at the altimeter, and then the distance to the airport. Then at his descent rate. *Shit.* The turn was taking more altitude than he'd expected. *I'm not going to make the runway.*

He'd put her down west of SeaTac Airport, in Puget Sound, abeam Des Moines Marina. It wasn't what he'd planned, but if that was destiny so be it. Not that he couldn't handle a water landing, he just wasn't a copycat. The captain who'd landed on the river out East had taken that show, and would make Bill's landing old school.

The public didn't know that plane had flown itself, and was

virtually unable to stall—the power of the Airbus. He'd also had idle thrust on at least one of his engines and could have made the runway, yet they deemed him a hero. Timing, or an exit strategy? Bill didn't care either way. He'd proven the importance of the pilot. He realized, however, the reality of overnight hero status when a pilot saves a planeload of passengers. Bill's landing would be spectacular. His engines produced no power, and he'd flown his plane drugged.

The Boeing 757 continued to descend at a higher rate than anticipated. *Shit. I might not make the damn shoreline.* Maybe he should have headed West instead of turning south, but he'd thought he could make SeaTac. Now, Puget Sound was an option that looked less likely with each sinking minute.

Bill lifted the PA handset. "This is your captain speaking. We're making a water landing. Flight attendants, you have less than five minutes to prepare." There was no reason to tell them they may end up in a fireball, and ruin the last few minutes of life.

He rolled his wings level, and pointed his ship toward the shore. Timing was everything. He lowered the nose to keep her speed up. If he stalled her, there would be no altitude for recovery.

When he thought he could reach the shoreline, he pressed the alternate flaps switches to on, then turned the alternate flap knob to the 30 position, and the flaps began to move. Slowly. He wouldn't get them all out because they moved about a tenth of the normal speed without hydraulics, and there wasn't time or altitude.

Surprised at her weight, Bill reached over and pulled the manual stab trim levers to relieve some pressure. He'd also forgotten how slow the manual trim was, half the rate of what he was used to.

"Hey Ryan, give me a hand, buddy?" Bill said to the corpse sitting beside him.

He'd leave the gear up to avoid flipping. If he caught an engine, there was a chance that they'd flip anyway. But what the heck, he'd been drugged. He tossed a bottle of pills into Ryan's flight bag, and placed the other into his pocket. Then pulled his shoulder straps tight.

"Coastal Seven, emergency aircraft landing on Puget Sound."

Everyone had made a big deal about that baby bus, the A320's, water landing. Now it was Bill's turn, and his airplane wasn't as forgiving. In minutes he'd find out how unforgiving she was. The pitch shifted as the flaps extended, and he used the manual trim as needed. He slowed her to minimum maneuvering speed, making sure not to go below 130 knots or he'd lose the hydraulics to his flight controls. More importantly, at this weight he'd stall.

He slowed her just above the stall speed. The wind came from behind, as a quartering right tailwind, and the current was going against him. He gripped the control yoke tightly, and reached over and pulled more stab trim, then returned his hand to the controls. Veins bulged in both his arms.

The stick shaker clacked intermittently, and he glanced at his airspeed. Unfortunately if he lowered his nose, he wouldn't clear the trees just ahead of him, the final barrier to survival. He glanced at the flap gauge. They were passing through 5. The stall warning clacked, but he didn't have many options. There was only one thing to do.

He pulled hard, yanking back on the control yoke, and the plane gained momentary lift as it barely cleared the wall of trees, hopping over them. "Hot damn!" He quickly pushed the nose back down to regain his speed and avoid stalling. But he had maybe fifty feet to play with. Pushing the nose over that close to the ground was intuitively wrong. He was now in a dangerously nose low attitude, and had but seconds to react. He'd also lost too much airspeed.

He pulled her back to stop the descent, but not too far. *Yes! Right there baby.* He he held her off, just above the water, stick shaker screaming. He would hold her off for as long as he could. But it wasn't long enough. She'd lost too much speed and dropped. Thankfully they were kissing the water when she gave up flying.

The fuselage hit hard. His neck jerked and pain shot through his spine. A deafening crack exploded from somewhere in the cabin. He didn't know how bad she'd broken. But he continued to hold backpressure, speeding forward. If he let her fall, that would be the end. Ride cut short due to a minor technicality—drowning by all.

They sped across the bay, black water pounding against the windshield. They were down. The plane appeared to be in one piece. He continued to hold the nose off. With both hands on the controls, he held tight. Fire burned through his arms. He couldn't allow her to completely drop. Not yet. Not until she stopped.

Deafening noise filled the flight deck, as they raced across the Sound, water pounding on the aircraft, fighting to get in, trying to swallow plane and passengers. Bill held her out of the mouth of death for as long as he could.

A damn fantastic ride. He had never had this much fun. The battle now was to keep her upright, and it was a battle he wouldn't lose. "Come on, baby. Do this for daddy."

Holding the plane off the water took more strength than he'd expected. Working out had definitely been worth the effort. He'd planned well.

"Jesus Christ, hold on, baby," he yelled.

As the aircraft finally slowed he released the control yoke and she lunged, jerked and then stopped. He had no idea how long it would take for her to sink. But he knew the hand of God, with his dad by his side, would hold her up until everyone was off safely. He'd done well, and his father would be proud.

"Thanks for the help Dad."

CHAPTER 62

B ILL LIFTED THE P.A. handset and yelled, "Evacuate the aircraft! Evacuate the aircraft! Evacuate the aircraft!"

The EICAS should have indicated the doors were opening, but both screens were black. It didn't matter. He reached back and opened the cockpit door. They were evacuating, and water was flowing in. Too bad Ryan missed it all. His yellowed eyes were open wide. He'd overdosed. Bill said a silent prayer for the young man. "Your death is not in vain," Bill whispered.

Rescue boats were on them quickly and collected passengers. Everyone appeared calm. Nobody screamed, passengers or flight attendants. At least they had the confidence that a water landing could be safely made.

Bill read the emergency evacuation checklist. Not sure why, but it seemed like the thing to do. The engines had already been shut down, the bottles fired. There was not much more he could do. And then water reached the cockpit. Not more than a foot or so, but the force was strong, and raising rapidly.

He climbed out of his seat and walked down the aisle to make sure everyone was off the plane. The aircraft groaned as she settled into the sea. The silence after the roar of impact was haunting. Water was up to his thighs, flowing faster now. Outside, it crested the top of the windows. He had but minutes, and rushed back to the cockpit.

He swallowed four pills. They would take a blood test, and he needed to test positive. He unbuckled Ryan and pulled him out of his seat. He weighed what felt like a ton. "This is what they mean by dead weight," Bill said to his dad, and laughed.

Dragging Ryan out of the cockpit and down the aisle wasn't easy. The water level increased rapidly and was now chest high. Floating Ryan helped, but the force of the rushing water made it a struggle. It was hard for him to walk. He had to kick Ryan once when his leg caught between seats as he crossed to the over-wing exit. "Sorry, buddy."

Now less than two inches of daylight above the door existed, and was quickly being swallowed. The exit was submerged.

He'd planned on stepping onto the wing for the show, but they were already under water. He was swimming with an arm around Ryan. He sucked a deep breath from the last few inches of air captured at the top of the cabin, then ducked into the water with Ryan in tow and pushed through the emergency exit.

Shit. Ryan's foot caught again. Bill contemplated dropping him to save himself, but he was able to pull the first officer free. He owed him that much. He looked up and saw the shadow of a rescue boat. He kicked one final time and headed for the surface, his lungs burning. He popped out of the water, barely free of the plane that sank below him, gasping for air.

"I've got a him!" a voice yelled. A life ring was tossed to Bill, and he grabbed on. They pulled him to the boat, as he held tight to Ryan.

They pulled Ryan from him. He heard someone yell, "This one's dead," and "get the captain." They pulled Bill into the boat. His body shook violently, and someone wrapped a blanket around his shoulders.

"Captain, are you okay?"

He nodded then looked at Ryan's body covered with a blanket lying in the corner. Bill closed his eyes. When he opened them they were moist. Red. Sullen. He glanced at the marina that grew in size with each minute.

Everyone except for the overdosed first officer survived. His plane broke up, yes, but his landing had been better than the baby bus. He'd notified the flight attendants they were landing on water, and he'd pulled it off drugged. He'd become the new hero.

A seagull flew overhead. He didn't have the reflexes to duck when it dropped a load his direction, but the mess splattered on the seat beside him, another positive sign—they were all around him. Bill looked to shore. Hundreds of people stood waiting for him.

He thought he was going to vomit and took a deep breath.

Once Adams had been trained, hired and groomed, Bill had planned on Adams telling him which pilots were ready to kick the bucket, and use them. Why not have them take a plane in, since they were ending it all anyway? They could further his cause in the process. But the first pilot had backed out last minute and Bill couldn't risk him telling anyone. He had to be taken care of. That was when he'd decided to do it himself, with the help of his friends.

The process of readying them had taken eight years before he approached them. Time, playing with their schedules, getting drugs to their kids, setting their wives up—hell, Brian had been the toughest nut to crack. Bill had had to kill both of his kids to make his life bad enough to give it all up to murder a planeload of people. Bill had always convinced them that their problems were the airline's fault. It was easy, because it was true. He'd always been there for them, a shoulder to cry on in their times of desperation; he was their strongest support. Then he just gave them the home videos of their personal despair to nudge them over the edge.

The wind changed directions and salt water splashed across the bow of the boat, spraying all occupants, just as the rain began to fall—a sign from his father that they were on course. The same sign he'd sent two years prior. Bill closed his eyes remembering the moment when he and the guys made the pact to take back control of the industry.

THEY ALL STOOD in the graveyard staring into the hole that housed two caskets. The wind whipped through the trees, and the rain fell in sheets like razors. Brian sat in silence, broken, after everyone had gone—everyone expect for Bill, Aaron, Walt and Grant.

"I should have been home," Brian finally said. "I should have been here for them."

"It wasn't your fault man," Walt said. "You couldn't have done anything. Your hands were tied."

"I should have called in sick for Gods sake."

"The fucking company," Bill said, filling their glasses with Scotch, rain worked for the mixer. "You would've lost pay, and probably your job with all the sick calls you've had. How in the hell were you going to pay for their college without a job?"

Brian shook his head, but said nothing. His body began to shake as he choked on a sob. Bill knew that college tuition was the last of Brian's worries now. Those kids had meant everything to him. His life was worthless now.

"And you, Aaron, do you think it's your fault your wife is whoring around on you?" Bill drained his glass then said, "If you had a goddamned life— she'd be in your arms right now. And Walt. Grant. You both fucking lost your pensions. How are you going to survive retirement? You're not!" Bill refilled his glass. "It makes me so Goddamned mad."

"My wife found out about Jane," Grant spoke softly. "Nothing has been the same since, and it never will. I think my daughter knows. She's been so distant lately. But hell, what am I supposed to do? I'm on the road all the time, a man needs—"

"I know what I'm gong to do," Walt said. He downed his drink and added, "I bought a gun."

"What the fuck man?" Grant said.

"I'm ready to pull the fucking trigger myself," Aaron said. "I can't even pay for my son's rehab. He wouldn't be there if it wasn't for—"

"Guys," Bill said. "You're not alone. Adams told me there were eight pilot suicides last year. They all figured they were worth more dead than alive."

"I had no idea," Aaron said. "But I'll tell you, I wouldn't mind taking my life if I could take my CEO with me. What do I have left? Nothing."

"Here, here," Bill said. "At least your son could get the best care, and those little granddaughters of yours might have a chance at a decent life."

"Jacobs, you better damn well win that election in a couple years. You'll change things."

"That I will. But I don't think it will be enough. I could win, but then it would take me another five years to get to the national office. Can you guys survive for the next seven years? I don't think so. God forbid where we'll be then, where the entire industry will be. My father's rolling over in his grave as I speak."

Bill tossed back his drink. "We have to do something, and we have to do it now. Make a stand like never before. Show the public our value. Then our companies will have no choice but to realize that we are their bottom line. Their lifeline."

"Anything. I'll do fucking anything," Brian said, opening a

second bottle and refilling his glass. "I thought my life was over when my wife left me and took everything. But now my babies are in the dirt. Fuck!" He began to sob, again, and Bill knelt in the mud and wrapped his arms around him.

"If it's the last thing I do, I will make it right for you," Bill said, patting Brian's back.

"What in the hell can we do?" Walt asked.

"I know what we'll do," Bill said. "If they want to take our lives, then we'll fight—blood for blood. We'll show them who's flying their fucking planes!" Bill stood.

"What do you mean?" Aaron asked.

"We're fucking going to crash our planes! One by one—we'll show them who's in control. The companies have stripped us of everything. Hell, I watched my dad blow his face off because of what his airline did to him." Bill paced. "I'd thought the union would clean things up, and they did for a while. But since deregulation, the tide shifted. And what in the hell is the union doing now? Nothing! They're all in bed with management. What are the companies doing? Cutting our work-rules! Stealing our pay! Killing our families!"

"Kill the passengers?" Grant said.

"People die in war," Bill said. "It's not personal. Besides, there are far worse things than death." He placed a hand on Brian's shoulder.

"Bill, your life is great. You're at the strongest airline, you have a beautiful wife and your kids aren't fucked up like mine," Aaron said. "Why would you do this?"

"I told you thirty-seven years ago I wouldn't let you down. Hell, I convinced you all to become pilots. If it hadn't been for me, you might have found normal jobs, and been home every night… able to provide for your families. I owe it to you. I promised my life to you all, and I keep my word."

"You owe me nothing," Aaron said. "I owe you everything. I owe you my life."

"We all do," Walt said lifting his glass. "I have to admit, it's been a great ride,"

"It has," Grant said. "And, if it hadn't been for corporate greed, we'd still be riding high."

"Good things come to an end," Brian said, kicking dirt into the hole. "But killing the passengers?"

"Do you think anyone thought of the thousands killed in Nam?" Bill asked. "No. 'Casualties of war,' they said. Well, this is war. Do any of you have anything better to live for?"

"I don't," Brian said, standing taller. "It would be my honor to show them they have no right to destroy our lives."

"If you guys are serious, I'm in," Aaron said. "I've been living on borrowed time since Nam. I would never have made it out if it hadn't been for you, Bill."

"None of us would," Walt added.

"To Bill," Grant said, extending his arm. They all clinked glasses.

THEY HIT A WAKE and jolted Bill, and his stomach rolled. He leaned over the edge and vomited, and the driver slowed the boat to a stop.

They all owed him from Nam—that was true. And it was Bill who stood by them when the airlines destroyed their lives and took their families. He loved them all. They were his brothers, and brothers did anything for the other. They had all proven their loyalty to him.

Eight years. Destruction of their families. A dying economy. And an airline industry that had gone astray—they *were* worth more dead than alive. With patience and time, anything was possible. He'd miss them, but it wasn't as if they were involved in each other's daily lives. They'd all agreed to keep their friendship special and separate from their normal, everyday lives. They'd meet four times a year, or when necessity dictated. Bill wiped his mouth and his rescue boat continued to move across the now choppy waters.

The industry took their lives. Executives stole their pensions. They were left hopeless. Hell, any pilot could've crashed on his own, and in the first two accidents, they had. Pilots sitting reserve and not flying set that stage. Bill cringed at the thought, but it wasn't enough. Nobody cared.

How the hell could a pilot not fly for five months and maintain proficiency? They couldn't. Bounces in the simulator every three months, a currency joke, was like kissing your sister. The union loved it—more pilots meant more dues. The board of directors loved it—they'd always have pilots on call and never have to cancel a flight.

Management knew pilots needed to fly to be safe. They also needed more training than what was being provided by the airlines. Bill did the math—annual training cost millions more to their bottom line than a plane or two going down. The public was kept in the blind. A series of accidents at the hands of the pilots was exactly what was needed—it was the only way.

Bill controlled the next level of destiny and his friends died heroes. They'd left their families financially well off—those who had families remaining. Brian left his life insurance to Medicine on the Move, in Ghana. They stuck it to the airline executives that screwed them over, and made the world a safer place.

When his stomach was under control, he opened his eyes and glanced at what was left of his aircraft—the tail. Then he reached into his pocket for the bottle of pills.

Getting sick had not been anticipated, and he needed to test positive for the drugs. When nobody was looking he popped three pills into his mouth.

The power he felt when one of his planes crashed was unlike anything he'd ever experienced. He'd had no idea. After the first crash he wondered if his dad had felt the same sense of power in the final seconds before the bullet exploded through his face.

To have the lives of so many in his hands, and take them out with one blow, was nothing short of spectacular. Surprisingly, he felt an unusual sense of disappointment with the accidents ending. He knew his flight would be the best. He had looked forward to this day, since the day he'd conceived the concept. Little did his friends know that he would be both the victim *and* the hero.

His political opportunities were now unlimited—a thought that had grown with the downing of each plane.

The wind picked up and he shivered. Kristen had actually done him a great favor by quitting early. He looked up to heaven and silently thanked her. Then there was Simone. He needed to clean up every connection to his past life in order to move forward with time and energy to do what was needed.

The boat docked. Camera crews and police swarmed the parking lot. He dropped the blanket, displaying his four stripes. The rain was now nothing but a cold mist.

Walker approached him and extended his hand. "Thank you."

Bill shook it. "I was just doing my job, sir. I only wish I had been there…" Walker raised a hand for him to stop, and he complied with a knowing nod of the head.

"It's over now," Walker said. "Thanks to you and your bride."

Yes, it is, for the time being, he thought when Kathryn approached, and stood by his side. He wrapped an arm around her and held tight, then kissed her head. Her hair was damp from the rain, and he could still smell the sweet scent of blood. The media stuck microphones in his face, and the questions came at him from all directions.

He raised his hand and said, "Ladies and gentlemen, I'll meet you here tomorrow afternoon at 1400 and answer all your questions." He glanced at his plane and watched its last breath. Then he collapsed.

"Bill. Oh my God." Kathryn knelt at his side, and yelled, "Get an ambulance."

Bill held still. Listened and waited. Enjoying the drugs as they warmed his body and encouraged his eyelids to remain closed.

The entire crew would be taken to the hospital for routine blood tests. The national APO president would be flying in from Washington, D.C. to brief him, and the union attorneys would tell him what to say. He'd listen and agree, and then say whatever he wanted to, anyway. But for now, he played victim.

He was placed in an ambulance, and Kathryn joined him. Once the doors were closed and they were on their way to hospital, Bill opened his eyes.

"Lie still sir," a paramedic said.

Bill ignored him and sat upright, and reached for Kathryn's hand. He nodded to her head. "That must have hurt. What happened?"

"Adams killed Darby, then hit me." And then she began to cry. He was moved by her emotion, and wrapped her in his arms. It was the least he could do to give her comfort during her final hours. She'd been a good wife, and she'd played her part well. But Bill didn't need to be told about the result of his handiwork. He had called the hospital and confirmed Darby's death. There would be no loose ends.

Soon Kathryn would be visiting her mother for a job well done.

CHAPTER 63
THURSDAY

BILL AND KATHRYN were released from the hospital and arrived at the pier in time for Bill's press conference, despite their doctor's objections.

"Can you give me a moment?" Bill asked Kathryn. He walked the length of the pier and left his wife standing in the parking lot. He gazed out at where his airplane had gone down. The sun had finally broken free from an overcast day and was setting over Vashon Island. The bay made excellent footage as a backdrop.

Just as he'd anticipated, they'd taken him and his crew to the hospital to have their blood drawn. The doctor had required Bill to stay for observation overnight because of the drugs in his system. They'd given him a double room so Kathryn could stay with him after they determined she had a concussion.

It was nice to have her there. She'd been full of information and filled in the missing details of the previous day's events. Knowing he was a free man had created a far more relaxing night. And the theory about him supporting Adams in college, "out of guilt for his father killing Adams's dad," was priceless.

Weeks ago, Bill had told Walker to hire Kathryn, but not for another month. He also never told Walker to fire her, and McAllister never would have done that on his own. Not that it mattered now, but he didn't like whatever game Walker was playing. Bill's orders were to be obeyed, and Walker knew that better than anyone. But Walker had suffered enough, and Bill still held leverage over him—he would be useful in the future.

Kathryn also said that Darby's death was her fault and that she should've figured out the Adams connection sooner. He'd told her that everyone makes mistakes.

Bill heard activity behind him, but he didn't turn. Instead, he glanced toward the yachts and then he thought of Simone, the last piece. He'd already figured out how to dispose of her—everything was coming to a close nicely.

A hand touched his shoulder. He acknowledged with a nod and turned toward the crowd that had filled the dock behind him. Slowly walking the length of the pier, he stepped in front of the group. Kathryn stood silently to his left. A microphone was stuck in his hand, and he stepped forward to speak.

"Ladies and gentlemen, thank you for being here. I wish I had better news, but it appears that our psychiatrist was playing God with our pilots. We hired him to assist with emotional issues stemming from the financial crises of the airlines, but what we didn't know was that he had an emotional crisis of his own.

"In 1964 he watched his father die at the hands of the passengers on a flight my father piloted. When I discovered that it was my father who had been the captain on that flight... I tried to make amends. I personally paid for his education, and I supported him in the psychiatric field in hopes that the process would help heal his anger and that he could, in turn, help others. It worked. He had been the best."

Bill shook his head and dropped his shoulders for impact with the weight of the situation. "So I thought. He scored the top in his class, and I encouraged our union to hire him. He was a brother to me." Bill paused and straightened slightly. "Our union attorneys tell me that I am limited as to what I can say, but I would like to answer your questions the best that I can."

"Captain Jacobs, were you seeing Dr. Adams for assistance?" a reporter shouted from the back of the crowd.

"Yes, I was. Next?" Bill pointed to another reporter.

"Is it true that you've been paying for Adams's mother to live in an expensive nursing home?"

"Yes. As I stated, I felt responsible for my father's involvement on that flight. Because of his ignorance about epilepsy, a good man died. It was the least I could do. God bless both their souls."

He pointed to another hand. "Captain Jacobs, do you blame the industry for any of these crashes, or is it solely the hand of a psychopath?" Finally a question worth answering. It had only been a matter of time.

"The industry brought our pilots to Adams in a receptive mode, enabling him to take advantage of them. If our pilots hadn't been facing bankruptcy, excessive fatigue from their schedules, and concern for their jobs, all high stress issues that forced them to behave in ways they normally wouldn't have..." He paused and took Kathryn's hand. "We never would've needed, or sought, Adams's help. The answer to that question is yes. The industry is to blame for these accidents. Adams was the person who swung the blade, but it was the industry that gave him the axe."

"Is it true that the doctor used hypnosis as well as drugs on the pilots?"

"Yes. He gave us drugs dressed as supplements, which impacted our judgment and cognition, causing hallucinations. Not only did these drugs impact our abilities, but he also used aggressive forms of hypnotherapy, all of which were overtly effective due to fatigue, stress, and our weakened mindsets. I was placed under many times."

"How long do you think the effects of the hypnosis and drugs are going to be with you? Are you safe to fly?"

Bill laughed. "Well, ladies and gentlemen, I was able to land a 757 in Puget Sound with no engines and Temazepam and Psilocybin running through my veins. What do you think?"

The audience rumbled, and cameras flashed. Soon, they'd verify that he'd been the one to shut down two perfectly good engines, but the drugs in his system and his visits with the doctor would justify that behavior.

"Now, if there aren't any more questions, I'd like to take my bride home. We're picking up our daughters from camp tomorrow, and we'd like to spend the evening alone. Thank you."

Bill set the microphone on the railing and took Kathryn's hand and they walked together down the dock, toward their car. He knew the cameras rolled. He wanted the visual of them walking into the sunset to be broadcast on national television. He helped Kathryn into his car and then waved.

"I'm starving," he said as he backed the car out of the parking lot. "Think we could finally have that quiet dinner before the girls come home? We have a lot to discuss."

A short fifteen-minute drive later, and they pulled into their driveway. He put the car into park and turned the key to off, then turned toward her and took both her hands in his.

"Sweetheart, I am so sorry for everything I've put you through. There have been things that I'm embarrassed to say that I've done. I've never known why the behavior, but now...with Adams, well, lets just say that it's all going to stop now that he's gone. I love you and the girls more than you can imagine." Bill closed his eyes and when he opened them, they were moist. Then he began to cry.

He'd sensed Kathryn's distance at the press conference, and something emitted from her pores—suspicion. Fear. Hatred. He wasn't sure, but her silence on the drive home told him something was notably off. He had to take care of one little detail, and he'd be damned if he came home to find Kathryn and her suitcase gone. That was not going to work. There would be only one way she'd be able to leave him, and he already planned on that.

He wiped his eyes. "I'm sorry sweetheart. I don't know what came over me. I'm just sorry for everything. Please, give us a chance to talk. I owe you much more of an apology than in a car."

Bill placed his hand over Kathryn's and squeezed. "I'm going to run and get a couple steaks and a bottle of wine. Then I have to drop by the office for ten minutes—I promise not a minute longer. But I'll make *you* dinner tonight." He kissed her on the cheek and spoke softly. "Go inside, call Jackie and see how she's doing then climb into a hot bath and relax. I'll be back before you know it, then tomorrow we'll go get the girls together."

Chapter 64

Hot water filled the tub while Kathryn looked into the mirror and carefully removed the bandage from her head. If Adams had used the poker instead of the broom, her daughters would have lost their mother. Amazingly she had fallen safely to the floor with nothing but an open wound, and a minor concussion. But Darby was dead.

The tragedy that had befallen her friends tore a hole in her soul so wide she doubted it would ever mend. How could she live without the joy that Greg and Darby brought to her world? She fought tears, but failed as they escaped and slid from her lashes. She sucked in a deep breath and stood tall, then wiped both her cheeks. She had to hold it together for the girls, and for Chris and Jackie—she had to be strong for them all.

Kathryn climbed into the tub, and sank deep within the water. But the water's warmth didn't stop the trembling, or the ache inside her gut that burned its way to her heart. She raised both hands and covered her face, trying to maintain her composure.

"Darby. Greg. I am so sorry," she whispered, fighting the pain that sucked the air from her lungs. It was too much to take. The week of exhaustion and the death of her friends overtook her, and she allowed the weight of emotion to break free. Her tears came in gushes and her sobs in jagged heaves.

She cried for the children Darby would never have, and the

one that Greg had left behind. She wanted to scream for the lives ripped from her heart. Her tears flowed for the loss that her girls would face. As hard as she had tried, she couldn't protect them from death.

She never wanted them to face the sorrow that she had faced as a child, but she'd failed.

"Why?" she asked. But there was no answer to that question. Life was cruel. Damn cruel. She'd wasted years trying to figure out why things happened the way they did. Trying to make sense of a world that took no mercy. She'd married the perfect man and made the perfect life, but that, too, was false.

She had no control over anything. Nobody did. Life just sucked those you loved away, and spit you out to live with the heartache that followed.

Visions of Darby lying in the tub filled with bloody water mingled with those of finding her mother. She pulled her legs close to her body and hugged them tight, and cried even harder.

Today was the anniversary of her mother's suicide. Kathryn had survived another year.

Despite everything that had happened, she found a renewed strength with that thought. She took three deep breaths. Life was about to start anew, and she would ride it strong into the future. She'd be the mother her daughters deserved, and the strength that Jackie needed. If life wanted a fight, she wouldn't back down. As Darby would say, "The battle is on."

Kathryn reached over the tub to her phone, and dialed Jackie's number. "How are you doing?" she asked when Jackie answered.

Jackie was crying.

"Sweetie, is your Mom with you?"

"She is," Jackie said between sobs.

Kathryn closed her eyes and pinched the bridge of her nose, feeling her friend's pain. "Do you want Bill and I to pick up Chris tomorrow?" she asked, wishing she could do more.

"No. Thanks. Mom is going with me, and then we'll stay at her house." Jackie's voice broke, again. "I have no idea how to tell Chris. I miss Greg so much, and I can't believe Darby is gone, and... if I would've lost you—"

"But you didn't. I'm right here, and together we'll get through this." Kathryn was thankful Jackie had her mother with her for support. "We need to dry our eyes and be strong for our kids tomorrow."

"Yeah, we do." Jackie agreed.

After they said goodbye, Kathryn closed the phone and dropped it on the towel. She shut her eyes and said a prayer for Darby, then one for Greg, and another for Jackie and Chris.

How am I going to tell the girls what happened? She couldn't imagine. Thank God she didn't have to tell them their dad was dead too. Fresh tears stung her eyes, but this time she kept them at bay.

She had worked hard to not end up like her mother, depressed to the point of no return. Kathryn had blamed her dad for the divorce, but now she knew there was so much more. Neither the crash nor the divorce had been the reason for her mother taking her own life. Her uncle was possibly the reason her mother hadn't done it sooner. Unfortunately they would never know the truth.

With Uncle Derek gone, her mother didn't know how to go on. But she wasn't her mother. And she did know how to go on. It was time to forgive herself. Her mother's death wasn't her fault.

Kathryn touched the lump on her head and winced at the sting. She allowed anger to push the sorrow aside, and it pounded with each throb. *How could Adams have killed all those people? What kind of monster would do that?* She hated him with every part of her being. He was supposed to have helped the pilots deal with life, not end it. She thought of Darby.

But why would he have attacked Darby in her home? He was anything but stupid. Why wouldn't he have made sure she was on the flight? She was supposed to see him that morning, and fly the trip. Why would he go to her house and inject her with drugs to kill her? Something didn't add up.

Maybe Darby hadn't responded to the drugs he'd given everyone else. No. Darby wasn't on drugs of any kind. Kathryn would have known if she had been. There was also no way that doctor had hypnotized her. Besides, why would Dr. Adams have left evidence behind? Maybe she startled him when she pounded on the door. But he'd knocked her out. He would have cleaned up his mess— unless he heard the sirens approaching.

She shuddered when she thought of his body falling on top of her. As it turned out, the syringe on his desk was filled with a sedative, nothing lethal. Yet he had files saying she was crazy. There was only one place those could have come from—Bill.

She closed her eyes and thought about Bill's press conference. Thank God nobody asked about Kristen Walker. She still didn't know where Simone fit into the current picture, but she didn't care. Her marriage was dead. Despite whatever excuse Bill would create, or his professed love, they were done. Simone could have him.

Kathryn slid into the water until it reached her chin. She lifted her toe and stuck it into the dripping faucet. She thought about Adams's brain splattering on her face, then slid under the water and cringed when the water stung her head.

She emerged and wiped bubbles from her eyes. She was thankful she'd gotten to Bill in time, and that he hadn't taken as many drugs as the first officer, or hundreds of people would have been killed. Thousands if he'd crashed into the city.

She tried to wipe out the vision of the first officer being pulled from the water, with eyes open, and head hanging back. He was the only pilot of all the accident victims who'd actually overdosed on… What was it that Bill had called the drugs? Temaze something and Psilocyber, she couldn't remember exactly. "Oh shit!" She dried her hands then reached for her cell and dialed Samantha.

John had rehired Samantha after Kathryn had pleaded her case. Walker had been made a hero for solving the crimes, thanks to Kathryn, so he'd forgiven all transgressions against her and Sam.

"Hey, babe, you looked good on the tube today," Sam said. "Thanks for getting me my job back and— "

"Do you know if the drug tests came back from the crew?" Kathryn asked, interrupting her.

"I'm good, but not that good. They just invited me back today, and I haven't even gone to work yet. Why?"

"I want to know what Adams was giving the flight crews."

"Sure, I'll call you right back."

Kathryn ran the details of the conference through her mind. Moments later, her cell rang and startled her. "What'd you find?"

"They were given Temazepam or Psilocybin. You know that Psilocybin is nasty hallucinating shit, and the other crap just kind of makes you sleep, but too much and you don't wake up. Regardless, they had the tests done late this afternoon, about the time the press conference started."

"Thanks, Sam. I really appreciate your help," she said, glancing at the Tylenol bottle on the counter. She closed her phone and dropped it on the floor beside the tub.

"Hey honey," Bill said from the doorway.

Kathryn jumped. "My God, you scared me." How long had he been standing there? The way he watched her scared her on a level she'd never felt before.

He laughed. "I didn't mean to frighten you, sweetheart. I wanted to let you know dinner will be ready in fifteen minutes. I'm grilling steak." He handed her a glass of red wine.

His best friend, his lover, and Darby had all died in the last two days, and the man that he'd supported all of his adult life, Adams, had supposedly killed them along with hundreds of people, and Bill was more relaxed than she'd ever seen him.

He leaned against the counter and stared.

She took a sip, and he smiled. "Thank you," she said. "This is exactly what I need."

"Take your time, sweetheart. Dinner will be ready when you are."

After he left the room, she smelled the wine. It smelled like wine, not that it wouldn't. But if her suspicions were correct, she had ample reason to be afraid.

She set the glass outside the tub and sank into the water that was growing colder by the minute. Bill was a womanizer, yes, and a jerk, but a murderer? She lifted the glass and smelled the wine again. She held it up to the light then stepped out of her tub and poured the contents into the water, creating a crimson spot, then pulled the plug on the drain.

CHAPTER 65

KATHRYN DIDN'T BOTHER drying her hair, and pulled it into a ponytail. She slipped on an old U.C. sweatshirt and a pair of gray sweat pants with a University of Washington Husky on the butt. The pants were from Darby while the sweatshirt held memories from her college days, back when she had planned to conquer the world. These clothes had brought her both luck and courage over the years, but they'd also brought her the comfort of a security blanket.

She sat on the floor and pulled socks onto her feet. Her tennis shoes screamed at her to put them on, walk out the door, and run like hell for safety. The thought of going to Jackie's house crossed her mind, but she couldn't do that to her friend, not now. Kathryn contemplated calling Linda. No. Not yet—Linda would never believe her. She wasn't sure anybody would.

Kathryn was trapped with a husband who could be a mass murderer, the same man the entire world thought to be a hero. She needed to find the truth, and she wouldn't let anything stop her. If it was the last thing she did, she would make sure the right person paid for Darby and Greg's deaths.

Videos of Bill surfacing with his dead first officer and arriving onto the dock filled television screens worldwide. He'd blinded everyone from seeing the monster that he was. She paced her bedroom, contemplating what to do.

Dr. Adams and Bill had created a paper trail pronouncing her unstable. Bill had written a note that he was worried about her and didn't want her to do anything drastic. They had brought files to the hospital from Adams' office that indicated her instability and, with Bill's permission, they had a psychiatrist visit her for an assessment. Not to mention, half the airline saw her theatrics at the memorial and they'd all testify she was unstable.

Bullshit. It was all bullshit. She reached for, and opened, her bottle of Tylenol, then stopped, put the lid back on, and threw it across the room. She was taking that bastard down.

If she told anyone what she suspected, they would say she was just a woman scorned. Nobody would take her seriously, except for John. Maybe. Unfortunately, he, too, was enthralled with the hero of the hour.

Pacing the length of the room, she ran the options through her mind. She had no proof that Bill had known what Adams was up to, and he held too much respect among the pilot group worldwide. The Secretary of Homeland Security had personally congratulated him— the man he'd battled for years. His only enemy, Walker, now viewed him with admiration.

The thought of him being the world's hero made her want to vomit. He did save hundreds, if not thousands, of lives by landing his 757 safely on Puget Sound instead of the city. But that show was a little too staged. The noose was his knowledge of the drugs.

The reports hadn't been released until his press conference had started, and there was no way for him to know what drugs the pilots had been given unless he and Adams were in this together. Bill was involved; she had no doubt. But at what level, she wasn't sure.

She sat heavily on the bed. She wanted to scream. There was something she was missing. A connection. A clue. She knew if she asked the right questions the answers would come.

Kathryn breathed deep and cleared her mind. She breathed in three slow cleansing breaths, relaxing her mind and body as she did.

Why would Bill and Adams do this? How did drugged pilots get through security unnoticed? How could they possibly function? How in the world could they start up an airplane and take it into the sky if they were drugged? How could Bill and Adams pull this off?

Mind control was a powerful thing. But nothing made sense. She pushed the 'how' from her mind and focused on the 'who.' The pilots.

Their profession connected them. Their union connected them. They were all connected to the doctor. That's it! They were connected to Bill.

Kathryn dialed Linda's number.

CHAPTER 66

KATHRYN CREPT DOWN the stairs and past the kitchen. Bill was cooking, and something smelled wonderful. He was humming as she slipped quietly down the hall and into his office. Using only the light from the hallway, she located his flight bag. Linda had confirmed that her husband had been in Nam around the time Bill had—she needed to see that picture, again.

He hadn't taken his flight bag on the flight. But that meant nothing since he'd been called out unexpectedly. She knelt at the bag, selecting the numbers Darby had figured out, but the lock didn't open. *Shit.* She began spinning the numbers. Birthdays. Their anniversary. Nothing worked. Then she spun in 1004. October 4th, the date Bill landed on Puget Sound, and the lock popped open.

Darby had taken the pictures of the naked women but left the others behind. She reached into the side pocket and removed the envelope. She flipped through the photos until she came to the shot of Bill and four other men. Soldiers. They couldn't have been more than eighteen years old. Vietnam. Drafted. She turned the photo over. Five names were written on the back. Grant, Walt, Aaron, Brian, and Bill—the captains of each flight that had crashed. All dead, except for Bill.

She quietly closed the bag. This was all she needed to prove he was involved. All the accidents were connected. Connected to Bill. Then she heard him whistling. He was coming down the hall.

Holding her breath, she prayed. *Please, God, don't let him come in here.* But her prayer wasn't answered.

Bill walked into his office, his back to her, as he stopped at his desk six feet away. She crouched beside the bag and held her breath, motionless. But he never turned on the light, and he didn't see her. He grabbed something off his desk and returned to the kitchen. She let out her breath.

She needed to get this photo to John, but she was trapped. Her keys and purse were sitting on the kitchen table. She could climb out the back window and run to the neighbor's, but would the photo be enough proof in a court of law? If what she suspected was true, her daughters would be in danger without an airtight case against him.

Kathryn dialed John's number and he answered on the first ring.

"John," Kathryn whispered. "It's Bill. He's behind the crashes."

"Are you sure?"

"Yes."

"Where are you?"

"In Bill's office holding a photo of him from Vietnam. He's standing with four other men, in uniform—each of the captains from the last four crashes."

"They'll say it's a coincidence."

"Bill knew the name of the drugs during the press conference. Samantha told me that the report, identifying the drugs, wasn't available until just before the press conference had started. There's no way he could've known unless..."

"I knew it! I thought Adams was in too nice a package—syringe in Darby's bathroom, drugged pilots, and bottles with the doctor's name on the label. They weren't actually prescription bottles, so why the name on the label? The biggest problem I had was with Adams's filing system. He'd had files for each pilot, and those that had been involved in accidents were filed in a cabinet separate from the others. Bill and his first officer were both in that filing cabinet with the other pilots that had crashed, and—"

"How did Adams know that scheduling would call Bill if Darby no-showed."

"Exactly," John said. "Adams had to know before that last flight that Bill would be the captain. There's no way he'd have that information unless someone fed it to him. Where's Bill now?"

"Kitchen."

"Can you get out of there?"

"If you want to pick me up on the side street I could try to get past the kitchen and sneak out the back. But before I do, I want to know one thing— is this photo enough to convict Bill?"

"No."

"That's what I was afraid of."

"It's all circumstantial. But it may be enough to knock him down a few pegs and create suspicion to open an investigation. But other than that, it won't do anything. He's a powerful man. Kat... we have your house wired. We've been watching him, and—"

"*What?* You've been listening to—"

"I'm sorry. I'll explain everything later, but now I need you to listen to me. He'll say, or do something wrong, we'll get him. But you need to get out of there. "

Damn right we'll get him. But getting out was the last thing Kathryn needed to do, she needed to protect her daughters.

"John, I need you to call my dad and tell him the girls are at Camp Waskowitz, and go pick them up tonight. Tell them that I love them all."

"Kathryn, what in the hell are you doing?"

"What's your fax number? I'll send you the photo."

John gave her the number and then said, "Get out of there. Now!"

There was no way Kathryn would allow Bill to walk away from this. There was only one thing to do, and she knew exactly what that was.

"John, I have to go."

CHAPTER 67

KATHRYN COULD WAIT for Bill to go upstairs looking for her, then grab her keys and run out the kitchen door. She could be out of the driveway before he made it back downstairs. But if she did that, her daughters would be in harm's way. John was right—Bill was a powerful man. A powerful man who'd painted a picture of his wife's instability. Nobody would believe her, and he'd take the girls. She knew exactly what that meant.

She had only one option—get a confession on record.

Kathryn tiptoed to the desk and moved the chair close to the door. Then turned the light on, and closed and locked the door. She tucked the chair under the doorknob as quietly as she could. But it wasn't quiet enough.

Within minutes Bill was at the door pounding on it.

"Kathryn what are you doing in there?"

"I'll be out in a few minutes."

Bill wiggled the doorknob. "God dammit! Open this door!"

Kathryn had already typed John's Fax number into the machine, and was placing the photo face down when Bill quieted. She pressed send. The machine beeped, and then the digits clicked off through all seven numbers, and stopped. She picked up the receiver—dead.

He'd cut the phone line.

Kathryn pulled a book off his shelf and put the photo inside, and replaced it just before Bill was back at the door, fighting the lock.

"Honey, open the door. You can't get out."

"The police are on their way. You won't get away with this."

"Get away with what darling? I have absolutely no idea what you're talking about." Then he began to laugh.

"What in the hell did you do, Bill?"

"What did *I* do? Don't be so damned naïve. I made the world stand up and take notice. I started a chain reaction to take back our industry, and ultimately make the airline industry safer. Now open the god-damned door!"

"By crashing planes?"

"How in the hell did you think we could fix this problem? The government would never agree to anything. We had to take control."

"Crashing planes is not a way to fix the airline industry."

"Like hell it's not," Bill said, and then the locked popped open, but the chair held the door in place. "Open this fucking door!"

"So you bribed Adams to help you drug your friends?"

"You think Adams could've drugged the pilots?" Bill said, ramming his shoulder into the door. "No, darling, I molded and positioned him where he could be most useful. I fed him clients, and he fed me details. Then I set him up to take the fall. Like you, he was nothing but a great opportunity, putty in my hands. But every opportunity has its useful life."

Kathryn glanced around the room for something to defend herself with. Anything. She pulled drawers open and found a pair of scissors then grasped them tightly behind her back. "All those people... and Greg... How could you?"

"How could *I*? You forget there are things far worse than death, my dear. What I did was orchestrate a symphony that will eventually make this industry safer and give pride back to our profession. I took action against CEOs who suck our pilots' souls dry and spit out their empty carcasses daily. I created a business plan complete with myself as the leader. Greg needed to die."

Bill threw his body into the door and it cracked, and the chair shifted. Kathryn moved behind his desk to create a barrier between them. "Adams was always part of the exit strategy, just as Kristen was."

"What does your girlfriend have to do with any of this?"

"How in the hell do you think I could get Walker to kill Adams? I knew Daddy would take revenge on her murderer."

"It was you who killed Darby and hit me over the head?"

"One of my finer moments."

"You're not sick, you're the Devil!"

He laughed as he came crashing through the door. "You have it so wrong, my love. I am not the Devil. I'm God, walking in hand with my father."

"God? You think taking lives makes you God?" Kathryn moved sideways, as Bill sauntered toward his desk.

"I now have a platform for re-regulation and as it turns out, the key to the front door of the White House."

He's going to kill me, then my girls. "I won't say anything. Nobody would believe me, anyway." If she could keep him talking, maybe she'd have a chance to escape.

"You're right, nobody would believe you." Bill slowly moved right, and she moved left, the desk between them. "You're psychotic and clinically depressed. You were taking the Tylenol that everyone thinks Adams had given to me, which added to your hallucinations. Had you drunk your wine in the tub, we wouldn't even be having this little dance. You'd have fallen asleep, and when I found you, your wrists would've been cut, just like your mother's. Like mother, like daughter. Then the poor, grieving husband who found his wife after she killed herself would have all his problems solved."

"I'd never kill myself."

"Don't count on that. You've been depressed. Your husband had multiple affairs, and he humiliated you on national television. You failed miserably as a mother. You were fired from your job. Your best friend and lover were murdered. Of course you have nothing to live for. Lately, I've been very concerned for you. Even Adams had his concerns. Everything has been documented."

"Yeah, by a 'known' psychopath. Your alibi just killed my conviction. Besides, I have everything to live for. I have my daughters. And Greg was never my lover, you prick."

Bill moved further right, and she sidestepped left, ready to change directions at any moment. The desk between them provided her safety, but the path to the door was opening as Bill moved slowly behind the desk, pushing her to the front.

"It's time to take a bath, darling," Bill said.

She grabbed the lamp and threw it at him. He ducked giving her the opportunity to head for the door. She'd held on tight to the scissors as she ran.

Bill was like a wildcat and chased her. She made it to the kitchen and he pounced on her from behind, knocking her to the floor. She hit her face on the kitchen table on the way down then lay motionless. Bill stood then kicked her foot—she didn't move. She waited for her opportunity.

He knelt by her side then rolled her onto her back and she screamed, "You bastard!" And drove the scissors into his chest.

Bill fell back, then pulled them out and began to laugh, raising them high over his head. He was on the downward swing when Kathryn rolled, and kicked his hand knocking the scissors to the floor, then she kicked him in the face.

"I *take* exercise classes you bastard!" she said, as he fell backward, knocking his head against the side of the kitchen cabinet.

Kathryn scrambled to her feet. Bill was lying motionless on the floor, blood seeping from the hole in his chest, and she reached for her keys. But the room began to spin and she dropped to her knees. The last thing she heard was ringing her ears before blackness closed in and took control.

CHAPTER 68
MONDAY

KATHRYN RELAXED into the touch that gently stroked her forehead. The fingers were rough, and the subtle odor of aircraft oil mixed with Old Spice filled her senses and heart.

"*Daddy.*"

"I'm here, Princess."

Instinctively, her hand went to her face as she remembered the night before, and she flinched. Her head ached. She worked to open her eyes, but the lights hurt. She squinted, and then the most joyous sound she could have imagined filled her soul.

"Look, she's awake," Jennifer said. "Mommy."

"Yippee!" Jessica yelled. "I knew she'd be fine."

Her daughters were okay, and they were both with her. She was alive. Kathryn closed her eyes and said a silent prayer of gratitude.

Jenny laid her head on her chest and said, "I love you, mommy." She placed a hand on her daughter's back and rubbed. This was the same little girl who'd yelled that she hated her. She didn't have to imagine how those words would have impacted Jenny's life had she died.

Never for a moment did she believe Jenny hated her. With Jenny's head over her heart, she realized her own mother had known she was loved, even though Kathryn had said those hateful words, too.

"Girls," she said, first looking at Jennifer, and then at Jessica, "I love you both so much." She smiled and fought tears at the same time. She spread her arms wide, and Jessica melted into her embrace. "But how did…"

"Hey, sweetie," Jackie said. "Mom and I picked them up when we got Chris." She tucked a strand of hair behind Kathryn's ear. "How are you feeling? You've been out for three days, and we've all been really worried."

"I think I've had better days," Kathryn said. "Bill?" she mouthed over the girl's head.

"Alive."

Kathryn closed her eyes, and held her daughters close.

"Hey, girl," Sam said, sitting quietly on the windowsill.

"Sam, I…"

"If I'd known you were going to be so stupid, I wouldn't have told you shi…" She looked at the kids. "Um… I would have called John instead."

"Knock, knock. Can anyone join this parteee?"

"Darby!" Kathryn cried. Her head spun and if she hadn't known better, she'd thought she'd died and gone to heaven. "They told me you were dead. I knew it couldn't be true."

"Are you kidding me? It takes a lot more to knock me off than your psycho husband. Sorry, girls." She bent down and hugged Kathryn. "I'll tell you everything later," she whispered.

Chris stood by his mother's side, and Kathryn saw the image of Greg. "Oh, honey, I'm so sorry about your dad." Her words felt empty. Chris looked at his feet, his emotions raw, and her heart ached for him. Jackie placed her hand on his back and pulled him close. Chris was giving Jackie strength and a reason to survive.

She looked at her dad, her friends, her daughters, and she

couldn't believe they were all there. Together.

"Look who we have awake," John said entering the room. He bent down and kissed her forehead.

"John… thank you…" She choked back the frog caught in her throat. "I want you to meet my friends, and my daughters. Girls, this is…"

"Uncle John." Jenny ran into his arms.

John laughed. "These darling little girls kind of adopted me into the family, I hope you don't mind." John shook her dad's hand.

How could she mind? They could've had their grandpa, too. Looking at her dad, her eyes filled. "I'm sorry," she whispered. He smiled and nodded then reached for Jessica, who melted into his arms. He kissed the top of her head.

"I guess you already met my friends, too?" Kathryn said.

"Oh, we've all met him," Jackie said. "He's the one who found you. He probably saved your life."

"Why'd you tell me that Darby was dead?" Kathryn asked John.

"Hey, guys," Jackie said to the kids. "Let's go get some cocoa."

The girls promised to bring her back a cup before they skipped out of the room.

When they were out of earshot, John said, "I'm sorry for lying to you. At the time, we didn't know who'd attacked her. Thanks to you forcing the autopsy on Greg, we discovered he was murdered with potassium chloride, and Darby had been injected with the same. We thought it safest to call it a death to prevent someone from coming back and finishing the job."

"Bill had been drugging you," Darby said. "The headaches, nausea, and forgetfulness… Kat, you're going to be fine. You're not sick. You're actually really lucky."

"Walker wanted me to personally thank you. Thanks to your

call and getting Bill's confession on tape, we'll be able to send him away for a very long time. But it was really stupid to put yourself in harm's way.

"Walker also said that for someone who'd been working under such indefinable circumstances, you did a hell of a job."

Kathryn felt a wave of emotion. She'd wished she could have done more, but was thankful it was over.

"Now for the really good news," John said. "We have approval to bring you back into your old position, with your old seniority, twenty years' worth, at full salary, and with a rather large bonus. We want you back at the NTSB."

"Way to go, Kat," Darby said.

"What about the girls?" Jackie stood in the doorway, the girls squeezing beside her into the room, with vending machine hot chocolate in their hands.

Kathryn looked at everyone. This was her team, and she could read them all. Her dad smiled with pride. Darby beamed with the excitement that she'd have more to talk about than the latest cookie recipe. Sam was psyched about them working together again. Jackie's concern for her being a single working parent was etched into her face. The kids sipped their hot chocolate, eyes wide, and listened without reaction.

"John. Thank you. But I have to say no."

"Are you serious? This is exactly what you wanted," Darby said.

"I thought it was exactly what I wanted, too." She hugged Jenny, who climbed on the bed and spilled her hot chocolate in the process. "But the reality is, I don't want that anymore. I don't want to investigate *why* accidents happened. I want to stop them from happening."

All the while she'd been investigating, her frustration grew with the FAA and their reactive behavior. The only thing that would increase aviation safety would be to make the FAA more proactive, and less fearful of the mega airlines and their political connections.

"Bill was right about one thing—the system is broken," Kathryn said. "The accidents could've happened without anyone's assistance. Pilots handle too much stress in their profession, and there's always a breaking point, for anyone."

What the industry was doing to them was wrong. How far could Greg be pushed financially, emotionally and physically before he had broken on his own? How far would the airlines bleed before they went under? They operated in the red daily, and their highest daily expense, other than fuel, was the flight crews. Where was the company's fiduciary responsibility? To the stockholders. But at what point would they willingly sacrifice crews without regulation guiding them? They had already crossed that line.

"Our pilots are exhausted. They don't get enough sleep, and their bodies are attacked physiologically with each flight. We need to do something," Kathryn said.

The current system had always bugged Kathryn, but she'd wanted to be an investigator since she was a little girl when her uncle's plane crashed and killed him and her brother. She needed to know why so it would never happen again to anyone else. But the NTSB was not the answer. She knew that now.

"I don't want to clean up after one more airline accident that could have been avoided." Her dad placed a hand on her shoulder and squeezed, and she continued. "I don't want to work for the NTSB. I want to work for the FAA. I want to prevent the accidents from happening."

"We don't have the ability to offer you a position with the FAA," John said. "You'd have to apply, and start at an entry-level position.

You'd be giving up twenty years of seniority with a huge pay cut."

"Starting at the bottom sounds stupid, I know. But returning to what I used to do is not good enough for me. Not anymore. I am going to work for the FAA, clean up that organization, and then fix the industry. Improve safety. Work somewhere I can make a difference and impact change."

CHAPTER 69

KATHRYN HELPED JACKIE locate Greg's life insurance policy, and in the process she found a letter written to Jackie from Greg. Jackie opened the envelope and saw what it was, but couldn't bring herself to read it.

Kathryn sat with Linda, Jackie, Sam, and Darby, in Jackie's living room. Half-empty cartons of Chinese food filled the table in front of them. The kids watched videos in the family room.

"Would you mind reading it?" Jackie asked Kathryn, pulling the comforter over her lap.

Kathryn opened the letter.

My dearest Jackie, I am writing this to you because I'm gutless to tell you what I've done. I only hope one day you'll forgive me.

I have a friend, I worked with at Saudi Airlines, and he's offered to help us. He's working on getting my old job back. But in the meantime, he's been loaning me money to make ends meet. I can't do that any longer. It's not right. So I agreed to sell him our home. He paid us a $350,000 down payment. And we have 5 years to refund that money, or the house is his, with an additional $250,000 payment upon receipt.

I still have faith we can make it work. Don't give up on me. Life hasn't turned out like I'd expected, but I know that there is nothing we can't accomplish if we stick together. I love you more today than ever, and each day I thank God you came into my life.

I renewed our insurance policy, and I'm sorry I didn't tell you. I know this is an added expense we can't afford. But if something were to happen to me, I couldn't bear the thought of leaving you in the hole I've dug. Just know that if something were to cut my life short, my days on this earth were perfect because of you.

I'll see you in a few days, and we can talk.

All my love, forever and four days, Greg."

EPILOGUE

KATHRYN KNELT in her flowerbed and stuck the trowel into the soft earth then closed her eyes. She tilted her face toward the warmth of the sun. It had been a year since they put Bill behind bars for three life terms. Despite the wake of destruction he'd left in his path, Bill filling in the missing pieces prevented him from receiving the death penalty. Kathryn didn't care if he lived or died, he was out of her life for good and he'd never harm anyone again.

Coastal Airlines merged with Colossal— if it could be called a merger. Colossal took their equipment, stapled the pilots to the bottom of their seniority list, and was in the process of closing the Seattle base. The best Darby could hope for was a First Officer position in New York. The flight attendant base stayed open, but Jackie had been talking to John—a lot—since he had moved to D.C. Kathryn feared that one day Jackie would head that way to be with him. But for now, Chris and the girls were a support system for each other.

Darby wasn't dating—exactly. She'd put Neil on probation for a year and told him that maybe she'd think about getting back together since he'd broken up with his wife. As Darby said, "He's cooling his jets."

Kathryn had been working for the FAA for a year, and loved the job, despite the frustration and the politics of it all. There was so much to be done, and not enough hours to do it all. Thankfully, when the President of the United States heard what she'd done, he saw to it she joined the FAA with her twenty years' seniority. That gave her a bit more power and ability to make change. It also gave her flexibility with the girls.

She opened her eyes and brushed a loose hair back from her face with the back of her hand.

"Hey, Mom, what are you doing?" Jennifer asked, stepping into the backyard.

"I thought it was time I do some planting. We need a little color around here."

They'd all had a tough year. She'd done her best to protect the girls, but for months the news centered only on Bill and what he'd done. His trial was a circus, and the girls had been put through hell. But they were surviving, together.

"Can I help?" Jennifer asked.

"I'd love it. Where's your sister?"

"Telephone, where else?"

Kathryn smiled. She loved weekends with her girls.

"Are you ready for the big game today?"

"I hope so."

Jessica and Jennifer had both joined the soccer team, and they were good. Playing soccer gave them confidence and strength. And Francine had become their assistant coach. Linda had gone back to school and was working on a counseling degree. They'd both become welcomed members of Kathryn's family.

Jessica knelt by her mother and stuck the trowel into the ground and began to dig holes for the bulbs.

"Hey, Mom, what's this?" she asked, brushing off a piece of pink cloth.

"I don't know."

Kathryn and her daughter carefully unearthed a pillowcase. When they pulled it free, Kathryn broke the shoelace that held it closed and peered inside.

"Mom, what is it? Are you okay?"

ACKNOWLEDGEMENTS AND REFERENCES

It takes more than an airplane to fly around the world. It takes a team. And it took a team to bring *Flight For Control* to publication.

My gratitude extends to...

Linda Gray and Heather McCorkle—who have supported and encouraged me along this journey. Linda read my novel *four* times critiquing and editing along the way. Linda, your time, effort, and talent are greatly appreciated.

Pat—my pilot reader took the challenge of technical editor, and gave me great advice during *numerous* early readings—this will be a fresh and fun read. 25 revisions later, much has changed.

Daniel Sallee—Pilot and friend, thank you for your 757 technical information in the final hours.

Christine—a future pilot, controller, friend, and editor did an early line edit and gave my novel wings.

Robert Dugoni and Mike Lawson, an extra special thanks to you both. These national bestselling authors had enough faith in me to read my novel and they provided much more than endorsements. They gave me clarity on character motivation. Their feedback and willingness for open discussion took *Flight For Control* to new heights.

William Bernhardt taught me how to walk before I could fly. His week of intensive training in Hawaii taught me how to write fiction. He gave me the insight to believability, and pointed me down the right path.

Nathan Everett, award-winning author and designer at NWE Signatures (www.NWESignatures.com), shared his wisdom and experience to help me design my book and bring it to life.

My team would not be complete without Darby. Thank you Darby for your inspiration, humor, and willingness to let me share snippets of your life. Truth is often more fun than fiction, and life is definitely more colorful with you in it—just ask anyone.

Thanks to my daughter Kayla for creating an *outstanding* cover.

An extra special thanks to my husband—Dick Petitt, the man who puts up with me writing instead of cleaning, who discusses plot points when the baseball game is on T.V., and who is turning into quite the editor. Dick has *always* encouraged my dreams and given me the wings to fly. Thank you my love. Forever and four days.

References

Flight Podcast: www.flightpodcast.com Interviews with pilots and aviaiton experts focusing on safety.

Flying Training: www.flyingtraining.net Meet your on-line flight instructors: Marty Khoury, Ken Pascoe, and Karlene Petitt.

Crew Resource Management: www.crewresourcemanagement.com Human Factors and Safety in Aviation.

Flight To Success: www.KarlenePetitt.com creating aviation safety through education, inspiration, and sharing the gift of flight.

Pacific Northwest Writers Association: www.pnwa.org The PNWA is must for anyone with the desire to write a book.

DISCUSSION QUESTIONS

1. The future threat to aviation includes advanced technology—what happens when it breaks? Will the pilots of the future know what to do if they are faced with flying their planes manually?

2. With this advancement of automation, training and checking events focus on managing the computers under normal operations, due to the high reliability of they systems. What can pilots do to maintain their flying skills in preparation for when systems fail? What can pilots do to maintain their flying skills under normal operations when they don't fly?

3. How is it possible for pilots to be rested on international flights, flying the backside of the clock and sleeping on the plane? The FAA's pending regulation change includes enabling pilots to be on duty for 17 hours with four crewmembers. Two of theses pilots take their rest at the beginning of their trip. Quite often, just hours after they awoke from a good night sleep. Therefore, not resting at all. 17 hours awake is equivalent to an alcohol level of .05. How many pilots are flying drunk from fatigue? Is it possible to schedule the flight crews in a way to not be fatigued?

4. The FAA currently mandates that pilots perform 3 takeoffs and 3 landings in the previous 90 days. This regulation was instituted because of the augmented crewed airplanes, and the pilots inability to maintain takeoff and landing currency on the long haul flights. Four pilots, and only one gets a takeoff and landing. However, many pilots sit reserve and never fly. All they do is visit the simulator for takeoffs and landings each 90 days. Was this the intent of the 90-day rule? More importantly, is it possible to be proficient if a pilot doesn't fly?

5. Operational and personal stress, pension loss, furloughs, loss of seniority with mergers, etc., impact the emotional stability of a pilot. But the pilot's personality is such that they can do and handle anything. This is a positive outlook because we need confidence in the flight deck. However, there is a point where confidence and denial meet. How can a pilot's mental health be self-monitored, and what can pilots do to maintain a clear head to perform their best?

6. It appears that the aviation regulatory agencies are reactive in nature—they wait until an accident happens before they create regulation. What could be done, if anything, to make the FAA and the industry more proactive? What can airlines do? What can the pilots do?

7. When an accident happens because the pilots didn't know how to operate their plane after the automation failed, who is to blame? The pilots? They only know what they were taught. The company? They will train in the shortest footprint allowed— their fiduciary responsibility is to the stockholders. The FAA? Does this agency have the experience to know the ramifications of automation and the impact of failures? Is lack of knowledge, or ability, a problem with proficiency, or a lack of training?

8. Pilots today don't have the in-depth systems knowledge that their senior counterparts once had. There was a time when they needed to know how a molecule of air traveled through the engine and pneumatic system. They had to draw a diagram of the electrical system. Today, pilots depend upon the airplane telling them when a system is broken and they don't need to know how it works. Is safety being compromised by this lack of systems knowledge?

9. Does increasing the requirement for first officers total flight time increase safety? Do 3000 hours of flying a Cessna 152 in a traffic pattern equal 500 hours of bush flying in Alaska? What about 350 hours of flying a jet, while holding a type-rating? Or 600 hours of teaching instruments in a complex aircraft? What is the answer, quality time or total time?

10. Has the modernization of aircraft improved or decreased safety?

11. Where do you see aviation in the next 10 years? What about the next 20? What unique problems, if any, will pilots of the future face? Would you fly on an airplane without pilots?

12. What can you do to help improve safety?

Karlene Petitt is available to host aviation discussion groups, join your book club, or speak at your meetings.

Please email her at Karlene.Petitt@gmail.com to schedule your next event.

KARLENE PETITT IS AN INTERNATIONAL AIRLINE PILOT WHO IS TYPE-RATED AND HAS FLOWN AND/OR INSTRUCTED ON THE B744, B747, B767, B757, B737, B727 AND A330. PETITT IS A 33-YEAR VETERAN OF FLYING, AND HAS WORKED FOR COASTAL AIRWAYS, EVERGREEN, BRANIFF, PREMAIR, AMERICA WEST, GUYANA, TOWER AIR, NORTHWEST AIRLINES AND CURRENTLY FLIES AN AIRBUS FOR AN INTERNATIONAL AIRLINE. SHE IS THE MOTHER OF THREE, GRANDMOTHER OF SIX, AND HOLDS MBA AND MHS DEGREES.

www.KarlenePetitt.com

CPSIA information can be obtained at www.ICGtesting.com
Printed in the USA
LVOW120628010912

296946LV00008B/34/P